MATHEMATICS
for AQA GCSE
STUDENT SUPPORT BOOK
Higher Tier

Tony Banks and David Alcorn

CPL

Causeway Press Limited

Published by Causeway Press Ltd
P.O. Box 13, Ormskirk, Lancashire L39 5HP

First published 2002
Reprinted 2004

British Library Cataloguing-in-Publication Data.
A catalogue record for this book is available from the British Library.

ISBN 1-902796-36-5

Acknowledgements
Past exam questions, provided by the *Assessment and Qualifications Alliance*, are denoted by the letters AQA. The answers to all questions are entirely the responsibility of the authors/publisher and have neither been provided nor approved by AQA.

Every effort has been made to locate the copyright owners of material used in this book. Any omissions brought to the notice of the publisher are regretted and will be credited in subsequent printings.

Page design
Billy Johnson

Reader
Anne Alcock

Artwork
David Alcorn

Cover design
Waring-Collins Partnership

Typesetting by Billy Johnson, San Francisco, California, USA

Printed and bound by Scotprint, Haddington, Scotland

preface

This book provides detailed revision notes, worked examples and examination questions to support students in their preparation for AQA GCSE Mathematics at the Higher Tier of Entry.

The book has been designed so that it can be used in conjunction with the companion book *Mathematics for AQA GCSE - Higher Tier* or as a stand-alone revision book for self study and provides full coverage of AQA Specification A and AQA Specification B (Modular).

In preparing the text, full account has been made of the requirements for students to be able to use and apply mathematics in written examination papers and be able to solve problems in mathematics both with and without a calculator.

The detailed revision notes, worked examples and examination questions have been organised into 40 self-contained sections which meet the requirements of the National Curriculum and provide efficient coverage of the specifications.

Sections 1 - 9   Number
Sections 10 - 22   Algebra
Sections 23 - 34   Shape, Space and Measures
Sections 35 - 40   Handling Data

At the end of the sections on Number, Algebra, Shape, Space and Measures and Handling Data, section reviews are provided to give further opportunities to consolidate skills.

At the end of the book there is a final examination questions section with a further compilation of exam and exam-style questions, organised for non-calculator and calculator practice, in preparation for the exams.

contents

Number

Algebra

Shape, Space and Measures

Handling Data

Whole Numbers

What you need to know

- You should be able to read and write numbers expressed in figures and words.

- Be able to recognise the place value of each digit in a number.

  Eg 1 In the number 5384 the digit 8 is worth 80, but in the number 4853 the digit 8 is worth 800.

- Know the Multiplication Tables up to 10×10.

- Use non-calculator methods for addition, subtraction, multiplication and division.

- Know the order of operations in a calculation.

First	Brackets and Division line
Second	Divide and Multiply
Third	Addition and Subtraction

  Eg 2 $4 + 2 \times 6 = 4 + 12 = 16$

  Eg 3 $9 \times (7 - 2) + 3 = 9 \times 5 + 3 = 45 + 3 = 48$

- Add $(+)$, subtract $(-)$, multiply $(\times)$ and divide $(\div)$ with negative numbers.
  To **add** or **subtract** negative numbers:
  Replace double signs with a single sign.

  Use these rules to **multiply** or **divide** negative numbers.

$+ \; +$ can be replaced by $+$
$- \; -$ can be replaced by $+$
$+ \; -$ can be replaced by $-$
$- \; +$ can be replaced by $-$

When multiplying:
$+ \times + = +$
$- \times - = +$
$+ \times - = -$
$- \times + = -$

When dividing:
$+ \div + = +$
$- \div - = +$
$+ \div - = -$
$- \div + = -$

  Eg 4 Work out.
  (a) $(-5) - (-8)$ (b) $(-2) \times (-3)$ (c) $\dfrac{(-8) \times (+2) + (-4)}{(-5) \times (-1)} = \dfrac{-16 - 4}{5} = \dfrac{-20}{5} = -4$
  $= -5 + 8$ $= 6$
  $= 3$

Exercise 1

Do not use a calculator for this exercise.

1. (a) Write one million five thousand and ten in figures.
   (b) Given that $235 \times 640 = 150\,400$, work out $1\,504\,000 \div 64$.

2. Work out. (a) $7096 + 2974$ (b) $8042 - 1357$ (c) 731×137 (d) $2002 \div 13$

3. (a) Using each of the digits 9, 2, 3 and 6 write down
      (i) the largest odd number, (ii) the smallest even number.
   (b) What is the answer when the smallest even number is subtracted from the largest odd number?

4. Last year Mr Alderton had the following household bills.

Gas	£364	Electricity	£158	Telephone	£187
Water	£244	Insurance	£236	Council Tax	£983

   He paid the bills by 12 equal monthly payments. How much was each monthly payment?

5. Naomi has collected £357 from her friends for concert tickets. The tickets cost £17 each. How many people have paid for tickets?

6 James packs teddy bears into boxes. He packs 283 teddy bears every hour.
James works 47 hours in one week.
How many teddy bears does James pack in this week?

AQA

7 Mrs. Preece is printing an examination for all Year 11 students.
Each examination uses 14 sheets of paper.
  (a) There are 235 students in Year 11.
      How many sheets of paper does she need?
  (b) A ream contains 500 sheets of paper.
      How many reams of paper does she need to print all the examinations?

AQA

8 (a) A travel company takes a party of people to a hockey match at Wembley.
      17 coaches are used. Each coach has seats for 46 passengers.
      There are 12 empty seats altogether.
      How many people are in the party?
  (b) 998 football supporters use another travel company to go to a football match at Wembley.
      Each coach has seats for 53 passengers.
      (i) How many coaches are needed?   (ii) How many empty seats are there?

AQA

9 Work out.
  (a) $12 - 6 + 2$ (b) $12 \div 6 \times 2$ (c) $(27 + 8) \times 3$ (d) $\dfrac{9 - 4 + 3 \times 5}{2 \times 3 + 4}$

10 Chris is 10 cm taller than Steven. Their heights add up to 310 cm. How tall is Steven?

AQA

11 (a) Copy and complete this magic square, so that every row,
      column and diagonal adds up to 3.
  (b) Paul says, "If I multiply each number in the square by -6,
      the new total for each row, column and diagonal will be -18."
      Show **clearly** that this is true for the first row of numbers.

2	–3	4
3	1	
–2		0

AQA

12 Work out.
  (a) $(-9) - (-5) + (-3)$ (b) $\dfrac{(-7) \times (-3) - (-6)}{(-9)}$ (c) $\dfrac{(-3) \times (-5) - (-7) \times (+3)}{(-4) + (-2)}$

13 A quiz consists of ten questions. Beth, John and Sue take part.
These are their results.

A correct answer scores 3 points.
An incorrect answer scores -2 points.
A question not attempted scores 0 points.

	Beth	John	Sue
Number of answers correct	4	6	5
Number of answers incorrect	4	3	1
Number of questions not attempted	2	1	4

Who scores the most points? Show your working.

AQA

14 The number of bacteria in a certain colony doubles every day.
At the start of an experiment there are 96 bacteria.
How many bacteria will there be 10 days later?

15 The prizes paid out in last Saturday's Lottery are shown in the table.

Number of winners	Value of each prize
1	£6 469 676
27	£73 728
708	£1 757
41 422	£66
812 558	£10

How much was paid out in prizes in last Saturday's Lottery?

Decimals and Fractions

What you need to know

- You should be able to use non-calculator methods for addition, subtraction, multiplication and division of decimals.

  Eg 1 Work out.

  (a) 5.1×0.43

  $$
  \begin{array}{r}
  5.1 \quad (1\,\text{d.p.}) \\
  \times \ \ 0.4\,3 \quad (2\,\text{d.p.}) \\
  \hline
  1\,5\,3 \leftarrow 51 \times 3 \\
  + \ 2\,0\,4\,0 \leftarrow 51 \times 40 \\
  \hline
  2.1\,9\,3 \quad (3\,\text{d.p.})
  \end{array}
  $$

  (b) $1.64 \div 0.2$

  $\frac{1.64}{0.2} = \frac{16.4}{2} = 8.2$

  > When a number is **multiplied** by a number between 0 and 1 the result will be **smaller** than the original number.
  > When a number is **divided** by a number between 0 and 1 the result will be **larger** than the original number.

- The top number of a fraction is called the **numerator**, the bottom number is called the **denominator**.

- $2\frac{1}{2}$ is an example of a **mixed number**. It is a mixture of whole numbers and fractions.

- $\frac{5}{2}$ is an **improper** (or '**top heavy**') fraction.

- Fractions must have the **same denominator** before **adding** or **subtracting**.

  Eg 2 Work out.

  (a) $\frac{3}{4} + \frac{2}{3} = \frac{9}{12} + \frac{8}{12} = \frac{17}{12} = 1\frac{5}{12}$

  (b) $\frac{4}{5} - \frac{1}{2} = \frac{8}{10} - \frac{5}{10} = \frac{3}{10}$

  > Add (or subtract) the numerators only. When the answer is an improper fraction change it into a mixed number.

- Mixed numbers must be changed to **improper fractions** before **multiplying** or **dividing**.

  Eg 3 Work out.

  (a) $1\frac{1}{4} \times 2\frac{1}{5} = \frac{\overset{1}{\cancel{5}}}{4} \times \frac{11}{\cancel{5}} = \frac{11}{4} = 2\frac{3}{4}$

  > The working can be simplified by dividing a numerator and a denominator by the same number.

  (b) $1\frac{1}{3} \div 1\frac{3}{5} = \frac{4}{3} \div \frac{8}{5} = \frac{\overset{1}{\cancel{4}}}{3} \times \frac{5}{\underset{2}{\cancel{8}}} = \frac{5}{6}$

  > Notice that dividing by $\frac{8}{5}$ is the same as multiplying by $\frac{5}{8}$.

- All fractions can be written as decimals.

  > To change a fraction to a decimal divide the **numerator** by the **denominator**.

  Eg 4 Change $\frac{4}{5}$ to a decimal.

  $\frac{4}{5} = 4 \div 5 = 0.8$

- Some decimals have **recurring digits**. These are shown by:

  a single dot above a single recurring digit,

  Eg 5 $\frac{2}{3} = 0.6666\ldots = 0.\dot{6}$

  a dot above the first and last digit of a set of recurring digits.

  Eg 6 $\frac{5}{11} = 0.454545\ldots = 0.\dot{4}\dot{5}$

Exercise 2

Do not use a calculator for questions 1 to 13.

1 (a) Lucy works out 0.2×0.4. She gets the answer 0.8. Explain why her answer must be wrong.

  (b) Work out   (i) 0.3×0.4,   (ii) 0.3×0.2.

2 Paddy worked out that $\frac{30}{0.05} = 60$.

His friend did a quick mental calculation and told him he had made a mistake.
Show how Paddy's friend could have done this calculation mentally.

3 Work out. (a) $5 - 2.36$ (b) 4.8×2.5 (c) $0.294 \div 12$ (d) $\frac{54.4 \div 0.4}{0.2 \times 0.5}$

4 Two pieces of wood of length 0.75 m and 2.68 m are sawn from a plank 5 m long.
What length of wood is left?

5 The following rule can be used to predict a child's height when it becomes an adult.

> **Step 1**: Add 12.5 cm to the mother's height.
> **Step 2**: Add this figure to the father's height and then divide by 2.

The child's adult height will be within ±8.5 cm of this value.

(a) Salma's mother is 157.5 cm tall. Salma's father is 180.0 cm tall.
Use the rule to find Salma's greatest height as an adult.
(b) Bob is 180 cm tall as an adult. His father is 175 cm tall.
Use the rule to find the least height his mother could have been.   AQA

6 Write these fractions in order of size, with the smallest first. $\frac{2}{3}$ $\frac{5}{8}$ $\frac{7}{12}$ $\frac{3}{4}$ AQA

7 (a) Write down a fraction that lies halfway between $\frac{1}{3}$ and $\frac{1}{2}$.
(b) An examination is marked out of 48. Ashley scored 32 marks.
What fraction of the total did he score? Give your answer in its simplest form.

8 Evaluate. (a) $3 - 1\frac{1}{5}$ (b) $4 \times 1\frac{1}{3}$ (c) $7\frac{1}{2} \div 1\frac{1}{2}$ AQA

9 Work out $\frac{81 \times \frac{1}{3}}{\frac{1}{16} \times 8}$.   AQA

10 (a) Change $\frac{1}{6}$ to a decimal. Give the answer correct to 3 d.p.
(b) Write these numbers in order of size, starting with the largest.

     1.067   1.7   1.66 $1\frac{1}{6}$ 1.67

(c) Change 0.65 to a fraction in its simplest form.

11 Work out. (a) $2\frac{2}{3} + 3\frac{3}{4}$ (b) $4\frac{3}{10} - 2\frac{1}{2}$ (c) $1\frac{3}{7} \times 2\frac{4}{5}$ (d) $2\frac{5}{6} \div 1\frac{2}{3}$

12 Three-fifths of the people at a party are boys. Three-quarters of the boys are wearing fancy dress.
What fraction of the people at the party are boys wearing fancy dress?

13 In a sale the price of a microwave is reduced by $\frac{1}{5}$.
The sale price is £96.
What was the price of the microwave before the sale?

Sale Price
£96

14 David buys 0.6 kg of grapes and 0.5 kg of apples. He pays £1.36 altogether.
The grapes cost £1.45 per kilogram. How much per kilogram are apples?   AQA

15 A shopkeeper changed from selling sweets in ounces to selling them in grams.
He used to charge 56p for 4 ounces of sweets.   1 ounce = 28.4 grams

How much should he now charge for 125 g of these sweets?   AQA

16 Work out $\frac{12.9 \times 7.3}{3.9 + 1.4}$. Write down your full calculator display.

Approximation and Estimation

What you need to know

- How to **round** to the nearest 10, 100, 1000.
- How to approximate using **decimal places**.

> Write the number using one more decimal place than asked for.
> Look at the last decimal place and
> - if the figure is 5 or more round up,
> - if the figure is less than 5 round down.

Eg 1 Write the number 3.649 to
(a) 2 decimal places,
(b) 1 decimal place.

(a) 3.65
(b) 3.6

- How to approximate using **significant figures**.

> Start from the most significant figure and count the required number of figures.
> Look at the next figure to the right of this and
> - if the figure is 5 or more round up,
> - if the figure is less than 5 round down.
> Add noughts, as necessary, to locate the decimal point and preserve the place value.

Eg 2 Write each of these numbers correct to 2 significant figures.
(a) 365
(b) 0.0423

(a) 370
(b) 0.042

- You should be able to choose a suitable degree of accuracy.

> The result of a calculation involving measurement should not be given to a greater degree of accuracy than the measurements used in the calculation.

- You should be able to use approximations to estimate that the actual answer to a calculation is of the right order of magnitude.

Eg 3 Use approximations to estimate $\dfrac{5.1 \times 57.2}{9.8}$

$\dfrac{5 \times 60}{10} = 30$

> Estimation is done by approximating every number in the calculation to 1 significant figure.
> The calculation is then done using the approximated values.

Exercise 3

Do not use a calculator for questions 1 to 13.

1 Write the result shown on the calculator display
(a) to the nearest whole number,
(b) to the nearest ten,
(c) to the nearest hundred.

| 626.47 |

2 A newspaper's headline states: "20 000 people attend concert".
The number in the newspaper is given to the nearest thousand.
What is the smallest possible attendance?

3 (a) 43 × 18 is about 800   Use approximation to show that this is correct.

(b) (i) Show how you could find an estimate for 2019 ÷ 37.
(ii) What is your estimated answer?

4 A snack bar sells coffee at 48 pence per cup. In one day 838 cups are sold.
By rounding each number to one significant figure, estimate the total amount received from the sale of coffee, giving your answer in pounds.

AQA

5 One dollar is worth about 62 pence. Mr Jones buys a watch that costs 89 dollars.
Estimate how much the watch is worth in pounds.

AQA

6 (a) To estimate 97×49 Charlie uses the approximations 100×50.
Explain why his estimate will be larger than the actual answer.
(b) To estimate $1067 \div 48$ Patsy uses the approximations $1000 \div 50$.
Will her estimate be larger or smaller than the actual answer?
Give a reason for your answer.

7 Isobella pays for 68 photographs to be developed. Each photograph costs 34 pence.
Isobella calculates the total cost to be £231.20.
(a) Which two numbers would you multiply to find a quick estimate of the total cost?
(b) Use your numbers to show whether Isobella's calculation could be correct.
Comment on your answer.

AQA

8 Clint has to calculate $\dfrac{414 + 198}{36}$. He calculates the answer to be 419.5.
By rounding each number to one significant figure estimate whether his answer is about right.
Show all your working.

9 Find an approximate value of $\dfrac{2.15}{141.8 + 58.3}$

AQA

10 In 2001 Mr Symms drove 8873 kilometres.
His car does 11 kilometres per litre. Petrol costs 69.9 pence per litre.
Use approximations to estimate the amount he spent on petrol.

11 Melanie needs 200 crackers for an office party.
The crackers are sold in boxes of 12.
How many boxes must she buy?

12 CRACKERS

12 Garth calculates $734\,990 \div 0.067$. He gets the answer $1\,097\,000$.
Use approximations to check whether his answer is of the right magnitude.

13 Use approximations to estimate the value of the following.
(a) $\dfrac{6.12}{11.3 + 19.8}$
(b) $\dfrac{0.613}{297}$
(c) $\dfrac{897 \times 5.03}{0.304}$

14 Calculate $97.2 \div 6.5$.
Give your answer correct to (a) two decimal places, (b) one decimal place.

15 Calculate 78.4×8.7.
Give your answer correct to (a) two significant figures, (b) one significant figure.

16 Andrew says, "Answers given to two decimal places are more accurate than answers given to two significant figures."
Is he right? Explain your answer.

17 Use your calculator to evaluate the following. $\dfrac{13.2 + 24.7}{21.3 - 17.2}$
Give your answer correct to one decimal place.

AQA

18 (a) Calculate $\dfrac{89.6 \times 10.3}{19.7 + 9.8}$.
(b) By using approximations show that your answer to (a) is about right.
You **must** show all your working.

AQA

Percentages and Money

What you need to know

- 10% is read as '10 percent'. 'Per cent' means out of 100. 10% means 10 out of 100.

- A percentage can be written as a fraction, 10% can be written as $\frac{10}{100}$.

- To change a decimal or a fraction to a percentage: **multiply by 100**.

- To change a percentage to a fraction or a decimal: **divide by 100**.

- How to express one quantity as a percentage of another.

  Eg 1 Write 30p as a percentage of £2.

  $\frac{30}{200} \times 100 = 30 \times 100 \div 200 = 15\%$

  > Write the numbers as a fraction, using the same units.
  > Change the fraction to a percentage.

- You should be able to use percentages to solve a variety of problems.

- Be able to find a percentage of a quantity.

  Eg 2 Find 20% of £64.
  £64 ÷ 100 = £0.64
  £0.64 × 20 = £12.80

  > 1. Divide by 100 to find 1%.
  > 2. Multiply by the percentage to be found.

- Be able to find a percentage increase (or decrease).

  Eg 3 Find the percentage loss on a micro-scooter bought for £25 and sold for £18.

  Percentage loss = $\frac{7}{25} \times 100 = 28\%$

  > Percentage decrease = $\frac{\text{actual decrease}}{\text{initial value}} \times 100\%$
  >
  > Percentage increase = $\frac{\text{actual increase}}{\text{initial value}} \times 100\%$

- Be able to solve reverse percentage problems.

  Eg 4 Find the original price of a car which is sold at a loss of 20% for £1200.

  80% of original price = £1200
  1% of original price = £1200 ÷ 80 = £15
  Original price = £15 × 100 = £1500

  > First find 1% of the original value by dividing the selling price by (100 − % loss), then multiply by 100.

- **Hourly pay** is paid at a **basic rate** for a fixed number of hours.
  Overtime pay is usually paid at a higher rate such as time and a half, which means each hour's work is worth 1.5 times the basic rate.

- Everyone is allowed to earn some money which is not taxed. This is called a **tax allowance**.

- Tax is only paid on income earned in excess of the tax allowance. This is called a **taxable income**.

  Eg 5 Tom earns £5800 per year. His tax allowance is £4385 per year and he pays tax at 10p in the £ on his taxable income. Find how much income tax Tom pays per year.

  Taxable income = £5800 − £4385 = £1415
  Income tax payable = £1415 × 0.10 = £141.50

  > First find the taxable income, then multiply taxable income by rate in £.

- **Value added tax**, or **VAT**, is a tax on some goods and services and is added to the bill.

- When considering a **best buy**, compare quantities by using the same units.
  For example, find which product gives more grams per penny.

④

- Money invested in a savings account at a bank or building society earns **interest**.

- With **Simple Interest**, the interest is paid out each year and not added to your account.

$$\text{Simple Interest} = \frac{\text{Amount invested}}{} \times \frac{\text{Time in years}}{} \times \frac{\text{Rate of interest per year}}{}$$

Eg 6 Find the Simple Interest paid on £600 invested for 6 months at 8% per year.

Simple Interest $= 600 \times \frac{6}{12} \times \frac{8}{100} = 600 \times 0.5 \times 0.08 = £24$

- With **Compound Interest**, the interest earned each year is added to your account and also earns interest the following year.

Eg 7 Find the **Compound Interest** paid on £600 invested for 2 years at 6% per year.

1st year		2nd year	
Investment	= £600	Investment	= £636
Interest: £600 × 0.06	= £ 36	Interest: £636 × 0.06	= £ 38.16
Value after one year	= £636	Value after two years	= £674.16

Compound Interest = Final value − Original value = £674.16 − £600 = £74.16

Exercise 4

Do not use a calculator for questions 1 to 5.

1. (a) Work out (i) 25% of 60 kg, (ii) 5% of £900.
   (b) What is (i) 60 pence as a percentage of £3, (ii) 15 seconds as a percentage of 1 minute?

2. A test is marked out of 80. Colin scored 35% of the marks.
   How many marks did Colin score?

3. A jacket normally costs £48. The price is reduced by 15% in a sale.
   What is the price of the jacket in the sale?

4. Angela is paid £7.40 per hour for a basic 35-hour week. Overtime is paid at time and a half.
   Last week Angela was paid £303.40.
   How many hours did she work last week?

5. Mrs Tilsed wishes to buy a car priced at £2400.

   Two options are available.
   Option 1 – A deposit of 20% of £2400 and 24 monthly payments of £95.
   Option 2 – For a single payment the dealer offers a discount of 5% on £2400.

   £2400

   How much more does it cost to buy the car if option 1 is chosen rather than option 2?

6. Terry receives a bill for £284 for repairs to his car. VAT at $17\frac{1}{2}$% is then added to this amount.
   Calculate the total amount which Terry pays.   AQA

7. In a local election 3750 people could have voted. 2150 people actually voted.
   What percentage of the people voted?   AQA

8. Toffee is sold in bars of two sizes.
   A large bar weighs 450 g and costs £1.69. A small bar weighs 275 g and costs 99p.
   Which size of bar is better value for money?
   You must show all your working.

9. A pogo stick is bought for £12.50 and sold for £8.
   What is the percentage loss?

10 A farmer has 200 sheep. 90% of the sheep have lambs.
Of the sheep which have lambs 45% have two lambs.
How many of the sheep have two lambs?

11 Simon invests £360 at 6.4% per annum simple interest.
How much interest does he get at the end of 6 months? *AQA*

12 Last year Sara had a tax allowance of £4385 and paid £3540 in tax.
The rates of tax were:

> 10p in the £ on the first £1520 of taxable income and
> 22p in the £ on all her remaining taxable income.

How much did Sara earn last year? *AQA*

13 Nadia invests £400 in an account which pays 6.5% interest per year.
The interest is added to her investment at the end of each year.
Nadia does not withdraw any money.
Calculate the number of years Nadia must invest her money so that the total investment has a value of more than £480. You must show all your working. *AQA*

14 (a) Vanessa has a Vauxhall Corsa.
She is given a no claims discount.
After taking off her no claims discount she has to pay £390 to insure her car.
Calculate her no claims discount as a percentage of £650.

> **1st STOP Car Insurance**
> **Typical insurance:**
> Vauxhall Corsa - £650 per year
> No Claims Discount Available

(b) Cedric has a BMW car.
He is given a 65% no claims discount.
After the discount he has to pay £336 to insure his car.
Calculate the price of the insurance before the discount.

15 This report appeared in a motoring magazine.

> In the first year of ownership a new car loses 20% of its value
> and in the second year it loses 15% of its one-year old value.

If this report is true, what is the percentage loss in the value of a new car in its first 2 years?

16 Questionnaires were sent to a number of people. 72 people replied.
This was only 18% of all the people that had been sent questionnaires.
How many people had been sent questionnaires?

17 A computer is advertised at £1116.25 including $17\frac{1}{2}$% VAT.
How much is the computer before VAT is added?

AQA

18 (a) Afzal invests £4000 at 7.5% per annum compound interest.
Calculate the value of his investment at the end of 2 years.
(b) Leroy gets 5% per annum interest on his investment.
After one year his investment has grown to £504. How much did he invest? *AQA*

19 A garden centre buys plants and resells them at a profit of 28%.
How much was the original price of a rose bush which is sold for £4.80? *AQA*

20 Jayne invests her money at 6% per annum compound interest.
What is the percentage increase in the value of her investment after 3 years?

● ● ● ● ● ● ● ● ● ● ● ● ● ● ● ● ● ● ●

What you need to know

- The ratio 3 : 2 is read '3 to 2'.
- A ratio is used only to **compare** quantities.
  A ratio does not give information about the exact values of quantities being compared.
- In its **simplest form**, a ratio contains whole numbers which have no common factor other than 1.

  Eg 1 Write £2.40 : 40p in its simplest form.
  £2.40 : 40p = 240p : 40p
  $\qquad\qquad$ = 240 : 40
  $\qquad\qquad$ = 6 : 1

  > All quantities in a ratio must be in the **same units** before the ratio can be simplified.

- You should be able to solve a variety of problems involving ratio.

  Eg 2 The ratio of bats to balls in a box is 3 : 5.
  There are 12 bats in the box.
  How many balls are there?

  12 ÷ 3 = 4
  3 × 4 : 5 × 4 = 12 : 20
  There are 20 balls in the box.

  > For every 3 bats there are 5 balls.
  > To find an **equivalent ratio** to 3 : 5, in which the first number is 12, multiply each number in the ratio by 4.

  Eg 3 A wall costs £660 to build.
  The costs of materials to labour are in the ratio 4 : 7.
  What is the cost of labour?

  4 + 7 = 11
  £660 ÷ 11 = £60
  Cost of labour = £60 × 7 = £420

  > The numbers in the ratio add to 11.
  > For every £11 of the total cost, £4 pays for materials and £7 pays for labour.
  > So, **divide** by 11 and then **multiply** by 7.

- When two different quantities are always in the **same ratio** the two quantities are in **direct proportion**.

  Eg 4 20 litres of petrol cost £14.
  Find the cost of 25 litres of petrol.

  20 litres cost £14
  1 litre costs £14 ÷ 20 = £0.70
  25 litres cost £0.70 × 25 = £17.50

  > This is sometimes called the **unitary method**.
  > **Divide** by 20 to find the cost of 1 litre.
  > **Multiply** by 25 to find the cost of 25 litres.

- When as one quantity increases the other decreases, the quantities are in **inverse proportion**.

  Eg 5 3 people take 8 hours to deliver some leaflets.
  How long would it take 4 people?

  3 people take 8 hours.
  1 person takes 8 hours × 3 = 24 hours
  4 people take 24 hours ÷ 4 = 6 hours
  So 4 people would take 6 hours.

  > This assumes that time is **inversely proportional** to the number of people.
  > **Multiply** by 3 to find how long 1 person would take.
  > **Divide** by 4 to find how long 4 people would take.

Exercise 5

Do not use a calculator for questions 1 to 6.

1 A toy box contains large bricks and small bricks in the ratio 1 : 4.
The box contains 40 bricks. How many large bricks are in the box?

2 To make mortar a builder mixes sand and cement in the ratio 3 : 1.
The builder uses 2.5 kg of cement. How much sand does he use?

3 In a drama club the ratio of boys to girls is 2 : 3.
    (a)   What fraction of club members are girls?
    (b)   What percentage of club members are boys?

4 The ratio of men to women playing golf one day is 5 : 3.
There are 20 men playing. How many women are playing?

5 A gardener wants to make a display of red and yellow tulips.
He orders red and yellow tulip bulbs in the ratio of 3 : 5. He orders a total of 2000 bulbs.
How many of each colour bulb will he get?   AQA

6 Dec shares a prize of £435 with Annabel in the ratio 3 : 2.
What is the difference in the amount of money they each receive?

7 A town has a population of 45 000 people. 1 in every 180 people are disabled.
How many disabled people are there in the town?   AQA

8 Two students are talking about their school outing.

> My class went to Tower Bridge last week.
> There are 30 people in my class.
> The total cost was £82.50

> There are 45 people in my group.
> What will be the total cost for my group?

9 A farmer estimates it will take 2 combine harvesters 6 days to harvest his crop.
Estimate how many days it will take 3 combine harvesters to harvest his crop.

10 When petrol is 70 pence a litre it costs £24.50 to fill the tank of my car with petrol.
How much will it cost to fill the tank of my car with petrol when petrol is 80 pence per litre?

11 A Munch Crunch bar weighs 21 g.
The table shows the nutrients that each bar contains.

Protein	1.9 g
Fat	4.7 g
Carbohydrate	13.3 g
Fibre	1.1 g

    (a)   What percentage of the bar is fat?
              Give your answer to an appropriate degree of accuracy.
    (b)   What is the ratio of protein to carbohydrate?
              Give your answer in the form $1 : n$.   AQA

12 On a map the distance between two towns is 5 cm.
The actual distance between the towns is 1 kilometre.
What is the scale of the map in the form of $1 : n$?

13 A car is 2.86 m long. Two scale models are made of the car.

> Model A is made to a scale of 1 : 30.   Model B is 38 mm long.

What is the difference between the length of model A and the length of model B?
Give your answer to an appropriate degree of accuracy.   AQA

14 Three friends agree to buy a hi-fi set for £792. Lauren contributes £110, Jack contributes £250
and Chloe contributes the rest. Three years later, they sell the hi-fi for £352.
They agree to divide the money in the ratio in which they contributed.
How much does Chloe receive?   AQA

15 At 80 km/h it takes 30 minutes to complete a journey.
How long would it take to complete the journey at 50 km/h?

Working with Number

What you need to know

- **Multiples** of a number are found by multiplying the number by   1,   2,   3,   4,   …

  Eg 1   The multiples of 8 are $1 \times 8 = 8$, $2 \times 8 = 16$, $3 \times 8 = 24$, $4 \times 8 = 32$,   …

- **Factors** of a number are found by listing all the products that give the number.

  Eg 2 $1 \times 6 = 6$ and $2 \times 3 = 6$.   So, the factors of 6 are: 1,   2,   3   and   6.

- A **prime number** is a number with only two factors, 1 and the number itself.
  The first few prime numbers are: 2,   3,   5,   7,   11,   13,   17,   19,   …
  The number 1 is not a prime number because it has only one factor.

- The **prime factors** of a number are those factors of the number which are themselves prime numbers.

  Eg 3   The factors of 18 are: 1,   2,   3,   6,   9   and   18.
  The prime factors of 18 are: 2   and   3.

- The **Least Common Multiple** of two numbers is the smallest number that is a multiple of them both.

  Eg 4   The Least Common Multiple of 4 and 5 is 20.

- The **Highest Common Factor** of two numbers is the largest number that is a factor of them both.

  Eg 5   The Highest Common Factor of 8 and 12 is 4.

- An expression such as $3 \times 3 \times 3 \times 3 \times 3$ can be written in a shorthand way as 3^5.
  This is read as '3 to the power of 5'. The number 3 is the **base** of the expression. 5 is the **power**.

- Powers can be used to help write any number as the **product of its prime factors**.

  Eg 6 $72 = 2 \times 2 \times 2 \times 3 \times 3 = 2^3 \times 3^2$

- Numbers raised to the power of 2 are **squared**.

  Squares can be calculated using the $\boxed{x^2}$ button on a calculator.

  > **Square numbers** are whole numbers squared.
  > The first few square numbers are: 1,   4,   9,   16,   25,   36,   …

  The opposite of squaring a number is called finding the **square root**.

  Square roots can be calculated using the $\boxed{\sqrt{}}$ button on a calculator.

  The square root of a number can be positive or negative.

  Eg 7   The square root of 9 can be written as $\sqrt{9}$ or $9^{\frac{1}{2}}$, and is equal to $+3$ or -3.

- Numbers raised to the power of 3 are **cubed**.

  > **Cube numbers** are whole numbers cubed.
  > The first few cube numbers are: 1,   8,   27,   64,   125,   …

  The opposite of cubing a number is called finding the **cube root**.

  Cube roots can be calculated using the $\boxed{\sqrt[3]{}}$ button on a calculator.

  Eg 8   The cube root of 27 can be written as $\sqrt[3]{27}$ or $27^{\frac{1}{3}}$, and is equal to 3.

● **Powers**

The squares and cubes of numbers can be worked out on a calculator by using the $\boxed{x^y}$ button. The $\boxed{x^y}$ button can be used to calculate the value of a number x raised to the power of y.

Eg 9 Calculate 2.6^4.
Enter the sequence: $\boxed{2}$ $\boxed{.}$ $\boxed{6}$ $\boxed{x^y}$ $\boxed{4}$ $\boxed{=}$.   So $2.6^4 = 45.6976$.

● The **reciprocal** of a number is the value obtained when the number is divided into 1.
The reciprocal of a number can be found on a calculator by using the $\boxed{\frac{1}{x}}$ button.

> A number times its reciprocal equals 1.
> Zero has no reciprocal.
> The reciprocal of a number can be shown using an index of -1.

Eg 10 Find the reciprocal of 5.
The reciprocal of $5 = 5^{-1} = \frac{1}{5} = 0.2$

Using a calculator, press: $\boxed{5}$ $\boxed{\frac{1}{x}}$

● **Roots** can be calculated using the $\boxed{x^{1/y}}$ button.

Eg 11 Calculate $\sqrt[7]{128}$.
Enter the sequence: $\boxed{1}$ $\boxed{2}$ $\boxed{8}$ $\boxed{x^{1/y}}$ $\boxed{7}$ $\boxed{=}$.   So $\sqrt[7]{128} = 2$.

● **The rules of indices**

Multiplying powers with the same base	$a^m \times a^n = a^{m+n}$
Dividing powers with the same base	$a^m \div a^n = a^{m-n}$
Raising a power to a power	$(a^m)^n = a^{mn}$
Raising any number to the power zero	$a^0 = 1$ (also $a^1 = a$)
Negative powers and reciprocals	$a^{-m} = \dfrac{1}{a^m}$ a^{-m} is the reciprocal of a^m
Fractional powers and roots	$a^{\frac{1}{n}} = \sqrt[n]{a}$ and $a^{\frac{m}{n}} = \left(a^{\frac{1}{n}}\right)^m = \left(\sqrt[n]{a}\right)^m$

Eg 12 Simplify. Leave your answers in index form.
(a) $2^9 \times 2^4 = 2^{9+4} = 2^{13}$ (b) $2^9 \div 2^4 = 2^{9-4} = 2^5$ (c) $(4^9)^3 = 4^{9 \times 3} = 4^{27}$

● You should be able to use the function keys on a calculator to solve a variety of problems.

Exercise 6   Do not use a calculator for questions 1 to 17.

1 (a) Write down all the factors of 18.
   (b) Write down a multiple of 7 between 30 and 40.
   (c) Explain why 15 is not a prime number.

2 A number of counters can be grouped into 2's, 3's, 4's and 5's.
Find the smallest possible number of counters.

3 (a) Work out the value of (i) 5^3 (ii) $\sqrt{64}$
   (b) Between which two consecutive whole numbers does $\sqrt{30}$ lie?   AQA

4 Look at these numbers.

| 2   15   27   36   44   51   64 |

   (a) Which of these numbers is a prime number?
   (b) Which of these numbers is both a square number and a cube number?

5 (a) Write 36 as a product of its prime factors.
   (b) Write 45 as a product of its prime factors.
   (c) What is the highest common factor of 36 and 45?
   (d) What is the least common multiple of 36 and 45?

6 Use examples to show that the sum of the squares of two prime numbers can be odd or even.

7 A white light flashes every 10 seconds. A red light flashes every 6 seconds.
The two lights flash at the same time.
After how many seconds will the lights next flash at the same time?

8 In this question a and b represent **positive integers**. $a \neq b$.

(a) $a\mathbf{H}b$ means the Highest Common Factor of a and b.

Find (i) $15\mathbf{H}35$, (ii) $(15\mathbf{H}45)\mathbf{H}21$.

(b) $a\mathbf{L}b$ means the Least Common Multiple of a and b.

Find (i) $15\mathbf{L}25$, (ii) $(15\mathbf{L}45)\mathbf{L}60$.

(c) p is a prime number.
  (i) You are given $ap\mathbf{H}bp = p$. What can you say about the integers a and b?
  (ii) You are given $ap\mathbf{L}bp = bp$. What can you say about the integers a and b? AQA

9 Work out. (a) $2^3 \times 3^2$ (b) $\left(\sqrt{9} \times \sqrt{25}\right)^2$ (c) $2^3 \times \sqrt[3]{64}$

10 Which is smaller $\sqrt{225}$ or 2^4? Show your working.

11 Work out the value of $2^1 - 2^0 + 2^{-1}$. AQA

12 Find the value of x in each of the following.
(a) $7^6 \times 7^3 = 7^x$ (b) $7^6 \div 7^3 = 7^x$ (c) $(7^6)^3 = 7^x$ (d) $7^0 = x$

13 Find the value of n when: (a) $10^3 \times 10^{-5} = 10^n$
(b) $(4 \times 10^5) \times (5 \times 10^{-3}) = 2 \times 10^n$
(c) $(4 \times 10^5) \div (5 \times 10^{-3}) = 8 \times 10^n$

14 Evaluate: (a) 2^{-2} (b) $32^{\frac{1}{5}}$ AQA

15 Evaluate: (a) $9^{\frac{1}{2}}$ (b) $64^{-\frac{1}{2}}$ (c) $25^{\frac{3}{2}}$ (d) $16^{-\frac{3}{4}}$

16 Solve the following equations.
(a) $8^{\frac{1}{x}} = 2$ (b) $16^{\frac{1}{4}} = 2^x$ (c) $32^y = 2$ (d) $125^x = \frac{1}{5}$ AQA

17 Simplify, leaving your answers in fractional form.
(a) $64^{\frac{1}{2}} \times 125^{-\frac{1}{3}}$ (b) $27^{\frac{2}{3}} \times 3^{-4}$ (c) $\left(\frac{1}{2}\right)^{-3} \div \left(\frac{1}{5}\right)^{-2}$

18 Find the reciprocal of 7. Give your answer correct to two decimal places.

19 Calculate $\sqrt{\dfrac{3.9}{(0.6)^3}}$ AQA

20 (a) Use your calculator to find $3.5^3 + \sqrt{18.4}$. Give all the figures on your calculator.
(b) Write your answer to 3 significant figures. AQA

21 (a) Calculate the value of $\sqrt{3.1 + \dfrac{6}{3.1} - \dfrac{9}{3.1^2}}$

(b) Show how to check that your answer is of the right order of magnitude. AQA

22 Calculate the value of $\sqrt{\dfrac{72.6}{8.3^2 - 8.89}}$ AQA

23 Calculate the value of:

(a) $5^{\frac{2}{5}}$ (b) $\dfrac{1}{(0.7)^5}$ (c) $\sqrt[3]{\dfrac{920\,000}{5^4}}$ (d) $\left(\dfrac{5.9}{\sqrt[5]{15}}\right)^{-3}$

Give your answers correct to two significant figures.

What you need to know

- **Standard index form**, or **standard form**, is a shorthand way of writing very large and very small numbers.

- In **standard form** a number is written as: **a number between 1 and 10 × a power of 10**
  Large numbers (ten, or more) have a **positive** power of 10.

  Eg 1 Write 370 000 in standard form.
  $370\ 000 = 3.7 \times 100\ 000 = 3.7 \times 10^5$

  Eg 2 Write 5.6×10^7 as an ordinary number.
  $5.6 \times 10^7 = 5.6 \times 10\ 000\ 000 = 56\ 000\ 000$

  Small positive numbers (less than one) have a **negative** power of 10.

  Eg 3 Write 0.000 73 in standard form.
  $0.000\ 73 = 7.3 \times 0.000\ 1 = 7.3 \times 10^{-4}$

  Eg 4 Write 2.9×10^{-6} as an ordinary number.
  $2.9 \times 10^{-6} = 2.9 \times 0.000\ 001 = 0.000\ 002\ 9$

- You should be able to interpret the display on a calculator.

  Eg 5 The calculator display shows the answer to 0.007×0.09
  In standard form, the answer is 6.3×10^{-4}
  As an ordinary number, the answer is 0.000 63

6.3	−04

- You should be able to solve problems involving numbers given in standard form.

Exercise 7

Do not use a calculator for questions 1 to 7.

1. Write one million in standard form.

2. Look at these numbers. | 2.6×10^4 | 6.2×10^3 | 9.8×10^{-4} | 8.9×10^{-5} |

   (a) (i) Which number is the largest? (ii) Write your answer as an ordinary number.
   (b) (i) Which number is the smallest? (ii) Write your answer as an ordinary number.

3. (a) Write 57 000 000 in standard index form. (b) Write 0.000 057 in standard index form.

4. The table shows the average speed of planets that orbit the Sun.

Planet	Average speed of orbit (km/h)
Jupiter	4.7×10^4
Mercury	1.7×10^5
Neptune	1.2×10^4
Pluto	1.7×10^4
Saturn	3.5×10^4
Uranus	2.5×10^5

   (a) Which planet is travelling the fastest?
   (b) What is the difference between the average speeds of Neptune and Pluto?
   Give your answer in standard form.

   AQA

5 Work out.
(a) $(6 \times 10^3) + (5 \times 10^4)$ (b) $(6 \times 10^3) \times (5 \times 10^4)$ (c) $(6 \times 10^3) \div (5 \times 10^4)$
Give your answers in standard form.

6 (a) A company buys 2 340 000 packs of paper.
Write this number in standard form.
(b) A pack of paper has a thickness of 4.8 cm.
There are 500 sheets of paper in each pack.
Calculate the thickness of one sheet of paper in centimetres.
Give your answer in standard form.

AQA

7 The population of Spain is 3.6×10^7 and there are 1.2×10^5 doctors in Spain.
Calculate the average number of people per doctor.

AQA

8 (a) Calculate $\dfrac{7.2 \times 10^6}{0.0045}$.
Give your answer in standard form.

(b) Calculate $\dfrac{530}{6.7 \times 10^5}$.
Give your answer as an ordinary number correct to two significant figures.

9 In England £1.012×10^{10} is spent on healthcare per year.
There are 4.71×10^7 people in England.
How much per person is spent on healthcare in England per year?

AQA

10 Very large distances in the Universe are measured in **parsecs** and **light-years**.
One parsec is 3.0857×10^{13} kilometres.
One parsec is 3.26 light-years.
How many kilometres are in 1 light-year?
Give your answer in standard form to an appropriate degree of accuracy.

AQA

11 Work out $\dfrac{3.5 \times 10^{-3}}{4.1 \times 10^2}$.

Give your answer as an ordinary number correct to 2 significant figures.

12 Approximate figures for the amount of carbon dioxide entering the atmosphere from artificial sources are shown below.

Total amount (world wide)	7.4×10^9 tonnes
Amount from the United Kingdom	1.59×10^8 tonnes

(a) What percentage of the total amount of carbon dioxide entering the atmosphere comes from the United Kingdom?
(b) Approximately 19% of the amount of carbon dioxide from the United Kingdom comes from road transport.
How many million tonnes of carbon dioxide is this?

AQA

13 In the United Kingdom:

4.53×10^{11} aluminium cans are used and 0.15% of them are recycled,

1.2×10^{10} steel cans are used and 11.7% of them are recycled.

What percentage of the total number of cans used are recycled?

AQA

8 Speed and Other Compound Measures

What you need to know

- **Speed** is a compound measure because it involves **two** other measures.

- **Speed** is a measurement of how fast something is travelling.
  It involves two other measures, **distance** and **time**.
  In situations where speed is not constant, **average speed** is used.

  $$\text{Speed} = \frac{\text{Distance}}{\text{Time}}$$ $$\text{Average speed} = \frac{\text{Total distance travelled}}{\text{Total time taken}}$$

  The formula linking speed, distance and time can be rearranged and remembered as:
  $$S = D \div T$$
  $$D = S \times T$$
  $$T = D \div S$$

- You should be able to solve problems involving speed, distance and time.

  Eg 1 A greyhound takes 32 seconds to run 400 metres.
  Calculate its speed in metres per second.

  $$\text{Speed} = \frac{\text{Distance}}{\text{Time}} = \frac{400}{32} = 12.5 \text{ metres per second}$$

  Eg 2 Norrie says, "If I drive at an average speed of 60 km/h it will take me $2\frac{1}{2}$ hours to complete my journey." What distance is his journey?

  $$\text{Distance} = \text{Speed} \times \text{Time} = 60 \times 2\frac{1}{2} = 150 \text{ km}$$

  Eg 3 Ellen cycles 5 km at an average speed of 12 km/h.
  How many minutes does she take?

  $$\text{Time} = \frac{\text{Distance}}{\text{Speed}} = \frac{5}{12} \text{ hours} = \frac{5}{12} \times 60 = 25 \text{ minutes}$$

  To change hours to minutes: **multiply by 60**

- **Density** is a compound measure which involves the measures **mass** and **volume**.

  Eg 4 A block of metal has mass 500 g and volume 400 cm³.

  $$\text{Density} = \frac{\text{Mass}}{\text{Volume}} = \frac{500}{400} = 1.25 \text{ g/cm}^3$$

  $$\text{Density} = \frac{\text{Mass}}{\text{Volume}}$$

- **Population density** is a measure of how populated an area is.

  Eg 5 The population of Cumbria is 489 700.
  The area of Cumbria is 6824 km².

  $$\text{Population density} = \frac{\text{Population}}{\text{Area}}$$

  $$\text{Population density} = \frac{\text{Population}}{\text{Area}} = \frac{489\,700}{6824} = 71.8 \text{ people/km}^2.$$

Exercise 8

Do not use a calculator for questions 1 to 5.

1. Sean cycled 24 km at an average speed of 16 km/h.
   How long did he take to complete the journey?

2. Ahmed takes $2\frac{1}{2}$ hours to drive from New Milton to London.
   He averages 66 km/h. What distance does he drive?

3. A motorist travels a distance of 156 miles in $3\frac{1}{4}$ hours.
   Calculate the average speed of the motorist in miles per hour.

4. Kay walks 2.7 km in 45 minutes.
   Calculate her average walking speed in kilometres per hour.

5 The distance between Heysham and the Isle of Man is 80 km.
A hovercraft travels at 50 km per hour. How long does the journey take?

AQA

6 Sheila lives 6 kilometres from the beach.
She jogs from her home to the beach at an average speed of 10 km/h.
She gets to the beach at 1000. Calculate the time when she left home.

AQA

7 The diagram shows the distances, in miles, between some junctions on a motorway.

West   **12**   **8**   East
◄—— (25) —————————— (26) —————————— (27) ——►

A coach is travelling west. At 1040 it passes junction 27 and at 1052 it passes junction 26.
(a) Calculate the average speed of the coach in miles per hour.

Between junctions 26 and 25 the coach travels at an average speed of 30 miles per hour.
(b) Calculate the time when the coach passes junction 25.

8 A train travels at an average speed of 80 miles per hour.
At 0940 the train is 65 miles from Glasgow. The train is due to arrive in Glasgow at 1030.
Will it arrive on time? Show your working.

9 A horse gallops at an average speed of 24 km/h for $4\frac{1}{2}$ minutes.
Calculate the distance it travels.

10 On Monday it took Helen 40 minutes to drive to work.
On Tuesday it took Helen 25 minutes to drive to work.
Her average speed on Monday was 18 miles per hour.
What was her average speed on Tuesday?

11 Henry completes a 200 m race in 25 seconds. What is his average speed in kilometres per hour?

AQA

12 A jet-ski travels 0.9 kilometres in 1.5 minutes.
Calculate the average speed of the jet-ski in metres per second.

13 The distance from the Earth to the Moon is 3.81×10^5 kilometres.
Light travels at a speed of 3×10^8 metres per second.
How long does it take light to travel from the Earth to the Moon?

14 (a) A goods train, 150 metres long, is travelling at 45 km/h.
How many seconds does it take to pass a signal?
(b) The goods train takes 5 seconds to pass a passenger train, 90 metres long, travelling in the opposite direction.
Calculate the speed of the passenger train in kilometres per hour.

15 A copper statue has a mass of 1080 g and a volume of 120 cm³. Work out the density of copper.

16 A silver medal has a mass of 200 g. The density of silver is 10.5 g/cm³.
What is the volume of the medal?

17 The population of Jamaica is 2.8 million people. The area of Jamaica is 10 800 km².
What is the population density of Jamaica?

18 The table gives some information about North America.

Country	Area (km²)	Population	Population density (people/km²)
Canada	9 860 000		2.98
United States		2.68×10^8	28.9

(a) Calculate the population of Canada.   (b) Calculate the area of the United States.
Give your answers to 3 significant figures.

Speed and Other Compound Measures

Extending the Number System

What you need to know

- **Rational numbers** can be written in the form $\frac{a}{b}$, where a and b are integers ($b \neq 0$).

  Examples of rational numbers are: 2, -5, $\frac{2}{5}$,   0.6,   3.47, $1\frac{3}{4}$.

- All fractions can be written as decimals.
  For example, $\frac{1}{3} = 0.3333333... = 0.\dot{3}$, $\frac{123}{999} = 0.123123123... = 0.\dot{1}2\dot{3}$

- You should be able to convert a recurring decimal to a fraction.

  Eg 1 Find the fraction which is equal to $0.\dot{2}\dot{7}$, in its simplest form.

$x = 0.2727...$
2 digits recur, so multiply by 100.
$100x = 27.2727...$
$99x = 27$
$x = \frac{27}{99} = \frac{3}{11}$
$0.\dot{2}\dot{7} = \frac{3}{11}$

  Let x = the recurring decimal.
  Multiply both sides by a power of 10:
  - by $10^1 = 10$ if only 1 digit recurs,
  - by $10^2 = 100$ if 2 digits recur, and so on.

  Subtract the original equation from the new equation.
  Solve the resulting equation for x.
  If necessary, write the fraction in its simplest form.

- All **terminating** and **recurring decimals** are rational numbers.

- A **surd** is the root of a rational number which is not rational.
  A surd is an **irrational number**.

  These are examples of surds: $\sqrt{2}$ $\sqrt{0.37}$ $3 + \sqrt{2}$

  $\sqrt{9}$ is not a surd because $\sqrt{9} = 3$ which is rational. $\sqrt{a}$ means the positive square root of a.

- Rules for manipulating and simplifying surds:

  $$\sqrt{ab} = \sqrt{a} \times \sqrt{b} \qquad m\sqrt{a} + n\sqrt{a} = (m + n)\sqrt{a} \qquad \sqrt{\frac{a}{b}} = \frac{\sqrt{a}}{\sqrt{b}}$$

  Eg 2 Simplify the following leaving the answers in surd form.

  (a) $\sqrt{32} = \sqrt{16} \times \sqrt{2} = 4\sqrt{2}$ Look for factors that are square numbers.

  (b) $\sqrt{8} + \sqrt{18} = \sqrt{4} \times \sqrt{2} + \sqrt{9} \times \sqrt{2} = 2\sqrt{2} + 3\sqrt{2} = 5\sqrt{2}$

  (c) $\sqrt{\frac{72}{20}} = \frac{\sqrt{72}}{\sqrt{20}} = \frac{\sqrt{36}\sqrt{2}}{\sqrt{4}\sqrt{5}} = \frac{6\sqrt{2}}{2\sqrt{5}} = \frac{3\sqrt{2}}{\sqrt{5}}$

- To **rationalise** the denominator of a fraction of the form $\frac{a}{\sqrt{b}}$ multiply both the numerator (top) and the denominator (bottom) of the fraction by $\sqrt{b}$.

  Eg 3 Rationalise the denominator and simplify where possible: $\frac{3\sqrt{2}}{\sqrt{6}}$.

  $$\frac{3\sqrt{2}}{\sqrt{6}} = \frac{3\sqrt{2}}{\sqrt{6}} \times \frac{\sqrt{6}}{\sqrt{6}} = \frac{3\sqrt{2}\sqrt{6}}{6} = \frac{3\sqrt{2}\sqrt{2}\sqrt{3}}{6} = \frac{6\sqrt{3}}{6} = \sqrt{3}$$

- You should be able to use surds in calculations.

  To keep an answer exact it is necessary to keep numbers like $\sqrt{3}$ in surd form.

1 (a) Change $\frac{5}{7}$ into a decimal.

   (b) Find the fraction which is equal to $0.\dot{2}$.
       Give your answer in its simplest terms.

2 Simplify. (a) $2\sqrt{5} + 3\sqrt{5}$ (b) $\sqrt{3} \times \sqrt{3}$ (c) $\sqrt{2} \times \sqrt{3} \times \sqrt{6}$ (d) $\sqrt{\dfrac{9}{16}}$

3 (a) Write the number $0.4\dot{5}$ as a fraction in its simplest form.

   (b) Jim says, "When you multiply two irrational numbers together the answer is always an irrational number."
       Is Jim correct? Give a reason for your answer.

4 $x = 0.\dot{3}7\dot{8}$ (read as $x = 0.378378378\ldots$)

   (a) (i) Write down the value of $1000x$.

       (ii) Hence express x as a fraction in its simplest form.

   (b) y is an irrational number. Is $\dfrac{1 + y}{1 - y^2}$ a rational or an irrational number?
       Justify your answer.   AQA

5 Write $\sqrt{18}$ in the form of $a\sqrt{b}$ where a and b are prime numbers.

6 Simplify, leaving your answers where appropriate in surd form.

   (a) $5\sqrt{3} - \sqrt{3}$ (b) $\sqrt{3} \times 3\sqrt{3}$ (c) $\dfrac{\sqrt{27}}{3}$ (d) $\sqrt{12} \times \sqrt{75}$

7 Simplify fully.

   (a) $\sqrt{\dfrac{16}{25}}$ (b) $\sqrt{75}$ (c) $\sqrt{75} + \sqrt{12}$ (d) $\dfrac{6}{\sqrt{3}}$ AQA

8 (a) Express 20 as the product of its prime factors.

   (b) a and b are prime numbers.

       (i) $\sqrt{20}$ can be written in the form $a\sqrt{b}$. Calculate the values of a and b.

       (ii) $\dfrac{1}{\sqrt{20}}$ can be written in the form $\dfrac{b^x}{a}$ where x is a rational number.
            Calculate the value of x.   AQA

9 Simplify the expression $\sqrt{24}(\sqrt{50} - \sqrt{8})$.

10 (a) Write $\sqrt{45}$ in the form $a\sqrt{b}$ where a and b are prime numbers.

   (b) Find the value of $(\sqrt{45} - \sqrt{20})^2$.   AQA

11 You are given that $u = \sqrt{3} + 1$ and $v = \sqrt{3} - 1$.

   (a) $u + v = \sqrt{n}$. Find the value of n.   (b) Find the value of $\dfrac{uv}{u - v}$.   AQA

12 Express each of the following in its simplest form with a rational denominator.

   (a) $\dfrac{6}{\sqrt{3}}$ (b) $\dfrac{15}{2\sqrt{5}}$

13 (a) You are given that $2^x = 16^{-\frac{3}{4}} \times \sqrt{2}$. Find the value of x.

   (b) Express $\sqrt{8}(\sqrt{2} + 3)$ in the form $a + b\sqrt{c}$ where a and b are positive integers and
       c is a prime number.   AQA

Section Review - Number

Do not use a calculator for questions 1 to 26.

1 Use these numbers to answer the following questions: | 2 | 12 | 27 | 36 | 80 | 88 |
(a) Which number is a factor of 16?
(b) Which number is a multiple of 16?
(c) Which number is a prime number?
(d) Which number is a square number?
(e) Which number is a cube number?

2 (a) Work out (i) $5 - 0.26$, (ii) 0.2×0.4, (iii) $24 \div 0.3$.
(b) A turkey costs £2.40 per kilogram.
What is the cost of a turkey which weighs 6.5 kilograms?

3 (a) Write these fractions in ascending order: $\frac{1}{2}$ $\frac{2}{3}$ $\frac{3}{5}$ $\frac{5}{8}$ $\frac{3}{4}$

(b) Write down a fraction that lies halfway between $\frac{1}{5}$ and $\frac{1}{4}$.

(c) Work out $\frac{2}{5}$ of 12.

(d) Work out. (i) $2\frac{2}{3} + 1\frac{4}{5}$ (ii) $2\frac{2}{3} - 1\frac{4}{5}$ (iii) $2\frac{2}{3} \times 1\frac{4}{5}$

4 A plane flies from Paris to Guadeloupe, a distance of 4200 miles.
The plane has an average speed of 500 miles per hour.
How long does the plane take for the journey?
Give your answer in hours and minutes. *AQA*

5 A teacher drives 19 miles to school each morning and the same distance home in the evening.
He works 5 days each week. There are 39 weeks in a school year.
(a) **Estimate** the number of miles the teacher drives to and from school each year.
(b) The teacher drives approximately 12 000 miles each year altogether.
  (i) Approximately what percentage of his annual mileage is driving to and from school?
  (ii) The total cost of running his car is 42p a mile.
  Estimate the cost of his annual mileage. *AQA*

6 Four cabbages cost £2.88. How much will five cabbages cost? *AQA*

7 Two cucumbers and three lettuces cost £2.64.
A cucumber costs 25% more than a lettuce. Find the cost of a lettuce.

8 (a) Which is smaller 3^5 or 5^3? Show all your working.
(b) Work out. (i) $2^5 \times 3^2$ (ii) $30^3 \div 6^2$

9 A crowd of 54 000 people watch a carnival.
$\frac{2}{3}$ of the crowd are children and $\frac{3}{5}$ of the children are girls.
What percentage of the crowd are girls?

10 In a school the ratio of teachers to pupils is 2 : 35. There are 980 pupils.
How many teachers are there? *AQA*

11 (a) Conrad cycles 24 km in $1\frac{1}{2}$ hours. What is his cycling speed in kilometres per hour?
(b) Cas cycles 24 km at 15 km/h. She sets off at 0930. At what time does she finish?

12 (a) Given that $59 \times 347 = 20\ 473$, find the exact value of $\frac{20\ 473}{590}$.

(b) Use approximations to estimate the value of $\frac{97.3 \times 3049}{0.49}$. Show all your working.
(c) Work out $\sqrt{0.25} \times 0.1^2$.

13 Write these numbers in standard form.
    (a) 38 600 000   (b) 0.000 054

14 Jean uses 36 balls of wool to knit a black and white jumper.
The ratio of black wool to white wool is 7 : 2.
How many balls of black wool are used?

15 (a) Write 72 as a product of its prime factors.
    (b) Write 96 as a product of its prime factors.
    (c) Hence find   (i)   the least common multiple of 72 and 96,
                     (ii) the highest common factor of 72 and 96.

16 (a) Liam and Nora share 15% of £240 in the ratio 2 : 3.
          How much does Liam get?
    (b) What percentage of £240 does Nora get?

17 Felix and Jan are in cars travelling in opposite directions along a motorway.
At 1015 they are 30 km apart and travelling towards each other.
Felix is travelling at an average speed of 70 km/h.
If they pass each other at 1027, what is Jan's average speed?

18 Here are the first four terms of a sequence of numbers written in standard form.

$$6 \times 10^{-1}, \quad 6 \times 10^{-3}, \quad 6 \times 10^{-5}, \quad 6 \times 10^{-7}, \quad \ldots$$

  (a) Write down the 10th term of the sequence.
  (b) (i)   Write down the 1st term of the sequence as a decimal.
        (ii) Write down the **sum** of the first four terms as a decimal.
                                                      AQA

19 The ratio of male to female passengers on a bus is 3 : 5.
At the next stop 5 females get off and 2 males get on.
The ratio of male to female passengers is now 4 : 5.
How many male passengers are now on the bus?

20 The sale price of a pair of roller blades is £48.
What was the original price of the roller blades?

SALE
Sports Equipment
20% OFF

Sale
Price
£48

                                                       AQA

21 (a) Write 240 as the product of its prime factors.
    (b) Hence find the smallest whole number 240 must be multiplied by to give a perfect square.

22 It takes 15 minutes to fill a paddling pool at the rate of 12 litres per minute.
How long will it take to fill the pool at the rate of 20 litres per minute?

23 (a) Use approximations to estimate $\sqrt{\dfrac{40\,095}{(9.87^2)}}$

    (b) Work out $3 \times 10^5 \times 5 \times 10^{-2}$. Give your answer in standard form.
    (c) The value of a house has increased by 10% in one year. It is now valued at £55 000.
          What was the value of the house a year ago?
                                                      AQA

24 (a) What is the reciprocal of 2.5?
    (b) Write these numbers in descending order.

$$5^{-1} \qquad \left(\tfrac{1}{4}\right)^{\frac{1}{2}} \qquad 2^{-3} \qquad 3^{-2} \qquad \left(\tfrac{1}{2}\right)^2$$

    (c) Find the value of x when:
        (i) $2^4 \times 2^3 = 2^x$,   (ii) $3^{-2} \div 3^{-4} = 3^x$,   (iii) $216^{\frac{1}{3}} = 6^x$.
    (d) Work out $9^{-\frac{3}{2}}$. Give your answer as a fraction.

Section Review · · · · Section Review · · · · Section Review · · · ·

25 (a) (i) Simplify the following expression, leaving your answer in surd form. $\sqrt{27} + \sqrt{75}$

(ii) **Hence** simplify the expression $\dfrac{\sqrt{27} + \sqrt{75}}{\sqrt{12}}$.

(b) Calculate $64^{\frac{2}{3}}$.

(c) Calculate $81^{-\frac{1}{4}}$, giving your answer as a fraction.

26 (a) Write the number $0.\dot{2}\dot{1}$ as a fraction in its simplest form.

(b) A rational number, R, is given by the formula $R = (3 - \sqrt{2})^2 + x$.
Calculate a possible value of x.

27 Petrol costs 78.9 pence per litre. A car can travel 8.5 miles on one litre of petrol.
Calculate the cost of travelling 1000 miles in the car.
Give your answer to a suitable degree of accuracy.

AQA

28 (a) What is the reciprocal of 0.35? Give your answer correct to two decimal places.

(b) Work out $\dfrac{3.2^2}{\sqrt{0.04}}$.

29 A caravan is for sale at £7200.
Stuart buys the caravan on credit.
The credit terms are:

deposit 25% of sale price and 36 monthly payments of £175.

FOR SALE £7200

Express the extra amount paid for credit, compared with the cash price,
as a percentage of the cash price.

30 Karina says, "For some numbers the square root of the number is larger than the number itself."
For what numbers is this true?

31 At 20 miles per hour a bus journey takes 40 minutes.
A taxi does the same journey at 25 miles per hour.
How many minutes does the taxi take?

32 A puppy weighed 1.50 kg when it was born.
(a) Its weight increased by 28% during the first month.
Calculate the puppy's weight at the end of the first month.
(b) In the second month the puppy's weight increased by 15% of its **new** weight.
Calculate its weight at the end of the second month.
(c) The puppy's weight continues to increase by 15% each month.
How many months old is the puppy when it has doubled its birth weight?
Show your working.

AQA

33 Hannah wishes to insure the contents of her house for £7500.
She is quoted a premium of £1.30 for every £100 of contents.
(a) Find the premium which she is quoted.
(b) Hannah can receive a 20% discount for agreeing to pay the first £100 of any claim.
She can then receive a further 8% discount because her house is in a neighbourhood
watch area. Find the premium which Hannah actually pays.

AQA

34 £1 can buy 1.54 euros. £1 can buy 1.37 dollars.
How many dollars can be bought with 1000 euros?

35 $p = 3^2 \times 5 \times 7$ and $q = 2 \times 3 \times 5^2$. Find the least common multiple of p and q.

36 The population of China is 1.2×10^9. The area of China is 9.5×10^6 square kilometres.
What is the population density of China?

37   (a)   Place the following numbers in descending order. $\sqrt{6.9}$ 2.58 1.6^2 $2\frac{4}{7}$

     (b)   (i)   Calculate $\dfrac{612 \times 29.6}{81.3 - 18.9}$.

              Give your answer correct to 3 significant figures.

          (ii)   Use approximations to show that your answer is about right.

              Show all your working.

38   (a)   You are given the formula $k = \frac{3}{4} m^2$.

          Calculate the exact value of k, when $m = 4.8 \times 10^3$.   Give your answer in standard form.

     (b)   Calculate $\sqrt{\dfrac{5.2 \times 10^{-3}}{(0.039)^2}}$,   correct to two decimal places.

39   (a)   Jools invests £2000 at 6.5% per annum compound interest.

          Calculate the value of his investment at the end of 3 years.

     (b)   Jennifer gets 6% per annum on her investment.

          After one year the value of her investment is £1272.

          How much did she invest?

40   Last year Alf had a tax allowance of £4385 and paid £4332 in tax. The rates of tax were:

> 10p in the £ on the first £1520 of taxable income and
> 22p in the £ on all the remaining taxable income.

   How much did Alf earn last year?

41   In 1998 the average cost of printing 24 photographs was £3.42.

     (a)   In 1998 British tourists took 1.6×10^6 photographs.

          Calculate the cost of printing all these photographs.

     (b)   The price of printing photographs in 1998 was 5% less than in 1988.

          Calculate the cost of printing 24 photographs in 1988.   AQA

42   The world harvest of garlic is 20 000 tonnes every day.

     (a)   How much garlic is harvested in one year? Take a year to be 365 days.

          Give your answer in standard form.

   France produces 5.29×10^4 tonnes of garlic in a year.

     (b)   What percentage of the world total is produced by France?   AQA

43   Charlie is building a house. She estimates the cost of concrete for the base.

   When the lorry delivers the concrete, Charlie finds that she needs an extra 30% of concrete.

   Because she has bought extra concrete, she is given a 15% discount on the full price of all the concrete.

   What is the percentage increase in the cost of the concrete which she has bought, compared with her initial estimate?   AQA

44   (a)   Write $\sqrt{45}$ in the form $a\sqrt{b}$ where a and b are prime numbers.

     (b)   Write $\dfrac{5}{\sqrt{10}}$ in the form $\dfrac{\sqrt{a}}{b}$ where a and b are whole numbers.

     (c)   Express $\sqrt{32}$ as a power of 2.

     (d)   Simplify $4^0 + 4^{-1} + 4^{-2}$.

     (e)   Write $0.2\dot{7}$ as a fraction in its simplest form.

45   The sum of all the terms in a sequence is $0.\dot{0}\dot{4}$. Express this recurring decimal as a fraction.

                                                                      AQA

46   Calculate the value of $(5.8 \times 10^{-5})^{\frac{1}{3}}$.

   Give your answer in standard form correct to 2 significant figures.

Introduction to Algebra

What you need to know

- You should be able to write **algebraic expressions**.

  Eg 1 An expression for the cost of 6 pens at n pence each is $6n$ pence.

  Eg 2 An expression for 2 pence more than n pence is $n + 2$ pence.

- Be able to **simplify expressions** by collecting **like terms** together.

  Eg 3 (a) $2d + 3d = 5d$ (b) $3x + 2 - x + 4 = 2x + 6$ (c) $x + 2x + x^2 = 3x + x^2$

- Be able to **multiply expressions** together.

  Eg 4 (a) $2a \times a = 2a^2$ (b) $y \times y \times y = y^3$ (c) $3m \times 2n = 6mn$

- Recall and use these properties of powers:
  Powers of the same base are **added** when terms are **multiplied**.
  Powers of the same base are **subtracted** when terms are **divided**.
  Powers are **multiplied** when a power is raised to a power.

  $$a^m \times a^n = a^{m+n}$$
  $$a^m \div a^n = a^{m-n}$$
  $$(a^m)^n = a^{m \times n}$$

  Eg 5 (a) $x^3 \times x^2 = x^5$ (b) $a^5 \div a^2 = a^3$ (c) $6m^6 \div 2m^2 = 3m^4$ (d) $(2y^2)^3 = 8y^6$

- How to **multiply out brackets**.

  Eg 6 (a) $2(x - 5) = 2x - 10$ (b) $x(x - 5) = x^2 - 5x$ (c) $2m(m + 3) = 2m^2 + 6m$

- How to **factorise expressions**.

  Eg 7 (a) $3x - 6 = 3(x - 2)$ (b) $m^2 + 5m = m(m + 5)$ (c) $3a^2 - 6a = 3a(a - 2)$

Exercise 10

1. Godfrey is 5 years older than Mary.
   Write expressions for the following.
   (a) Godfrey's age when Mary is t years old.
   (b) Mary's age when Godfrey is x years old.

2. A cup of coffee costs x pence and a cup of tea costs y pence.
   Write an expression for the cost of 3 cups of coffee and 2 cups of tea.

3. Simplify (a) $m + 2m + 3m$,   (b) $2m + 2 - m$,   (c) $m \times m \times m$.

4. Write an expression, in terms of x,
   for the sum of the angles in this shape.

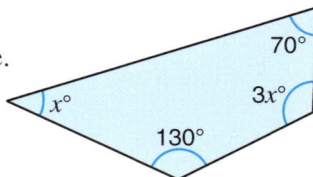

5. A muffin costs $d + 3$ pence.
   Write an expression for the cost of 5 muffins.

6. Which algebraic expressions are equivalent?

$2y$	y^2	$2(y + 1)$	$y \times y$	$y + y$
$2y + 2$	$2y + y$	$2y^2$	$3y$	$2y + 1$

AQA

7 (a) Simplify (i) $2x + 3 + x$, (ii) $2x + y - x + y$.
   (b) Multiply out (i) $2(x + 3)$, (ii) $x(x - 1)$.
   (c) Multiply out and simplify (i) $2(x - 1) - 3$, (ii) $7 + 3(2 + x)$.
   (d) Factorise (i) $2a - 6$, (ii) $x^2 + 2x$.

8 (a) Ken works x hours a week for £y per hour.
     Write an expression for the amount he earns each week.
   (b) Sue works 5 hours less than Ken each week and earns £y per hour.
     Write an expression for the amount Sue earns each week.

9 Lorna buys some 1st class stamps and some 2nd class stamps.
She buys 12 stamps altogether.
   (a) She buys x 1st class stamps.
     Write an expression for the number of 2nd class stamps she buys.
   (b) 2nd class stamps cost d pence.
     A 1st class stamp costs 5 pence more than a 2nd class stamp.
     Write an expression for the cost of a 1st class stamp.
   (c) Write an expression, in terms of x and d, for the amount Lorna has to pay for her 12 stamps.

10 (a) Simplify $8a + ab - a + 2b + 3ab$.
   (b) Expand and simplify $5(x + 3) - x$.
                                                   AQA

11 Multiply out and simplify $3(4x - 1) + 2x - 6$.
                                                          AQA

12 Simplify. (a) $y^3 \times y^2$ (b) $x^6 \div x^3$ (c) $\dfrac{z^4 \times z}{z^3}$ (d) $\dfrac{x^2 y}{xy^2}$

13 (a) Simplify (i) $2a^5 \times 3a^2$, (ii) $36a^6 \div 9a^2$.
   (b) Factorise completely $3x^2 - 9x$.
                                                AQA

14 Simplify. (a) $3a^5 \times 4a^2$ (b) $6a^4 \div 2a$ AQA

15 (a) Simplify $5 - 3(2n - 1)$.
   (b) Multiply out $(-3m) \times (-2m)$.
   (c) Factorise fully $8mn - 2m$.

16 Expand and simplify $3(2x + 3) - 2(5 + x)$.

17 (a) Simplify (i) $2a^3 \times 3a$, (ii) $6x^8 \div 3x^2$, (iii) $\dfrac{3m^2 \times 4n^6}{6mn^2}$, (iv) $4x^3y \times 5x^2y$.
   (b) Expand (i) $(3m^3)^2$, (ii) $(2a^2b)^3$.

18 (a) Expand the brackets. (i) $2x(x - 3y)$ (ii) $3a(3a + a^2)$
   (b) Factorise. (i) $4xy - 2y^2$ (ii) $3m^2 - 12m$
   (c) Simplify. $2x^2 - x(1 + x)$

19 Simplify fully $\dfrac{2a^3b^2 \times 6a^4b^2}{4ab^3}$.
                                                      AQA

20 (a) Multiply out $2x(2y - xy)$.
   (b) Factorise $6pq - 3pq^2$.
   (c) Simplify $21m^6 \div 7m^3$.

21 Simplify. (a) $\dfrac{6x^2z \times 2x^2y^2z}{3x^3y}$ (b) $\sqrt{\dfrac{1}{m^6}}$

22 Simplify $(3xy^2)^4$.
                                                            AQA

23 Simplify fully $\dfrac{3a^2}{bc} \times \dfrac{b^2}{6ac^2} \times \dfrac{2ac^2}{b}$.

Solving Equations ● ● ● ● ● ● ● ●

What you need to know

- The solution of an equation is the value of the unknown letter that fits the equation.

- You should be able to solve simple equations by **inspection**.

- Be able to solve simple problems by **working backwards**.

  Eg 1 I think of a number, multiply it by 3 and add 4. The answer is 19.

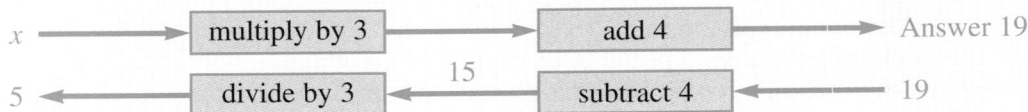

  x ⟶ | multiply by 3 | ⟶ | add 4 | ⟶ Answer 19

  5 ⟵ | divide by 3 | ⟵ 15 | subtract 4 | ⟵ 19

  The number I thought of is 5.

- Be able to use the **balance method** to solve equations.

  Eg 2 Solve these equations.

  (a) $d - 13 = -5$
  $d = -5 + 13$
  $d = 8$

  (b) $-4a = 20$
  $a = \frac{20}{-4}$
  $a = -5$

  (c) $5 - 4n = -1$
  $-4n = -6$
  $n = 1.5$

- Be able to solve equations with unknowns on both sides of the equals sign.

  Eg 3 Solve $3x + 1 = x + 7$.

  $3x = x + 6$
  $2x = 6$
  $x = 3$

- Be able to solve equations which include brackets.

  Eg 4 Solve $4(3 + 2x) = 5(x + 2)$.

  $12 + 8x = 5x + 10$
  $8x = 5x - 2$
  $3x = -2$
  $x = -\frac{2}{3}$

- Be able to solve equations which involve fractions.

  Eg 5 Solve $\frac{x}{2} + \frac{2x}{3} = 7$.

  $6 \times \frac{x}{2} + 6 \times \frac{2x}{3} = 6 \times 7$
  $3x + 4x = 42$
  $7x = 42$
  $x = 6$

  Eg 6 Solve $\frac{x - 1}{3} = \frac{x + 1}{4}$.

  $4(x - 1) = 3(x + 1)$
  $4x - 4 = 3x + 3$
  $4x = 3x + 7$
  $x = 7$

- You should be able to write, or form, equations using the information given in a problem.

Exercise **11**

1 Solve these equations. (a) $7 + x = 12$ (b) $5 - x = 3$ (c) $5x - 9 = 11$

2 (a) I think of a number, add 3, and then multiply by 2.
   The answer is 16. What is my number?
 (b) I think of a number, double it and then subtract 3.
   The answer is 5. What is my number?

3 Solve these equations.
 (a) $3x - 7 = 23$ (b) $5 + 7x = 47$ (c) $5(x - 2) = 20$ (d) $3x - 7 = x + 15$

4 The lengths of these rods are given, in centimetres, in terms of n.

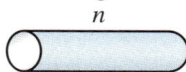

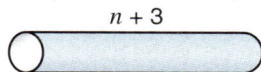

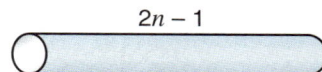

n $n + 3$ $2n - 1$

The total length of the rods is 30 cm.
By forming an equation, find the value of n.

5 Solve the equations. (a) $4x + 7 = 13$ (b) $3x + 7 = 3 - x$ AQA

6 Solve the equation $5x - 7 = 3x + 5$.   AQA

7 Solve these equations.
(a) $7x + 4 = 60$ (b) $3x - 7 = -4$ (c) $2(x + 3) = -2$ (d) $3x - 4 = 1 + x$

8 Solve the equations (a) $2x + 3 = 15$,   (b) $3(x - 1) = 6$,   (c) $x + 2 = 5 - x$.   AQA

9 A small paving slab weighs x kilograms.
A large paving slab weighs $(2x + 3)$ kilograms.
(a) Write an expression, in terms of x, for the total weight of 16 small slabs and 4 large slabs. Give your answer in its simplest form.

The total weight of the slabs is 132 kilograms.
(b) Write down an equation and find the value of x.   AQA

10 Solve these equations.
(a) $8x = 20$ (b) $3n - 7 = n + 5$ (c) $2m - 7 = -10$ (d) $3(2x + 3) = 2 - x$

11 Solve these equations.
(a) $\frac{x}{3} = -7$ (b) $2(x - 1) = 3$ (c) $5 - 2x = 3x + 2$ (d) $\frac{1}{4}x + 5 = 2$

12 Solve the equations (a) $\frac{x - 7}{5} = 2$,   (b) $5x + 6 = 24 - 10x$.   AQA

13 Solve these equations.
(a) $\frac{x + 5}{2} = 3$ (b) $\frac{1 - 2x}{3} = 2$ (c) $\frac{3}{2} = \frac{3x}{5}$ (d) $\frac{x}{2} + \frac{x}{3} = 5$

14 The diagram shows a rectangle and a right-angled triangle.

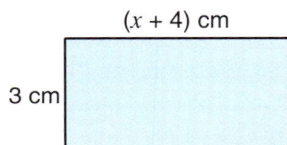

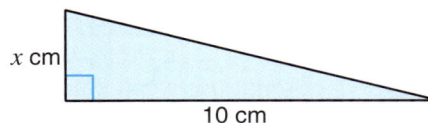

$(x + 4)$ cm

3 cm

x cm

10 cm

Not drawn accurately

The area of the rectangle is equal to the area of the triangle.
By forming an equation work out the value of x.   AQA

15 Solve these equations.
(a) $2(x - 3) + 3(x + 1) = 2$ (b) $3(2 + 3a) = 5(a - 2)$ (c) $x - 3(x + 1) = 2(5 - 2x)$

16 Solve the equations (a) $\frac{x - 3}{4} = 1 - x$,   (b) $\frac{x - 3}{2} = \frac{2x + 1}{3}$.

17 Solve the equation $\frac{1}{2}(3x + 1) = \frac{1}{4}(2x + 1)$.   AQA

18 Solve the equation $\frac{x - 1}{3} + \frac{x + 1}{2} = \frac{5}{6}$.

19 Solve the equation $\frac{3x - 1}{2} - \frac{2x - 1}{3} = 6$.   AQA

Formulae

What you need to know

- An **expression** is just an answer using letters and numbers.
  A **formula** is an algebraic rule. It always has an equals sign.

- You should be able to **write simple formulae**.

  Eg 1 A packet of crisps weighs 25 grams.
  Write a formula for the total weight,
  W grams, of n packets of crisps.
  $$W = 25n$$

  Eg 2 Start with t, add 5 and then multiply
  by 3. The result is p.
  Write a formula for p in terms of t.
  $$p = 3(t + 5)$$

- Be able to **substitute** values into given expressions and formulae.

  Eg 3 (a) $A = pq - r$
  Find the value
  of A when $p = 2$,
  $q = -2$ and $r = 3$.

  $A = pq - r$
  $= 2 \times (-2) - 3$
  $= -4 - 3$
  $= -7$

  (b) $M = 2n^2$
  Find the value
  of M when $n = 3$.

  $M = 2n^2$
  $= 2 \times 3^2$
  $= 2 \times 9$
  $= 18$

  (c) Find the value of $\dfrac{b^2c}{d}$
  when $b = \frac{1}{2}$, $c = 4.8$
  and $d = -3$.

  $\dfrac{b^2c}{d} = \dfrac{\left(\frac{1}{2}\right)^2 \times 4.8}{-3}$
  $= \dfrac{\frac{1}{4} \times 4.8}{-3} = \dfrac{1.2}{-3}$
  $= -0.4$

- Be able to **rearrange** a given formula to make another letter (variable) the subject.

  Eg 4 $y = 2x + a$

  Make x the subject of the formula.

  $y = 2x + a$
  $y - a = 2x$
  $\dfrac{y - a}{2} = x$
  So, $x = \dfrac{y - a}{2}$

  Eg 5 $T = ab^2$
  Rearrange the formula to give b
  in terms of T and a.

  $T = ab^2$
  $\dfrac{T}{a} = b^2$
  $b = \pm \sqrt{\dfrac{T}{a}}$

Exercise 12   Do not use a calculator for questions 1 to 12.

1 Given that $m = -3$ and $n = 5$, find the value of
   (a) $m + n$,   (b) $m - n$,   (c) $n - m$,   (d) mn.

2 If $p = 4$ and $q = -5$ find the value of   (a) $3pq$,   (b) $p^2 + 2q$.

3 $L = 5(p + q)$. Find the value of L when $p = 2$ and $q = -0.4$.

4 $A = b - cd$. Find the value of A when $b = -3$, $c = 2$ and $d = 4$.

5 What is the value of $10y^2$ when $y = 3$?

6 What is the value of $3x^3$ when $x = 2$?

7 $T = ab^2$. Find the value of T when $a = 4$ and $b = -5$.

8 $S = pq - 2r^2$. Find the value of S when $p = -5$, $q = -2$ and $r = -3$.

9 $T = \frac{uv}{w}$.   Find the value of T when $u = 3$, $v = -2$ and $w = \frac{1}{2}$.

10 $M = \sqrt{\frac{a}{b}}$.   Find the value of M when $a = 8$ and $b = \frac{1}{2}$.

11   Each year the High School has a disco for Year 7.
A teacher works out the number of cans of drink to buy,

using this rule: | 3 cans for every 2 tickets sold, plus 20 spare cans.

  (a)   This year, 160 tickets have been sold. How many cans will he buy?
  (b)   Using N for the number of cans and T for the number of tickets,
       write down the teacher's formula for N in terms of T.
  (c)   Last year, he bought 215 cans. How many tickets were sold last year?

AQA

12   Given that $m = \frac{1}{2}$, $p = \frac{3}{4}$, $t = -2$,   calculate   (a) $mp + t$ (b) $\frac{(m + p)}{t}$

AQA

13   A formula is given as $c = 3t - 5$.   Rearrange the formula to give t in terms of c.

14   A formula for calculating distance is $d = \frac{(u + v)t}{2}$.

  (a)   Find the value of d when $u = 9.4$, $v = 6.3$ and $t = 8$.
  (b)   Make t the subject of the formula.
  (c)   Find the value of t when $d = 60$, $u = 5.8$ and $v = 10.2$

AQA

15   You are given the formula $v = u + at$.

  (a)   Find v when $u = 17$, $a = -8$ and $t = \frac{3}{5}$.
  (b)   Rearrange the formula to give a in terms of v, u and t.

16   Make r the subject of the formula $p = \frac{gr}{s}$.

17   (a)   If $x = -4$,   calculate the value of $3x^2$.
  (b)   If $a = \frac{2}{3}$ and $b = \frac{2}{5}$,   calculate the exact value of $a^2\left(1 - \frac{1}{b}\right)$.

AQA

18   Scientists use the formula $\frac{1}{f} = \frac{1}{u} + \frac{1}{v}$ to calculate the focal length, f, of a lens.

The lengths u, v and f are all measured in centimetres.
Calculate f when $u = 2.4$ and $v = -3.2$.

AQA

19   You are given the formula $V = \sqrt{PR}$.
Rearrange the formula to give P in terms of V and R.

AQA

20 s is given by the formula $s = ut + \frac{1}{2}at^2$.
Find the value of s when $u = 2.8$, $t = 2$ and $a = -1.7$.

AQA

21   You are given the formula $g = \frac{3}{5}h^2$.
  (a)   Find the value of g when $h = 2.5 \times 10^3$.
  (b)   Rearrange the formula to give h in terms of g.

22   Rearrange the formula $p = \frac{q}{5 - q}$ to make q the subject.

23   Make v the subject of the formula $w = \frac{uv}{u + v}$.

24 $n = \frac{3 + m}{m - 5}$.   Rearrange the formula to give m in terms of n.

Direct and Inverse Proportion

What you need to know

- **Direct proportion**
  If x and y are quantities such that $y : x^n$ is always constant, then y varies **directly** with x^n.
  This can be expressed:
  - in **words**: y is **proportional** to x^n,
  - in **symbols**: $y \propto x^n$ (where $\propto$ means "is proportional to"),
  - as an **equation**: $y = kx^n$ (where k is the **constant of proportionality**).

  Eg 1 The cost, £C, of tiling a floor is proportional to the area of the floor, $a\,\text{m}^2$.
  It costs £60 to tile a floor of area $2\,\text{m}^2$.
  (a) Find the formula connecting C and a.
  (b) A floor costs £150 to be tiled. What is the area of the floor?

  (a) $C = ka$
  When $C = 60$, $a = 2$.
  $60 = 2 \times k$
  $k = 30$
  $C = 30a$

  (b) $C = 30a$
  When $C = 150$.
  $150 = 30a$
  $a = 5$
  Area of floor $= 5\,\text{m}^2$

  > Constant of proportionality, k.
  > This can be calculated when corresponding values of C and a are known.

- **Inverse proportion**
  If x and y are quantities such that $y : \dfrac{1}{x^n}$ is always constant, then y varies **inversely** with x^n.
  This can be expressed:
  - in **words**: y is **inversely proportional** to x^n,
  - in **symbols**: $y \propto \dfrac{1}{x^n}$,
  - as an **equation**: $y = \dfrac{k}{x^n}$ or $x^n y = k$.

  Eg 2 y is inversely proportional to x^2. When $x = 3$, $y = 4$.
  (a) Find the equation connecting y and x. (b) Find the value of y when $x = 2.4$.

  (a) $y = \dfrac{k}{x^2}$
  When $x = 3$, $y = 4$.
  $4 = \dfrac{k}{3^2}$ so $k = 36$
  $y = \dfrac{36}{x^2}$

  (b) $y = \dfrac{36}{x^2}$
  When $x = 2.4$.
  $y = \dfrac{36}{(2.4)^2}$
  $y = 6.25$

- The general form of a proportional relationship is $y \propto x^n$ or $y = kx^n$.

  Direct proportion, $y = kx^n$, $n > 0$

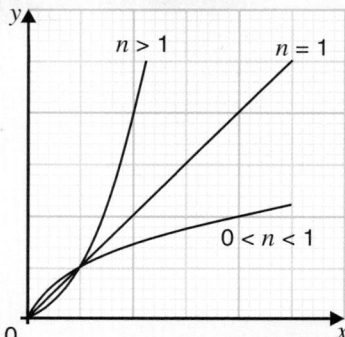

  Inverse proportion, $y = kx^n$, $n < 0$

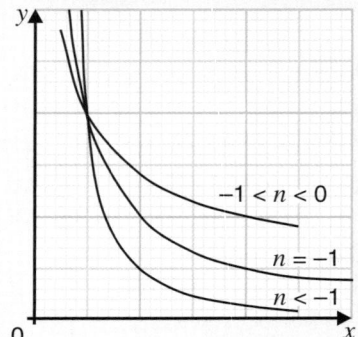

  When:
  $n = 1$: y increases at a constant rate.
  $0 < n < 1$: y increases at a rate that decreases.
  $n > 1$: y increases at a rate that increases.

  When:
  $n = -1$: the graph is symmetrical about the line $y = x$.

1 The table shows values of m and n.

Bay or sweets

Cake money

m	0.6	9	16.5
n	0.4	6	11

(a) Show that m is directly proportional to n.
(b) Find the value of (i) m when $n = 1.8$,
(ii) n when $m = 12.6$.

2 The table shows values of the variables x and y, where y is inversely proportional to x.

x	0.4	2.5	100
y	5.0	8	0.02

(a) Find an equation expressing y in terms of x.
(b) Copy and complete the table.

AQA

3 y is proportional to x^3.
When $x = 3$, $y = 54$.
Find the value of x when $y = 250$.

4 R is inversely proportional to the square of P.
When $R = 36$, $P = 2$.
Find R when $P = 6$.

AQA

5 m is proportional to the square root of n.
$m = 6$ when $n = 81$.
(a) Find the equation connecting m and n.
(b) Calculate (i) the value of m when $n = 36$,
(ii) the value of n when $m = 10$.

6 An artist hand-paints circular plates of different sizes.
The price, £C, of a hand-painted plate is proportional to the square of the radius, r cm,
of the plate.
The price of a plate of radius 6 cm is £9.
Calculate the price of a plate of radius 8 cm.

7 The wavelength, w metres, of radio waves is inversely proportional to the frequency, f kHz,
of the waves.
(a) A radio wavelength of 1000 metres has a frequency of 300 kHz.
The frequency is doubled to 600 kHz. What is the new wavelength?
(b) Calculate the frequency when the wavelength is 842 metres.
(c) Radio NEAB has a frequency in kHz which is numerically equal to its wavelength
in metres.
Calculate the wavelength of Radio NEAB.

AQA

8 y is proportional to x^n.
Sketch a graph of y against x when $x \geqslant 0$ and (a) $n = 2$, (b) $n = -2$.

9 You are given that $y = 6x^n$ and that $y = 3$ when $x = 8$.
Find the value of n.

10 y is proportional to x^3.
(a) When $x = 4$, $y = 80$. Find the value of y when $x = 8$.

Also, x is inversely proportional to the square root of z.
(b) When $y = 10$, $z = 16$. Find the value of z when $x = 4$.

AQA

Sequences ● ● ● ● ● ● ● ● ● ● ● ● ●

What you need to know

- A **sequence** is a list of numbers made according to some rule.
  The numbers in a sequence are called **terms**.

- You should be able to draw and continue number sequences represented by patterns of shapes.

- Be able to continue a sequence by following a given rule.

  Eg 1 The sequence 2, 7, 22, … is made using the rule:

  > multiply the last number by 3, then add 1.

  The next term in the sequence $= (22 \times 3) + 1 = 66 + 1 = 67$

- Be able to find a rule, and then use it, to continue a sequence.

  > **To continue a sequence:**
  > 1. Work out the rule to get from one term to the next.
  > 2. Apply the same rule to find further terms in the sequence.

  Eg 2 Describe the rule used to make the following sequences.
  Then use the rule to find the next term of each sequence.

(a) 5, 8, 11, 14, …	(b) 2, 4, 8, 16, …	(c) 1, 1, 2, 3, 5, 8, …
Rule:	Rule:	Rule:
add 3 to last term	multiply last term by 2	add the last two terms
Next term: 17	Next term: 32	Next term: 13

  > | **Special sequences** | **Square numbers:** | 1, 4, 9, 16, 25, … |
  > |---|---|---|
  > | | **Triangular numbers:** | 1, 3, 6, 10, 15, … |

- Find an expression for the nth term of a **linear sequence**.

  > A number sequence which increases (or decreases) by the same amount
  > from one term to the next is called a **linear sequence**.
  > The sequence 2, 8, 14, 20, 26, …   has a **common difference** of 6.

  Eg 3 Find the nth term of the sequence: 3, 5, 7, 9, …
  The sequence is linear, common difference $= 2$.
  To find the nth term add one to the multiples of 2.
  So, the nth term is $2n + 1$.

- Find an expression for the nth term of a **quadratic sequence**.

  Eg 4 Find the nth term of the sequence: 4, 7, 12, 19, …
  The sequence is not linear, because the differences between terms is increasing.
  Compare the sequence with the sequence of square numbers: 1, 4, 9, 16, …
  To find the nth term add 3 to the square numbers.
  So, the nth term is $n^2 + 3$.

Exercise **14**

1 What is the next number in each of these sequences?
  (a) 1, 2, 5, 10, ….   (b) 1, 3, 9, 27, ….   (c) 1, $\frac{1}{2}$, $\frac{1}{4}$, $\frac{1}{8}$, ….

2 Ahmed writes down the first four numbers of a sequence: 10,   8,   4,   −2,   …
(a)   What is the next number in this sequence?   (b)   Explain how you found your answer.

AQA

3 Look at this sequence of numbers.   2,   5,   8,   11,   ….
(a)   What is the next number in the sequence?
(b)   Is 30 a number in this sequence? Give a reason for your answer.

4 The rule for a sequence is: | Add the last two numbers and divide by 2. |

Write down the next three terms when the sequence begins: 3,   7,   …

5 A sequence begins: 1,   −2,   …
The next number in the sequence is found by using the rule:

   | ADD THE PREVIOUS TWO NUMBERS AND MULTIPLY BY TWO |

Use the rule to find the next **two** numbers in the sequence.

AQA

6 A sequence begins: 1,   6,   10,   8,   ….
The rule to continue the sequence is: **double the difference between the last two numbers**.
Ravi says if you continue the sequence it will end in 0. Is he correct? Explain your answer.

7 The first three patterns in a sequence are shown.
(a)   How many squares are in pattern 20?
Explain how you found your answer.
(b)   Write an expression for the number of
squares in the n th pattern.

Pattern 1   **Pattern 2**   **Pattern 3**

8 A sequence is given by   5,   12,   19,   26,   33,   …
(a)   What is the next term in this sequence? Explain how you got your answer.
(b)   Write down the n th term for the sequence.

AQA

9 Find the n th term of the following sequences.
(a)   5,   7,   9,   11,   …   (b)   1,   5,   9,   13,   …

10 (a)   Write down the first **three** terms of the sequence whose n th term is given by $n^2 + 4$.
(b)   Will the number 106 be in this sequence? Explain your answer.

AQA

11 Give the n th term of the following sequences.
(a)   1,   4,   9,   16,   25,   36,   …   (b)   2,   5,   10,   17,   26,   37,   …

AQA

12 The n th term of a sequence is $\dfrac{5n}{4n + 5}$.
(a)   Write down the first two terms of this sequence.
(b)   Which term of the sequence has the value 1?

AQA

13 Find, in terms of n, the n th term of the sequence: $\dfrac{1}{3}$, $\dfrac{2}{5}$, $\dfrac{3}{7}$, $\dfrac{4}{9}$, $\dfrac{5}{11}$,   …

14 (a)   Regular pentagons are used to form patterns, as shown.

Pattern 1   **Pattern 2**   **Pattern 3**   **Pattern 4**
5 sides   **8 sides**   **11 sides**   **14 sides**

Write, in terms of n, the number of sides in Pattern n.
(b)   A number pattern begins: 0,   3,   8,   15,   24,   …
Write, in terms of n, the n th term in this pattern.

AQA

15 Find the n th term of the sequence: 2,   6,   12,   20,   30,   …

Straight Line Graphs

What you need to know

- **Coordinates** (involving positive and negative numbers) are used to describe the position of a point on a graph.

- The x axis is the line $y = 0$.   The y axis is the line $x = 0$.

- The **gradient** of a line can be found by drawing a right-angled triangle.

$$\text{Gradient} = \frac{\text{distance up}}{\text{distance along}}$$

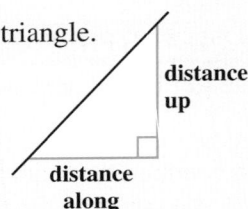

Gradients can be positive, zero or negative.

- You should be able to find the equation for a given line.

In general, the equation of any straight line can be written in the form

$$y = mx + c$$

where m is the **gradient** of the line
and c is the **y-intercept**.

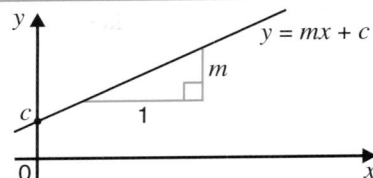

Eg 1 Find the equation of the line shown on this graph.

Gradient of line $= \dfrac{\text{distance up}}{\text{distance along}} = \dfrac{2}{1} = 2$

The graph crosses the y axis at the point $(0, -3)$,
so the y-intercept is -3.
The equation of the line is $y = 2x - 3$.

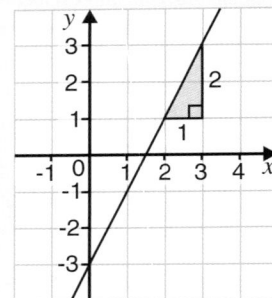

- The points where a line crosses the axes can be found:
  by reading the coordinates from a graph,
  by substituting $x = 0$ and $y = 0$ into the equation of the line.

Eg 2 The diagram shows a sketch of the line $2y = x + 3$.
Find the coordinates of the points P and Q.

When $x = 0$, $2y = 0 + 3$, $2y = 3$, $y = 1\frac{1}{2}$.
When $y = 0$, $0 = x + 3$, $x = -3$.
The points are $P\left(0, 1\frac{1}{2}\right)$ and $Q(-3, 0)$.

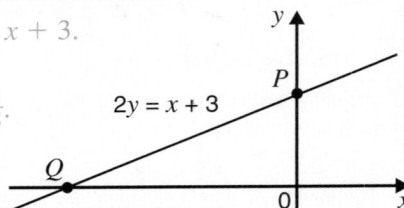

- You should be able to find the gradient of a line which is perpendicular to a given line.

If two lines are perpendicular to each other,
the product of their gradients $= -1$.

This can be written as: $m_{AB} \times m_{CD} = -1$

where m_{AB} is the gradient of the line AB,
and m_{CD} is the gradient of the line CD.

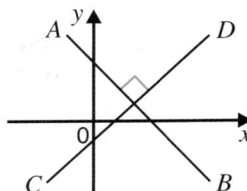

$$m_{AB} = \frac{-1}{m_{CD}}$$

Eg 3 Write down the gradient of the line which is perpendicular to the line with equation $y = -3x + 4$.
The gradient of the line $y = -3x + 4$ is -3.
The gradient of the line which is perpendicular to this line is $-1 \div (-3) = \frac{1}{3}$.

- Equations of the form $px + qy = r$ can be **rearranged** to the form $y = mx + c$.

Eg 4 The graph of a straight line is given by the equation $4y - 3x = 8$.
Write this equation in the form $y = mx + c$.
$4y - 3x = 8$
$4y = 3x + 8$
$y = \frac{3}{4}x + 2$

> The line has gradient $\frac{3}{4}$ and y-intercept 2.

- You should be able to solve equations and problems involving straight line graphs.

Exercise 15

1 (a) Copy and complete the table of values for $y = 1 - 2x$.
(b) Draw the line $y = 1 - 2x$ for values of x from -3 to 3.
(c) Use your graph to find the value of y when $x = -1.5$.

x	-3	0	3
y		1	

2 (a) On the same axes, draw the graphs of $y = -2$, $y = x$ and $x + y = 5$.
(b) Which of these lines has a negative gradient?

3 The diagram shows a sketch of the line $2y = 6 - x$.
(a) Find the coordinates of the points P and Q.
(b) The line $2y = 6 - x$ goes through $R(-5, m)$.
What is the value of m?

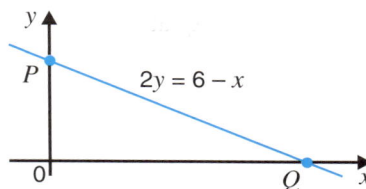

4 Points A, B and C are shown on the grid.
(a) Write down the equation of the line AB.
(b) (i) Use the grid to work out the gradient of the line CB.
(ii) Write down the equation of the line CB.

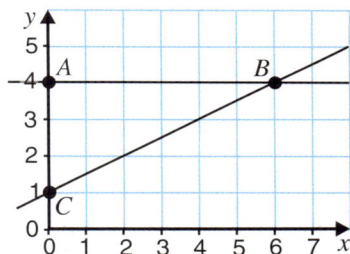

AQA

5 Match these equations to their graphs.

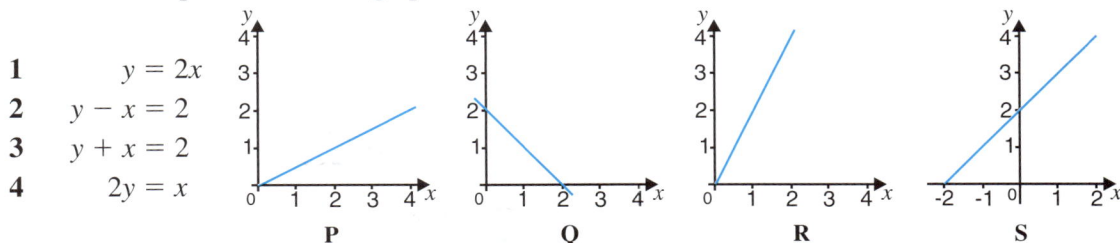

1 $y = 2x$
2 $y - x = 2$
3 $y + x = 2$
4 $2y = x$

P   Q   R   S

6 (a) Copy and complete the table of values for $2y = 3x - 6$.
(b) Draw the graph of $2y = 3x - 6$ for values of x from -2 to 4.
(c) What is the gradient of the line $2y = 3x - 6$?
(d) Use your graph to find the value of x when $y = 1.5$.

x	-2	0	4
y		-3	

7 The graph of a straight line is shown.
What is the equation of the line?

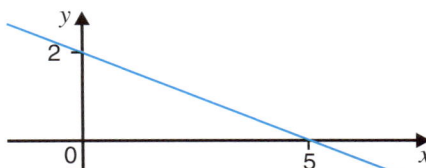

AQA

8 The table shows the largest quantity of salt, w grams, which can be dissolved in a beaker of water at temperature $t°C$.

$t°C$	10	20	25	30	40	50	60
w grams	54	58	60	62	66	70	74

(a) Draw a graph to illustrate this information.
(b) Use your graph to find
  (i) the lowest temperature at which 63 g of salt will dissolve in the water,
  (ii) the largest amount of salt that will dissolve in the water at 44°C.
(c) (i) The equation of the graph is of the form $w = at + b$.
    Use your graph to estimate the values of the constants a and b.
  (ii) Use the equation to calculate the largest amount of salt which will dissolve in the water at 95°C.

AQA

9 The total monthly bill for Ann's mobile phone is made up of two parts: the fixed network charge and the cost of calls.
The graph shows the monthly bill, £B, for calls up to a total of 60 minutes.

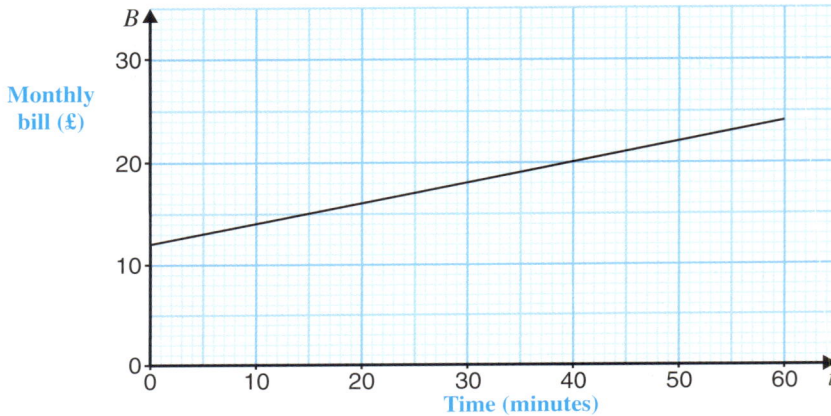

Find the equation of the line.

AQA

10 The equation of a line is $5y - 2x = 10$.
(a) Write this equation in the form $y = mx + c$.
(b) Write down the equation of the line, parallel to $5y - 2x = 10$, which passes through the point $(0, -1)$.

11 Show that the lines $5y = x + 4$ and $y = 6 - 5x$ are perpendicular to each other.

12 The diagram shows the graph of $2y = x + 4$.

Find the equation of the line through B which is perpendicular to the line $2y = x + 4$.

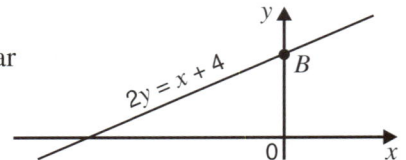

13 In the diagram, the lines AB and CD are perpendicular to each other and intersect at $(1, 3)$.
The line AB goes through $(0, 6)$.
The line CD goes through P.

Find the coordinates of P.

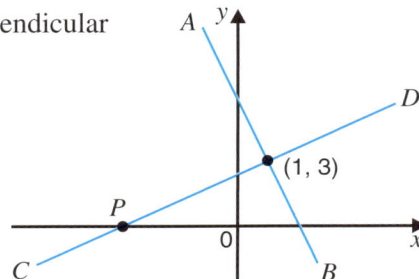

Using Graphs

What you need to know

- A **gradient** measures the **rate of change** of one quantity with respect to another.
  A **positive** gradient represents a **rate of increase**.
  A **negative** gradient represents a **rate of decrease**.

- The gradient of a **distance-time graph** gives the speed.

  > **Speed** is the rate of change of distance with respect to time.
  > When the distance-time graph is **linear** the **speed is constant**.
  > When the distance-time graph is **horizontal** the **speed is zero**.

  Eg 1 The graph shows a car journey.
  - (a) Between what times does the car travel fastest? Explain your answer.
  - (b) What is the speed of the car during this part of the journey?

  - (a) 1200 to 1230. Steepest gradient.

  - (b) $\text{Speed} = \dfrac{\text{Distance}}{\text{Time}} = \dfrac{20\,\text{km}}{\frac{1}{2}\,\text{hour}} = 40\,\text{km/h}$

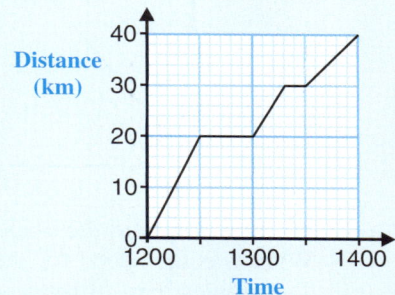

- The gradient of a **speed-time graph** gives the acceleration.

  > **Acceleration** is the rate of change of speed with respect to time.
  > When the speed-time graph is **linear** the **acceleration is constant**.
  > When the speed-time graph is **horizontal** the **speed is constant** and the **acceleration is zero**.

- The **area** enclosed by the graph on a speed-time graph represents the **distance** travelled.

  Eg 2 The graph shows the speed of a car against time between two roundabouts.
  - (a) Calculate the acceleration of the car.
  - (b) Calculate the distance travelled.

  - (a) $\text{Acceleration} = \dfrac{\text{Speed}}{\text{Time}} = \dfrac{10\,\text{m/s}}{15\,\text{s}} = 0.67\,\text{m/s}^2$

  - (b) Distance travelled $= \frac{1}{2}(15 + 35) \times 10 = 250$ metres

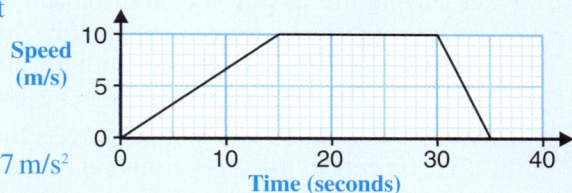

- You should be able to draw and interpret graphs which represent real-life situations.

Exercise 16

1. Water is poured into some containers at a constant rate.
   Copy the axes given and sketch the graph of the depth of the water against time for each container as it is filled.

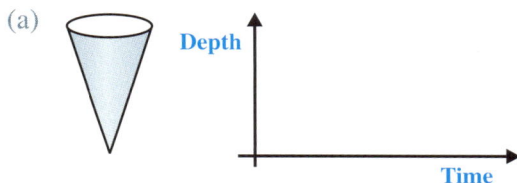

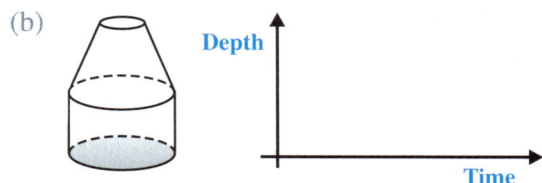

   (a) **Depth** / **Time**

   (b) **Depth** / **Time**

2 The graph shows the journey of a group of walkers.

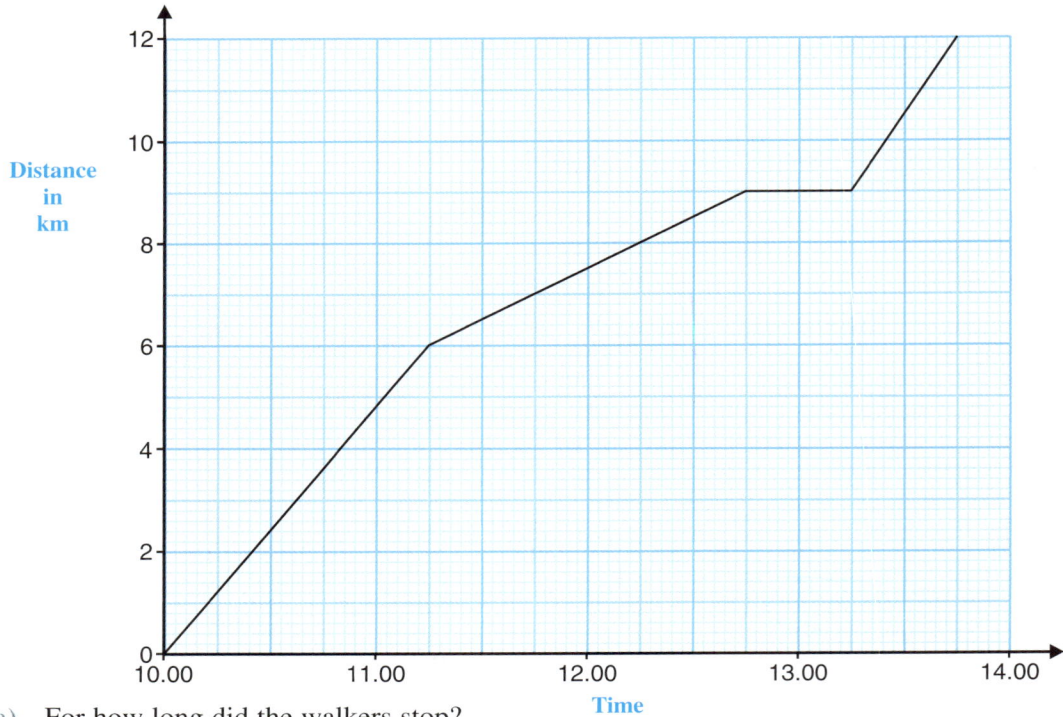

(a) For how long did the walkers stop?
(b) What was the speed for the first part of the journey?
(c) The slowest part of the journey was across boggy ground.
How far did they walk across the boggy ground?
(d) What was the average speed for the whole journey?   AQA

3 A coach leaves Gateshead at 0830 to travel to London.
It completes the first 270 km of the journey at 90 km/hour before stopping at a service station.
The coach stops at the service station for 30 minutes.
After leaving the service station the coach travels a further 180 km, arriving in London at 1500.
(a) Draw a distance-time graph for the coach journey.
Use a scale of 2 cm for 1 hour on the horizontal axis and 1 cm for 50 km on the vertical axis.
(b) What is the average speed of the coach from the service station to London?

Travis leaves London at 1000 and travels by car to Gateshead on the same route.
(c) Travis gets to the service station as the coach is about to leave.
At what average speed is Travis driving?

4 This diagram shows the speed-time graph of a
local train on a journey between station *A*
and station *B*.

(a) How far is it between station *A* and station *B*?

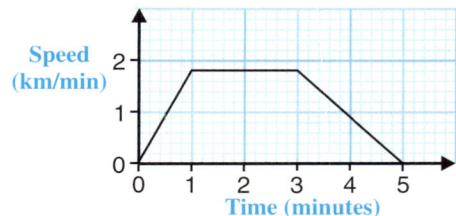

This diagram shows the speed-time graph of an
express train from the start of its journey at
station *A* as it travels beyond station *B*.

(b) How long does it take the express train
to travel between station *A* and station *B*?

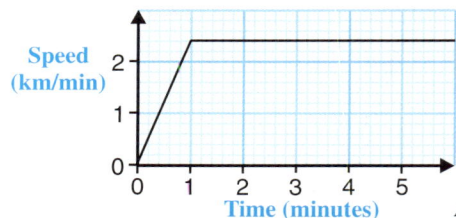

AQA

More or Less

What you need to know

- **Inequalities** can be described using words or numbers and symbols.

Sign	Meaning
$<$	is less than
$\leqslant$	is less than or equal to

Sign	Meaning
$>$	is greater than
$\geqslant$	is greater than or equal to

- Inequalities can be shown on a **number line**.

  Eg 1 This diagram shows the inequality: $-2 < x \leqslant 3$

  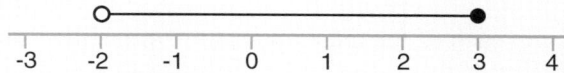

  > The circle is: **filled** if the inequality is **included** (i.e. $\leqslant$ or $\geqslant$),
  > **not filled** if the inequality is **not included** (i.e. $<$ or $>$).

- **Solving inequalities** means finding the values of x which make the inequality true.

  > The same rules for equations can be applied to inequalities, with one exception:
  > When you **multiply** (or **divide**) both sides of an inequality by a negative number
  > the inequality is reversed. For example, if $-3x < 6$ then $x > -2$.

  Eg 2 Solve these inequalities.

  (a) $7a \geqslant a + 9$

  $\quad 6a \geqslant 9$

  $\quad a \geqslant 1.5$

  (b) $-3x < 6$

  $\quad x > -2$

  > Divide both sides by -3.
  > Because we are dividing by a negative number the inequality is reversed.

  Eg 3 Find the integer values of n for which $\;-1 \leqslant 2n + 3 < 7$.

  $\quad -1 \leqslant 2n + 3 < 7$

  $\quad -4 \leqslant 2n < 4$

  $\quad -2 \leqslant n < 2$

  Integer values which satisfy the inequality $\;-1 \leqslant 2n + 3 < 7\;$ are: $\;-2, -1, 0, 1$

- Inequalities can be shown on a graph. A line divides the graph into two **regions**.

  > **To show an inequality on a graph:** Replace the inequality by '$=$' and draw the line.
  > For $>$ and $<$ the line is **broken**. For $\geqslant$ and $\leqslant$ the line is **solid**.
  > Test a point on each side of the line to see whether its coordinates satisfy the inequality.
  > Label the required region.

Eg 4 Show the region which satisfies these inequalities:

$$y < 3, \quad 1 < x < 4 \quad \text{and} \quad 2y > x.$$

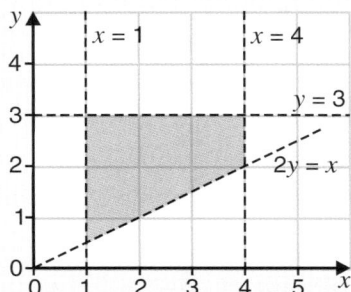

Eg 5 Use inequalities to describe the shaded region in this diagram.

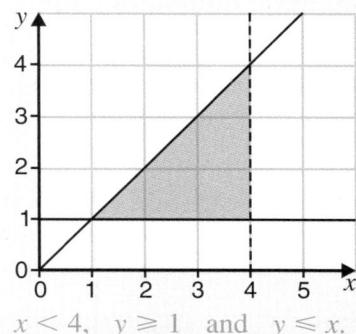

$x < 4, \quad y \geqslant 1 \quad \text{and} \quad y \leqslant x.$

1 Solve these inequalities.
   (a) $5x > 15$ (b) $x + 3 \geqslant 1$ (c) $2x \leqslant 6 - x$ (d) $3 - 2x > 7$

2 Draw number lines to show each of these inequalities.
   (a) $x \geqslant -2$ (b) $\frac{x}{3} < -1$ (c) $-1 < x \leqslant 3$ (d) $x \leqslant -1$ **and** $x > 3$

3 List the values of n, where n is an integer such that:
   (a) $-2 \leqslant 2n < 6$ (b) $-3 < n - 3 \leqslant -1$ (c) $-5 \leqslant 2n - 3 < 1$

4 Solve the inequalities.   (a) $2x - 5 > x + 2$ (b) $-9 < 5x + 1 \leqslant 6$

5 Solve the inequality $x + 20 < 12 - 3x$.   AQA

6 Solve the inequality $3(x - 2) < x + 7$.   AQA

7 Match each of the inequalities to its **unshaded** region.

   1 $x + y < 2$
   2 $y > 2$
   3 $y > x$
   4 $x < 2$

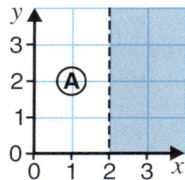

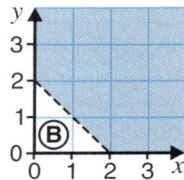

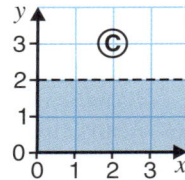

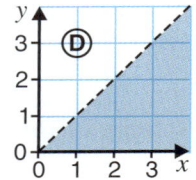

8 Draw and label axes for both x and y from 0 to 5.
   (a)   On your diagram draw and label the lines $x = 1$ and $x + y = 4$.
   (b)   Show clearly on the diagram the single region that is satisfied by all of these inequalities.
         $y \geqslant 0$ $x \geqslant 1$ $x + y \leqslant 4$.   Label this region R.   AQA

9 (a)   Draw and label axes for x from -1 to 6 and for y from -2 to 6.
            On your diagram draw and label the following lines. $y = 2x$ and $x + y = 5$
   (b)   Show clearly the single region that is satisfied by **all** of these inequalities.
         $x + y \leqslant 5$ $y \geqslant 2x$ $x \geqslant 0$.   Label this region R.   AQA

10 Write down three inequalities which describe the shaded region.

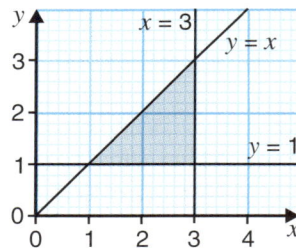

                                                                                    AQA

11 (a) x is an integer such that $-4 \leqslant x < 2$.
            (i)   Make a list of all the possible values of x.
            (ii)   What is the largest possible value of x^2?
   (b)   Every week Rucci has a test in Mathematics. It is marked out of 20.
         Rucci has always scored at least half the marks available.
         She has never quite managed to score full marks.
         Using x to represent Rucci's marks, write this information in the form of two inequalities.
                                                                                    AQA

12 (a)   Solve each of the following inequalities.   (i) $5x - 4 \leqslant 2x + 8$ (ii) $2(2x - 1) > 6$
   (b)   Write down the whole number values of x which satisfy both of the above inequalities
         simultaneously.
                                                                                    AQA

13 Solve the following inequalities.   (a) $2 > x - 4$ (b) $2(x + 3) > 3(2 - x)$ AQA

Further Graphs

What you need to know

- The graph of a **linear function** is a straight line.
  The general equation of a straight line is $y = mx + c$.

- The graph of a **quadratic function** is always a smooth curve and is called a **parabola**.

- The general form of a **quadratic function** is
  $y = ax^2 + bx + c$, where a cannot be zero.
  The graph of a quadratic function is symmetrical
  and has a **maximum** or **minimum** value.

  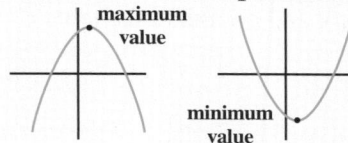

- The general form of a **cubic function** is $y = ax^3 + bx^2 + cx + d$, where a cannot be zero.

- The graph of the **reciprocal function** is of the
  form $y = \frac{a}{x}$, where x cannot be equal to zero.

  Eg 1

  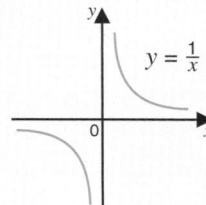
  $y = \frac{1}{x}$

- The graph of the **exponential function** is of the
  form $y = a^x$.

  Eg 2

  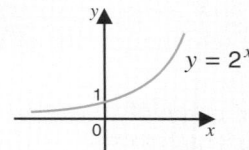
  $y = 2^x$

- The graph of a **circle**, centre $(0, 0)$, is of the
  form $x^2 + y^2 = r^2$, where r is the radius
  of the circle.

  Eg 3

  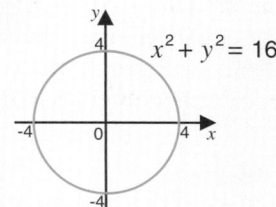
  $x^2 + y^2 = 16$

- The graph of a function can be used to solve a variety of equations.
  This may include drawing another graph and looking for points of intersection.

  Eg 4 (a) Draw the graph of $y = x^2 - 2x - 5$ for values of x from -2 to 4.
  (b) Use your graph to solve the equation $x^2 - 2x - 5 = 0$.

  (a)

  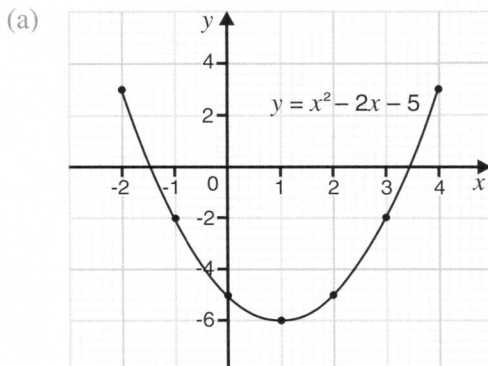
  $y = x^2 - 2x - 5$

  To draw a quadratic graph:
  Make a table of values connecting x and y.
  Plot the points.
  Join the points with a smooth curve.

x	-2	-1	0	1	2	3	4
y	3	-2	-5	-6	-5	-2	3

  To solve the equation, read the values of x
  where the graph of $y = x^2 - 2x - 5$
  crosses the x axis ($y = 0$).

  (b) $x = -1.4$ and 3.4, correct to one decimal place.

1 Match these equations to their graphs.

1 $y = 1 - x^2$
2 $y = x^3$
3 $y = x^2 - 1$
4 $y = 1 - 2x$

A   B   C   D

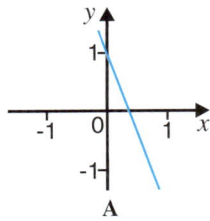

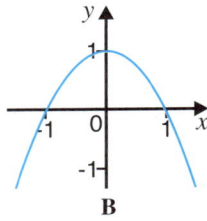

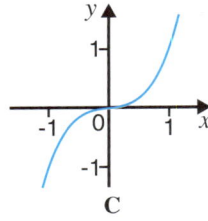

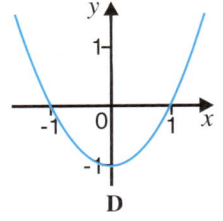

2 (a) Copy and complete the table of values for $y = x^2 - 4x + 2$.

x	-1	0	1	2	3	4
y			-1		-1	2

(b) Draw the graph of $y = x^2 - 4x + 2$ for values of x from -1 to 4.
(c) Hence, solve the equation $x^2 - 4x + 2 = 0$.   AQA

3 (a) Copy and complete the table of values for $y = 2x^2 - 3x + 2$.

x	-2	-1	0	1	2	3
y	16		2		4	

(b) Draw the graph of $y = 2x^2 - 3x + 2$ for values of x from -2 to 3.
(c) Explain how the graph shows that there are no values of x for which $2x^2 - 3x + 2 = 0$.
(d) State the minimum value of y.

4 (a) Draw the graph of $y = 5x - x^2$ for $-1 \leqslant x \leqslant 6$.
(b) Use your graph to solve
   (i) the equation $5x - x^2 = 0$,
   (ii) the equation $5x - x^2 = 3$.
(c) Find, from your graph, the value of x for which y is a maximum.
Hence, calculate the maximum value of y.

5 (a) Draw the graph of $y = x^3 - x$ for $-3 \leqslant x \leqslant 3$.
(b) Use your graph to find the value of x when $y = 10$.
(c) Use your graph to solve the equation $x^3 - x = 0$.

6 (a) Using the same axes, draw the graphs with equations $y = 3x$ and $y = x^2 + 1$.
(b) Explain how you can use these graphs to solve the equation $x^2 - 3x + 1 = 0$.
(c) Hence, solve the equation $x^2 - 3x + 1 = 0$.

7 On separate diagrams, sketch the graphs of these equations.
Label any point where the graphs cross the x or y axes.
(a) $y = -x^3$ (b) $xy = 1$ (c) $x^2 + y^2 = 9$ (d) $y = \left(\frac{1}{2}\right)^x$

8 (a) Draw the graph of $y = 4^x$ for values of x from -2 to 2.
(b) Use your graph to find the value of x when $y = 8$.

9 Draw the graph of $y = \frac{3}{x}$ for $-6 \leqslant x \leqslant 6$.

10 Find graphically the points of intersection of $x^2 + y^2 = 16$ and $2y = x - 1$.

Quadratic Equations ●●●●●●●

What you need to know

● Brackets, such as $(x + 2)(x + 3)$, can be multiplied out using the **diagram method**, or by **expanding**.

Eg 1 Multiply out $(x + 2)(x + 3)$.

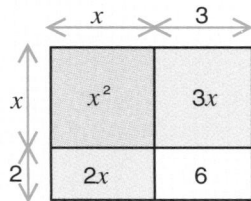

$$(x + 2)(x + 3) = x^2 + 3x + 2x + 6$$
$$= x^2 + 5x + 6$$

Eg 2 Expand $(x - 3)(2x + 1)$.

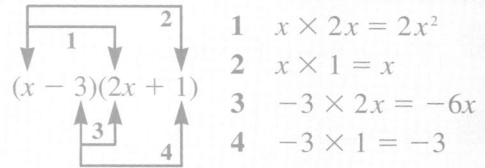

1 $x \times 2x = 2x^2$
2 $x \times 1 = x$
3 $-3 \times 2x = -6x$
4 $-3 \times 1 = -3$

$$(x - 3)(2x + 1) = 2x^2 + x - 6x - 3$$
$$= 2x^2 - 5x - 3$$

● **Factorising** is the opposite operation to removing brackets.

Eg 3 Factorise the following.
(a) $x^2 + 3x = x(x + 3)$
(b) $2x^2 - 8 = 2(x^2 - 4)$
$\qquad = 2(x - 2)(x + 2)$
(c) $x^2 + 2x - 15 = (x + 5)(x - 3)$

When factorising, work logically.
1. Does the expression have a **common factor**?
2. Is the expression a **difference of two squares**?
$\qquad a^2 - b^2 = (a - b)(a + b)$
3. Will the expression factorise into **two brackets**?

● **Quadratic equations** can be solved by factorising.

Eg 4 Solve these equations.
(a) $x^2 - 5x = 0$
$\quad x(x - 5) = 0$
$\quad x = 0 \quad \text{or} \quad x = 5$

(b) $m^2 + m - 6 = 0$
$\quad (m - 2)(m + 3) = 0$
$\quad m = 2 \quad \text{or} \quad m = -3$

(c) $2a^2 - 5a - 3 = 0$
$\quad (2a + 1)(a - 3) = 0$
$\quad a = -\frac{1}{2} \quad \text{or} \quad a = 3$

● The general form for a **quadratic equation** is $ax^2 + bx + c = 0$ where a cannot be zero.

● The solutions to a quadratic equation can be found using the **quadratic formula**.

$$\text{If} \quad ax^2 + bx + c = 0 \quad \text{and} \quad a \neq 0 \quad \text{then} \quad x = \frac{-b \pm \sqrt{b^2 - 4ac}}{2a}$$

Eg 5 Solve $x^2 - 3x - 2 = 0$.

$$x = \frac{-(-3) \pm \sqrt{(-3)^2 - 4(1)(-2)}}{2(1)}$$

$$x = \frac{3 \pm \sqrt{17}}{2}$$

$x = -0.56 \quad \text{or} \quad 3.56$, correct to two decimal places.

Substitute: $a = 1$, $b = -3$ and $c = -2$,
into $x = \dfrac{-b \pm \sqrt{b^2 - 4ac}}{2a}$

● Quadratic expressions, such as $x^2 + 8x + 20$, can be written in the form $(x + a)^2 + b$, where a and b are integers.

In **completed square form**, $(x + a)^2 + b$:
the value of a is half the coefficient of x, the
value of b is found by subtracting the value of a^2
from the constant term of the original expression.

Eg 6 $x^2 + 8x + 20 = (x + a)^2 + b$
$a = \frac{1}{2}(8) = 4$
$b = 20 - 4^2 = 4$
$x^2 + 8x + 20 = (x + 4)^2 + 4$

19

- Quadratic equations can be solved by **completing the square**.

Eg 7 Solve $x^2 + 4x = 5$.
$$(x + 2)^2 - 4 = 5$$
$$(x + 2)^2 = 9$$
$$x + 2 = \pm 3$$
$$x + 2 = 3 \quad \text{or} \quad x + 2 = -3$$
$$x = 1 \quad \text{or} \quad x = -5$$

> Write the left-hand side (LHS) of the equation in the form $(x + a)^2 + b$ by completing the square.
> $x^2 + 4x = (x + 2)^2 - 4$

- You should be able to form and solve quadratic equations.

Exercise 19

1 Multiply out and simplify.
   (a) $x(x - 7)$
   (b) $(x - 2)(x + 5)$
   (c) $(2x - 1)(x + 3)$
   (d) $(3x + 2y)^2$

2 Factorise.
   (a) $x^2 - 6x$
   (b) $x^2 + 2x - 15$
   (c) $x^2 - 4x + 3$
   (d) $x^2 - 9$

3 Solve these equations.
   (a) $x(x + 5) = 0$
   (b) $(x - 3)(x + 2) = 0$
   (c) $(2x + 3)(x - 1) = 0$

4 (a) Factorise $x^2 - x - 12$.
   (b) Hence, solve the equation $x^2 - x - 12 = 0$.   AQA

5 Solve these equations.
   (a) $x^2 - 3x = 0$
   (b) $x^2 - 3x + 2 = 0$
   (c) $x^2 + x - 6 = 0$

6 Solve, by factorisation, $x^2 - 2x - 3 = 0$.   AQA

7 Solve the equation $x^2 - 11x + 28 = 0$.

8 Factorise.   (a) $2x^2 - 7x - 15$
   (b) $x^2 - 25y^2$ AQA

9 (a) Factorise $2x^2 - 5x - 3 = 0$.
   (b) Hence, solve the equation $2x^2 - 5x - 3 = 0$.

10 Solve the equation $3x^2 - x - 2 = 0$.

11 The expression $x^2 + 6x - 5$ can be written in the form $(x + p)^2 + q$.
   Calculate the values of p and q.

12 (a) Write $x^2 - 4x - 8$ in the form $(x + a)^2 + b$.
   (b) Hence, solve the equation $x^2 - 4x - 8 = 0$, correct to 2 decimal places.

13 Solve the equation $x^2 + 3x - 5 = 0$.
   Give your answers correct to 2 decimal places.

14 Solve the equation $x^2 = 5x + 7$, giving your answers correct to 3 significant figures.   AQA

15 Solve the equation $2x^2 - 4x - 3 = 0$.   Give your answers correct to 2 decimal places.   AQA

16 The area of a rectangle, with dimensions x cm by $(x + 2)$ cm, is 18 cm^2.
   Calculate the value of x, correct to one decimal place.

17 A number, x, is equal to its reciprocal plus $\frac{1}{2}$.
   (a) Show that $2x^2 - x - 2 = 0$.
   (b) Solve the equation $2x^2 - x - 2 = 0$.
   Give your answers to an accuracy of **two** decimal places.   AQA

Simultaneous Equations

What you need to know

- A pair of **simultaneous equations** has the same unknown letters in each equation.

- To solve a pair of simultaneous equations find values for the unknown letters that fit **both** equations.

- Simultaneous equations can be solved either **graphically** or **algebraically**.

- Solving simultaneous equations **graphically** involves:
  drawing the graphs of both equations,
  finding the point(s) where the graphs cross.
  When the graphs of both equations are parallel, the equations have no solution.

  Eg 1 Solve the simultaneous equations $x + 2y = 5$ and $x - 2y = 1$ graphically.

  Draw the graph of $x + 2y = 5$.
  Draw the graph of $x - 2y = 1$.

  The lines cross at the point (3, 1).
  This gives the solution $x = 3$ and $y = 1$.

  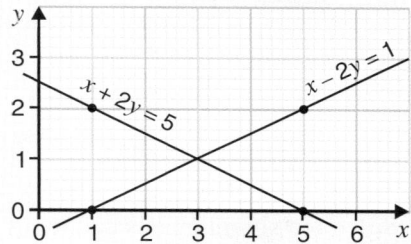

- Solving simultaneous equations **algebraically** involves using either:
  the **elimination** method, or the **substitution** method.

  Eg 2 Solve the simultaneous equations $5x + 2y = 11$ and $3x - 4y = 4$ algebraically.

$$5x + 2y = 11 \quad \text{A}$$
$$3x - 4y = 4 \quad \text{B}$$

A × 2 gives
$$10x + 4y = 22 \quad \text{C}$$
$$3x - 4y = 4 \quad \text{D}$$

C + D gives
$$13x = 26$$
$$x = 2$$

Substitute $x = 2$ into $5x + 2y = 11$.
$$10 + 2y = 11$$
$$2y = 1$$
$$y = 0.5$$

The solution is $x = 2$ and $y = 0.5$.

> To make the number of y's the same we can multiply equation A by 2.

> The number of y's is the **same** but the **signs** are **different**. To eliminate the y's the equations must be **added**.

> You can check the solution by substituting $x = 2$ and $y = 0.5$ into $3x - 4y = 4$.

- You should be able to solve simultaneous equations in which one equation is linear and one is quadratic.

  Eg 3 Solve the simultaneous equations $y = x - 2$ and $x^2 + 3y = 12$.

Substitute $y = x - 2$ into $x^2 + 3y = 12$.
$$x^2 + 3(x - 2) = 12$$
$$x^2 + 3x - 18 = 0$$
$$(x + 6)(x - 3) = 0$$
$$x = -6 \text{ or } x = 3$$

Using $y = x - 2$.
When $x = -6$.
$y = -6 - 2$
$y = -8$

When $x = 3$.
$y = 3 - 2$
$y = 1$

This gives the solution: $x = -6$, $y = -8$ **and** $x = 3$, $y = 1$.

Exercise 20

1 The graph of the equation $3y = x + 1$ is drawn on the grid.
Copy the diagram.

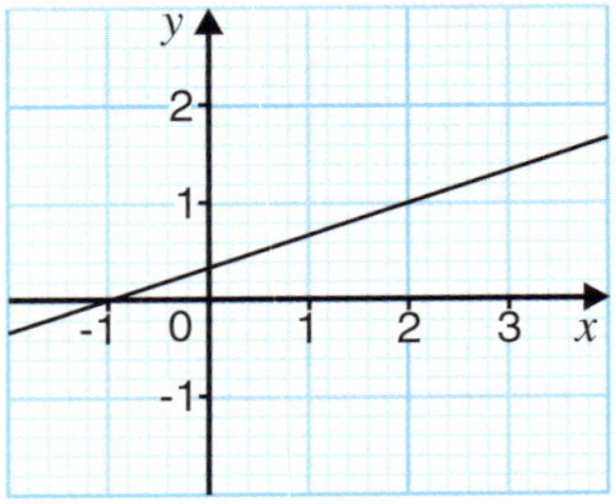

(a) On your diagram, draw the graph of the equation $y = 1 - x$.

(b) Use your graphs to solve the simultaneous equations $y = 1 - x$ and $3y = x + 1$.

AQA

2 (a) On the same axes, draw the graphs of $y + x = 4$ and $y - 3x = 2$ for values of x from -2 to 2.

(b) Hence, solve the simultaneous equations $y + x = 4$ and $y - 3x = 2$.

3 Solve graphically the simultaneous equations $y = 3 - x$ and $y = x - 2$.

4 The sketch shows the graph of $y = 2x - 1$.
Copy the diagram.

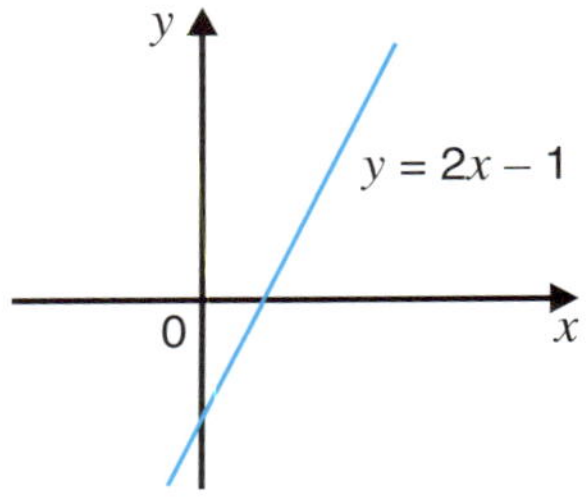

(a) On your diagram, sketch the graph of $y = 2x + 1$.

(b) Explain why the equations $y = 2x - 1$ and $y = 2x + 1$ cannot be solved simultaneously.

5 Solve these simultaneous equations. $6x + y = 15$
$8x - y = 6$

AQA

6 Solve the simultaneous equations $x + 3y = 13$ and $4x + 2y = 2$.

7 Solve the simultaneous equations. $2x + y = 2$
$4x - 3y = 9$

AQA

8 Heather sold 40 boxes of cards to raise money for charity.
She sold x small boxes at £4 each and y large boxes at £7 each.
She raised £184 altogether.

(a) Write down two equations connecting x and y.

(b) Solve these simultaneous equations to find how many of each size of box she sold.

9 Micro-scooters costs £x each and pogo sticks cost £y each.
2 micro-scooters and 4 pogo sticks cost £65.
1 micro-scooter and 3 pogo sticks cost £40.

(a) Write down two equations connecting x and y.

(b) Solve these simultaneous equations to find the cost of a micro-scooter and a pogo stick.

10 Solve these simultaneous equations. $4x - 3y = 17$ and $6x - 4y = 23$

AQA

11 Solve the simultaneous equations. $4x - 3y = 11$ and $6x + 2y = 10$

AQA

12 Use a graphical method to solve each of these pairs of simultaneous equations.

(a) $y = 4 - 2x$
$y = x^2 - 4$

(b) $y - x = 4$
$y = 6x - x^2$

(c) $y = 2x$
$x^2 + y^2 = 25$

13 Use an algebraic method to solve the simultaneous equations
$5y = 2x - 7$ and $xy = 6$.

14 Solve the simultaneous equations.

(a) $y - x = -11$
$x^2 = y + 13$

(b) $y = 3 - x$
$x^2 + y^2 = 17$

(c) $2x + y = 3$
$y = \dfrac{1}{x}$

What you need to know

- An **identity** is true for all values of x. It is the same expression written in another form.
  For example: $(2x + 3)^2 + (2x + 9)(2x + 5) = 2(4x^2 + 20x + 27)$.

  > To show that an identity is true, either:
  > start with the LHS and show that it is equal to the RHS, or
  > start with the RHS and show that it is equal to the LHS.

- **Algebraic fractions** have a numerator and a denominator.

  > To write an algebraic fraction in its **simplest form**:
  > factorise the numerator and denominator of the fraction,
  > divide the numerator and denominator by their highest
  > common factor.

Eg 1 Simplify.

(a) $\dfrac{2x - 4}{x^2 - 2x} = \dfrac{2(x - 2)}{x(x - 2)} = \dfrac{2}{x}$

(b) $\dfrac{x^2 - 9}{x^2 + 2x - 3} = \dfrac{(x + 3)(x - 3)}{(x + 3)(x - 1)} = \dfrac{(x - 3)}{(x - 1)}$

(c) $\dfrac{2}{x - 3} - \dfrac{1}{x} = \dfrac{2x - (x - 3)}{x(x - 3)} = \dfrac{x + 3}{x(x - 3)}$

> The same methods used for adding, subtracting, multiplying and
> dividing numeric fractions can be applied to algebraic fractions.

- You should be able to solve equations involving algebraic fractions.

- The solutions to a variety of equations can be found using a process called **iteration**.

Eg 2 Find a solution to the equation $x^2 - 4x - 3 = 0$,
correct to 2 decimal places, using iteration.

Use the iterative formula $x_{n + 1} = \sqrt{4x_n + 3}$.

$x_1 = 4$

$x_2 = \sqrt{4 \times 4 + 3} = 4.3588\ldots$

$x_3 = \sqrt{4 \times 4.3588\ldots + 3} = 4.5205\ldots$

$x_4 = \sqrt{4 \times 4.5205\ldots + 3} = 4.5915\ldots$

$x_5 = \sqrt{4 \times 4.5915\ldots + 3} = 4.6223\ldots$

$x_6 = \sqrt{4 \times 4.6223\ldots + 3} = 4.6356\ldots$

$x_7 = \sqrt{4 \times 4.6356\ldots + 3} = 4.6414\ldots$

$x_8 = \sqrt{4 \times 4.6414\ldots + 3} = 4.6438\ldots$

$x = 4.64$, correct to 2 d.p.

> The process of iteration has three stages.
>
> 1. Rearranging an equation to form an **iterative formula**.
>
> 2. Choosing a **starting value**, x_1.
>
> 3. **Substituting** the starting value, and then values of x_n into the iterative formula.
>
> Continuing the process until the required degree of accuracy is obtained.

21 ● **Trial and improvement** is a method used to solve equations. The accuracy of the value of the unknown letter is improved until the required degree of accuracy is obtained.

Eg 3 Use a trial and improvement method to find a solution to the equation $x^3 + x = 40$, correct to one decimal place.

x	$x^3 + x$	Comment
3	$27 + 3 = 30$	Too small
4	$64 + 4 = 68$	Too big
3.5	$42.8\ldots + 3.5 = 46.3\ldots$	Too big
3.3	$35.9\ldots + 3.3 = 39.2\ldots$	Too small
3.35	$37.5\ldots + 3.35 = 40.9\ldots$	Too big

For accuracy to 1 d.p.
check the second decimal place.
The solution lies between
3.3 and 3.35.

$x = 3.3$, correct to 1 d.p.

Exercise 21

1 Expand and simplify $(x + 3)^2 - (x - 3)^2$.

2 Show that $2x(x + y) - (x + y)^2 = x^2 - y^2$.

3 (a) Show that $(3x + 4)^2 - (3x + 2)^2 = 12x + 12$.
   (b) Hence, solve the equation $(3x + 4)^2 - (3x + 2)^2 = (x + 1)(4x - 1)$.   AQA

4 Simplify. (a) $\dfrac{x^2 - 3x}{x}$ (b) $\dfrac{2x^2 - 6x}{4x - 12}$ (c) $\dfrac{x^2 + 2x + 1}{x^2 - 2x - 3}$ (d) $\dfrac{x^2 + x}{x^2 - 1}$

5 Simplify fully the expression $\dfrac{2x - 8}{2x^2 - 7x - 4}$.   AQA

6 Simplify. (a) $\dfrac{1}{x} + \dfrac{1}{2x}$ (b) $\dfrac{2x}{x + 1} + \dfrac{1}{2}$ (c) $\dfrac{1}{x + 2} + \dfrac{2}{2x - 5}$

7 Solve the equation $\dfrac{x}{2} - \dfrac{3}{x + 5} = 1$ correct to 2 decimal places.

8 Solve the equation $\dfrac{2}{2x - 1} - 1 = \dfrac{2}{x + 1}$.

9 Solve the equation $\dfrac{1}{1 - x} - \dfrac{1}{1 + x} = 2$. Give your answer correct to two decimal places.   AQA

10 (a) (i) Factorise $3p^2 + 16p + 5$.   (ii) Hence, or otherwise, simplify $\dfrac{p^2 - 25}{3p^2 + 16p + 5}$.
   (b) Solve the equation $\dfrac{2}{x - 8} - \dfrac{1}{x - 3} = \dfrac{1}{x + 2}$.   AQA

11 (a) Expand and simplify $\left(x + \dfrac{1}{x}\right)\left(x + \dfrac{1}{x}\right)$. Write your answer in the form $x^2 + a + \dfrac{b}{x^2}$.
   (b) (i) Factorise $x^2 - 2 + \dfrac{1}{x^2}$.
      (ii) Hence, or otherwise, solve the equation $x^2 - 2 + \dfrac{1}{x^2} = 0$.   AQA

12 The iterative formula $x_{n+1} = \dfrac{3x_n + 10}{2x_n}$ can be used to solve a quadratic equation.

   (a) Write down the quadratic equation in the form $ax^2 + bx + c = 0$.
   (b) Use the iterative formula with $x_1 = 2$ to find the positive solution of the equation.
      Give your answer to an accuracy of one decimal place. You **must** show your iterations.   AQA

13 Use a trial and improvement method to solve the equation $x^3 + x^2 = 300$.
   Show all your trials. Give your answer correct to one decimal place.

What you need to know

● **Function notation** is a way of expressing a relationship between two variables.
For example

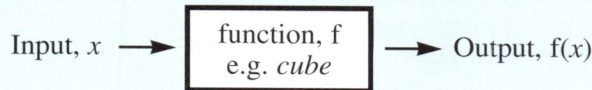

Input, x ⟶ | function, f e.g. *cube* | ⟶ Output, f(x)

This notation gives $f(x) = x^3$

$f(x)$ means 'a function of x'.
In the example above, $f(x) = x^3$ is equivalent to the equation $y = x^3$ where $y = f(x)$.

● **Transformations,** such as **translations** and **stretches**, can be used to change the position and size of a graph.
The equation of the transformed (new) graph is related to the equation of the original graph.

In general

Original	New graph	Transformation	Note
$y = f(x)$	$y = f(x) + a$	**translation**, vector $\begin{pmatrix} 0 \\ a \end{pmatrix}$.	If a is **positive**, curve moves a units **up**. If a is **negative**, curve moves a units **down**.
$y = f(x)$	$y = f(x + a)$	**translation**, vector $\begin{pmatrix} -a \\ 0 \end{pmatrix}$.	If a is **positive**, curve moves a units **left**. If a is **negative**, curve moves a units **right**.
$y = f(x)$	$y = af(x)$	**stretch**, from the x axis, parallel to the y axis, scale factor a.	The y coordinates on the graph of $y = f(x)$ are **multiplied** by a.
$y = f(x)$	$y = f(ax)$	**stretch**, from the y axis, parallel to the x axis, scale factor $\frac{1}{a}$.	The x coordinates on the graph of $y = f(x)$ are **divided** by a.
$y = f(x)$	$y = -f(x)$	**reflection** in the x axis.	The y coordinates on the graph of $y = f(x)$ **change signs**.
$y = f(x)$	$y = f(-x)$	**reflection** in the y axis.	The x coordinates on the graph of $y = f(x)$ **change signs**.

Eg 1 The diagram shows the graph of $y = f(x)$.
Draw the graphs of $y = f(x - 2)$ and $y = f(x) - 2$.

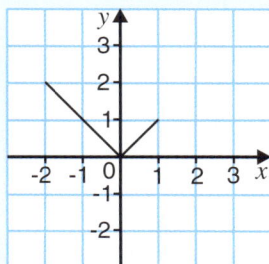

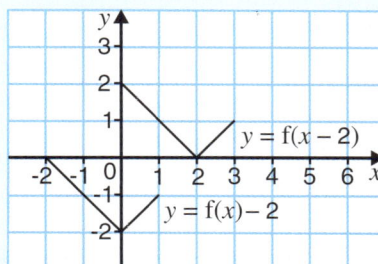

● You should be able to draw a suitable graph to find the relationship between a given set of variables.
Linear functions have straight line graphs, such as $y = ax + b$.
From the graph of **y against x**, the gradient $= a$ and the y-intercept $= b$.

Non-linear functions, such as $y = ax^n + b$, can be written as the linear function $y = az + b$ by substituting $z = x^n$.
From the graph of **y against x^n**, the gradient $= a$ and the y-intercept $= b$.

1 The graph of $y = f(x)$ for $-2 \le x \le 2$ is shown.
On separate diagrams draw the graphs of
$y = f(x)$ and:

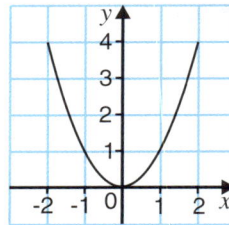

(a) $y = f(x + 2)$,   (b) $y = f(x) + 2$,
(c) $y = 2f(x)$,   (d) $y = -f(x)$.

2 The diagram shows a sketch of the graph of $y = f(x)$ for $-2 \le x \le 2$.
Each of the graphs below is a transformation of this graph.
Write down the equation of each graph.

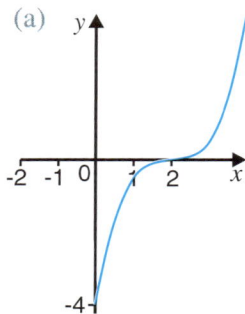

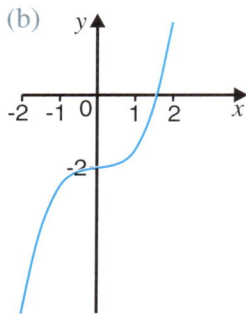

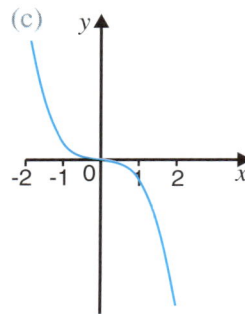

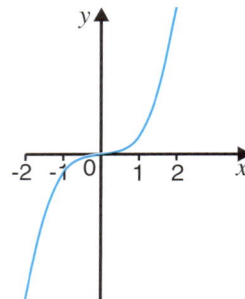

(a)   (b)   (c)

3 This is the graph of $y = \cos x$.

Below are shown three transformations
of the graph $y = \cos x$.
Give the equation of each graph.

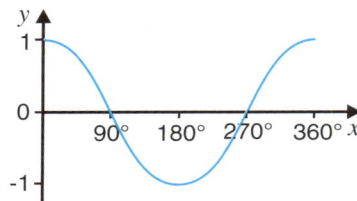

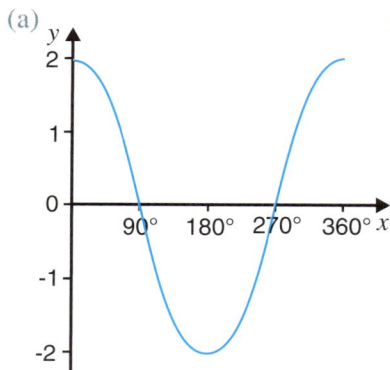

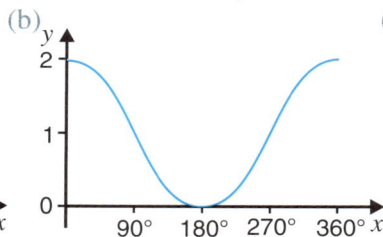

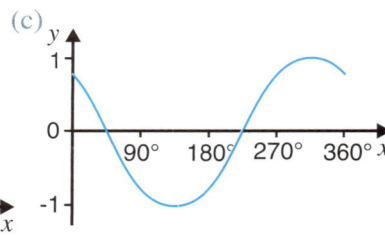

(a)   (b)   (c)

AQA

4 The table shows the results of an experiment.

x	5	12	20	24
y	5.5	6.9	8.5	9.3

(a) Draw a graph to show these results.
(b) The results are connected by the equation $y = ax + b$.
Find this equation and hence find the value of x when $y = 20$.

5 James has the following set of experimental results for values of x and y.

x	1	2.5	3	4	6	10
y	11.5	7.0	6.5	6.0	5.2	4.75

(a) Calculate the values of $\frac{1}{x}$ and plot the graph of y against $\frac{1}{x}$.

He knows that x and y are connected by the formula $y = \frac{a}{x} + b$, where a and b are constants.
(b) **Use your graph** to estimate the values of a and b.

AQA

Section Review - Algebra

1 (a) Simplify $3x + 5y - x - 4y$.

(b) Multiply out and simplify $5(2a - 3) - 3a + 7$.

2 A large cuddly toy cost £d.
A small cuddly toy costs £3 less than a large cuddly toy.
Write an expression for the cost of five small cuddly toys.

3 Here is a rule for working out a sequence of numbers.

| Choose a starting number S | → | Multiply by 3 | → | Subtract 4 | → | Write down the final number F. |

Write down an **equation** connecting the final number, F, and the starting number, S.

AQA

4 (a) Draw the line $y = 2x + 1$ for values of x from -1 to 2.

(b) The line $y = 2x + 1$ crosses the line $x = -5$ at P.
Give the coordinates of P.

5 Solve (a) $x + 7 = 4$, (b) $4x = 10$, (c) $2x + 5 = 11$, (d) $5 - 6x = 8$.

6 I think of a number. If I double my number and add 1, my answer is 35.

(a) Write down an equation to describe this.

(b) What number am I thinking of?

AQA

7 The graph shows the journey of a cyclist from Halton to Kendal.
The distance from Halton to Kendal is 30 miles.

(a) For how long did the cyclist stop during the journey?

(b) What was the average speed for the part of the journey from A to B?

(c) On which part of the journey was the cyclist travelling at his fastest speed?
Explain clearly how you got your answer.

(d) The cyclist stayed in Kendal for 2 hours.
He then returned to Halton, without stopping, at an average speed of 12 miles per hour.
Calculate the time he arrived back in Halton.

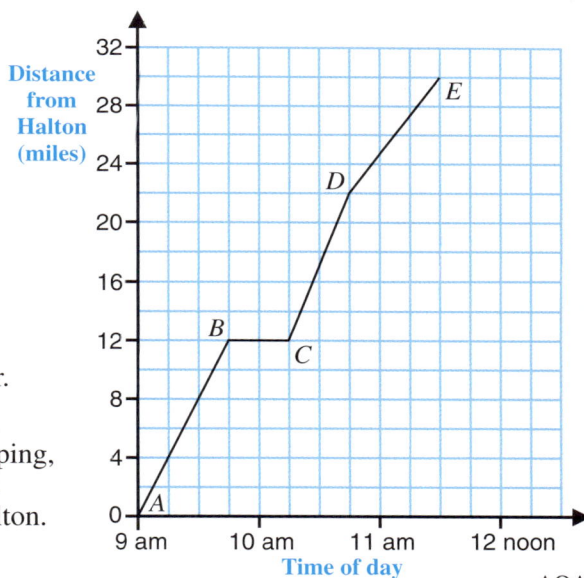

AQA

8 (a) Solve the equations (i) $4(a - 2) = 6$, (ii) $5t + 3 = -1 + t$.

(b) The sum of the numbers x, $x - 3$ and $x + 7$ is 25.
By forming an equation in x, find the value of x.

9 (a) This rule is used to produce a sequence of numbers.

> MULTIPLY THE LAST NUMBER BY 3 AND SUBTRACT 1.

The second number in the sequence is 20. What is the first number?

(b) Another sequence begins 2, 5, 8, 11, $\ldots$

(i) One number in the sequence is x.
Write, in terms of x, the next number in the sequence.

(ii) Write, in terms of n, the nth term of the sequence.

AQA

10 Given that $s = 2t^3$, find the value of t when $s = 250$.

11 $y = \frac{4}{5}(9 - x)$. Find the value of x when $y = 6$.

12 (a) Factorise   (i) $3a - 6$,   (ii) $k^2 - 2k$.
    (b) Multiply out   (i) $m(m - 4)$,   (ii) $3x(x + 5)$.

    (c) Solve   (i) $\dfrac{3x + 5}{2} = 7$,   (ii) $3 - 4x = x + 8$,   (iii) $3(2x + 1) = 6$.

13 (a) On the same diagram draw the graphs $2y = x + 4$ and $y = \frac{1}{2}x + 1$.
    (b) What do you notice about the two lines you have drawn?

14 A glass of milk costs x pence.
A milk shake costs 45 pence more than a glass of milk.
    (a) Write an expression for the cost of a milk shake.
    (b) Lou has to pay £4.55 for 3 milk shakes and a glass of milk.
        By forming an equation, find the price of a glass of milk.

15 (a) Copy and complete the table of values for $y = x^2 - 3$.

x	-2	-1	0	1	2	3
y		-2	-3			6

    (b) Draw the graph of $y = x^2 - 3$ for values of x from -2 to 3.
    (c) Use your graph to solve the equation $x^2 - 3 = 0$.

16 Use trial and improvement to find a solution to the equation $x^3 - 3x = 9$.
Give your answer correct to 1 decimal place.

17 (a) Expand and simplify. $3(2x - 1) + 2(4x - 5)$
    (b) Expand and simplify. $(3x + 2)(x + 4)$ AQA

18 (a) Solve the equation $3 - x = 4(x + 1)$.
    (b) Multiply out and simplify $2(5x - 3) - 3(x - 1)$.
    (c) Simplify   (i) $m^8 \div m^2$,   (ii) $n^2 \times n^3$.

19 (a) Multiply out and simplify $(3x - 1)(2x + 3)$.
    (b) Show how you could use your answer to (a) to work out 29×23.   AQA

20 Match these equations to their graphs.

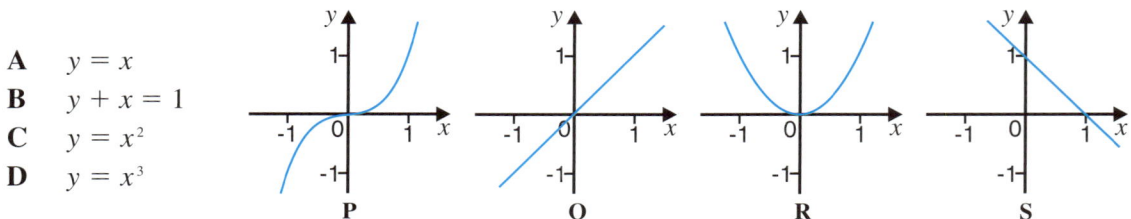

A $y = x$
B $y + x = 1$
C $y = x^2$
D $y = x^3$

                         P   Q   R   S

21 (a) Solve the inequality $3x < 6 - x$.
    (b) Solve the simultaneous equations $5x - y = 7$ and $3x + y = 1$.

22 Make x the subject of the formula $y = 2x - 5$.

23 (a) Draw the graph of $y = x^2 - 2x + 1$ for values of x from -1 to 3.
    (b) Use your graph to solve the equation $x^2 - 2x + 1 = 0$.
    (c) Use your graph to solve the equation $x^2 - 2x + 1 = 2$.

24 (a) Work out the value of $x^2 - 5x + 6$ when $x = -2$.
    (b) (i)   Factorise $x^2 - 5x + 6$.   (ii)   Hence, solve the equation $x^2 - 5x + 6 = 0$.

25 (a) Write down the equations of the lines labelled **A**, **B** and **C** in the diagram.

(b) Write down three inequalities to describe the shaded region.

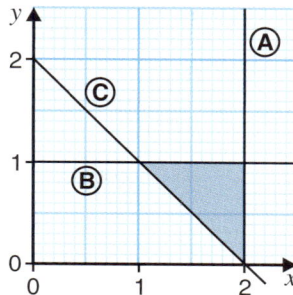

26 Write down the n th term of the following number sequences.
(a) 1, 4, 9, 16, 25, ... (b) 6, 9, 14, 21, 30, ...

AQA

27 (a) Find the gradients of these lines.

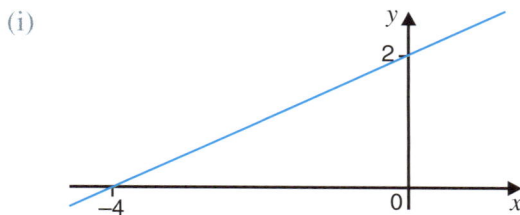

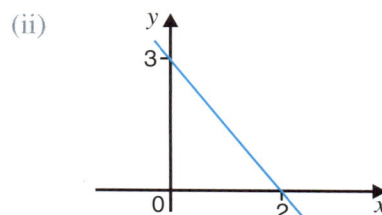

(i)

(ii)

(b) The equation of a different line is $4y - 3x = 8$.
What is the gradient of this line?

28 (a) Simplify, giving your answer in index form. (i) $\dfrac{a^8}{a^4}$ (ii) $(a^2)^3$
(b) Make q the subject of the formula $p = q^2 + r$.

AQA

29 (a) Solve the inequality $3x - 5 \leqslant 16$. (b) Multiply out and simplify $(y - 7)^2$.
(c) Simplify $2x^4 \times 3x^3$. (d) Factorise $p^2 + p - 12$.

AQA

30 (a) List all the values of n, where n is an integer, such that $-2 \leqslant n - 3 < 1$.
(b) Solve the simultaneous equations $x + 4y = 15$ and $3x - 2y = 10$.
(c) Factorise $xy - y^2$.
(d) Solve the equation $x^2 - 7x + 10 = 0$.

AQA

31 The dimensions of a rectangle are shown.
The rectangle has an area of 104 cm^2.
Form an equation for the area of the rectangle
and show that it can be written in the
form $2x^2 + x - 105 = 0$.

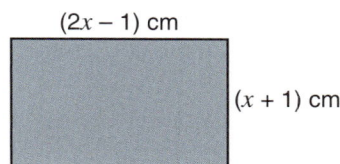

$(2x - 1)$ cm

$(x + 1)$ cm

32 You are given the formula $y = \sqrt{\dfrac{2x}{5}}$.

(a) Find the value of y when $x = 3.6 \times 10^{-4}$
(b) Rearrange the formula to give x in terms of y.

33 The diagram shows points $A\,(2, 0)$, $B\,(0, 2)$ and $C\,(3, 5)$.

Find the equations of the line segments.
(a) AB, (b) BC, (c) AC.

C (3, 5)

B (0, 2)

A (2, 0)

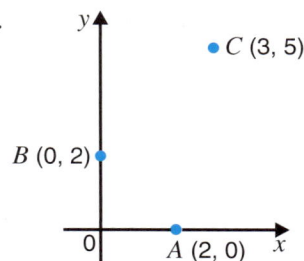

34 Solve the equation $\dfrac{5x - 3}{3} - \dfrac{1 + 2x}{2} = 3$

35 x is a number such that $x(x + 1)(x - 1) = 20$.
- (a) Find the two consecutive whole numbers between which x must lie.
- (b) Use the method of trial and improvement to find the solution correct to 3 significant figures.

AQA

36 Simplify. (a) $(3x^2 y)^3$ (b) $\dfrac{3a^2 b^3 \times 4a^5 b}{6a^3 b^2}$

37 Factorise the following. (a) $3x^2 - 75$ (b) $3x^2 - 8x + 5$

38 Solve the equation $x^2 + 2x - 5 = 0$.
Give your answers correct to two decimal places.

39 The volumes of these cuboids are the same.
- (a) Show that $3x^2 + 2x - 12 = 0$.
- (b) By solving the equation
$3x^2 + 2x - 12 = 0$ find the value of x.
Give your answer correct to one decimal place.

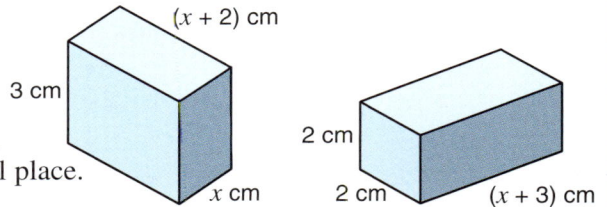

$(x + 2)$ cm   3 cm x cm   2 cm   2 cm $(x + 3)$ cm

40 On separate diagrams, sketch the graphs of:
- (a) $x^2 + y^2 = 9$,
- (b) $y = 2^x$, for $-3 \leqslant x \leqslant 3$.

41 The table shows the values of the variables p and q
where q is proportional to the square root of p.
- (a) Find the equation connecting p and q.
- (b) Copy and complete the table.

p	1	4	
q		0.8	1.2

42
- (a) Show that $(2x + 3)^2 - (2x + 1)^2 = 8(x + 1)$.
- (b) Hence, solve the equation $(2x + 3)^2 - (2x + 1)^2 = x^2 - 1$.

43
- (a) Simplify the expression $\dfrac{2x^2 - 8}{x + 2}$.
- (b) You are given the equation $a - c = ac$.
Rearrange this equation to give a formula for a in terms of c.
- (c) You are given that $(3x - b) = ax^2 - 12x + c$, for all values of x.
Find the values of a, b and c.

AQA

44 Rearrange the equation $x = \dfrac{y - 5}{3 - y}$ to make y the subject.

45 The speed-time graph of an underground train
travelling between two stations is shown.
- (a) What is the maximum speed of the train?
- (b) Calculate the acceleration of the train.
- (c) Calculate the distance between the stations.

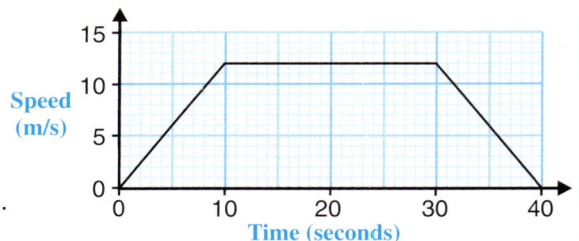

Speed (m/s)   15   10   5   0   0   10   20   30   40   Time (seconds)

46 Find the equation of the line which is perpendicular to $2y + x = 6$
and goes through the point $(4, 1)$.

47 Solve the equation $2x^2 = 5x - 1$.
Give your answers correct to two decimal places.

48 You are given that $y = 16x^n$ and that $y = 2$ when $x = 16$.
Find the value of n.

AQA

49 (a) Draw the graph of $y = \frac{2}{x}$ for $0 \leqslant x \leqslant 8$.

(b) On the same diagram draw the graph of $3y = 13 - 2x$.

The equation $3y = 13 - 2x$ can be written as $y = 4\frac{1}{3} - \frac{2}{3}x$.

(c) Show that $\frac{2}{x} = 4\frac{1}{3} - \frac{2}{3}x$ can be written as $2x^2 - 13x + 6 = 0$.

(d) Use your graphs, or otherwise, to solve the equation $2x^2 - 13x + 6 = 0$.

50 The n th term of a sequence is given by: $u_{n+1} = 2u_n - 2u_n^2$.

$u_1 = 0.8$ (a) Calculate u_2.   (b) What value does u_n approach as n gets very large? AQA

51 Two variables, p and Q, are connected by the rule $Q = \frac{a}{p^2} + b$, where a and b are constants.

The table shows values of Q when $p = 1$ and $p = 2$.

Plot the graph of Q against $\frac{1}{p^2}$. Hence, find the values of a and b.

p	1	2
Q	9	4.2

AQA

52 (a) Simplify fully the expression $\frac{2x^2 - 18}{2x^2 - 4x - 6}$.

(b) You are given the equation $xy = x + y$.
Rearrange the equation to give a formula for y in terms of x.

(c) You are given that $(2x - b)^2 - 5 = ax^2 - 4x + c$ for all values of x.
Find the values of a, b and c.

53 Solve the simultaneous equations $x + y = 4$ and $y = x^2 + 2x$.

54 (a) Show that the equation $x = \sqrt{\dfrac{3}{1 + x}}$ can be rearranged to give $x^3 + x^2 - 3 = 0$.

(b) Use the equation $x = \sqrt{\dfrac{3}{1 + x}}$

and an iterative method to find an approximate solution of $x^3 + x^2 - 3 = 0$,
giving your answer correct to 3 decimal places. AQA

55 (a) You are given that $(x + p)^2 + q = x^2 - 4x + 7$.
Find the values of p and q.

(b) Rearrange the equation $y(x - 3) = 1 + 2x$ to give a formula for x in terms of y.

56 Solve the equation $\dfrac{2}{x-1} - \dfrac{1}{x+1} = 1$. Give your answers correct to 2 decimal places.

57 The sketch shows the graph $y = x^3$.
Sketch the graphs indicated.

p is a positive integer greater than 1.

(a) $y = x^3 - p$ (b) $y = (x + p)^3$ (c) $y = \dfrac{x^3}{p}$

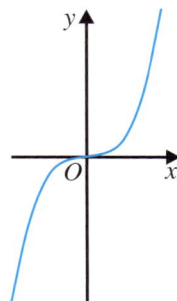

AQA

58 Solve the simultaneous equations $y = 2x + 1$ and $xy = 3$.

59 You are given that $\dfrac{1}{x+1} - \dfrac{3}{2x-1} = 2$.

Show that $4x^2 + 3x + 2 = 0$.

Angles, Parallel Lines and Polygons

What you need to know

- Types and names of angles.

Acute angle	**Right angle**	**Obtuse angle**	**Reflex angle**
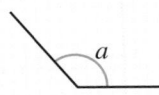		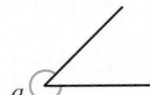	
$0° < a < 90°$	$a = 90°$	$90° < a < 180°$	$180° < a < 360°$

- Angle properties.

Angles at a point	**Complementary angles**	**Supplementary angles**	**Vertically opposite angles**
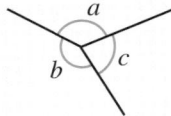	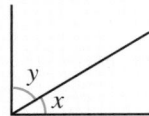	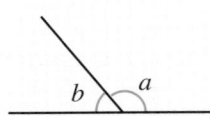	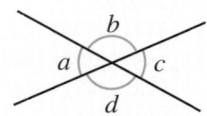
$a + b + c = 360°$	$x + y = 90°$	$a + b = 180°$	$a = c$ and $b = d$

- Lines which meet at right angles are **perpendicular** to each other.

- A straight line joining two points is called a **line segment**.

- Lines which never meet and are always the same distance apart are **parallel**.

- When two parallel lines are crossed by a **transversal** the following pairs of angles are formed.

Corresponding angles	**Alternate angles**	**Allied angles**
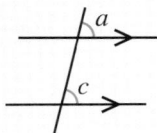	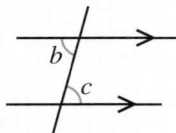	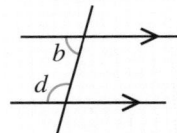
$a = c$	$b = c$	$b + d = 180°$

> Arrowheads are used to show that lines are **parallel**.

- A **triangle** is a shape made by three straight sides.

- Triangles can be: **acute-angled** (all angles less than 90°),
  obtuse-angled (one angle greater than 90°),
  right-angled (one angle equal to 90°).

- The sum of the angles in a triangle is 180°.
  $a + b + c = 180°$

- The exterior angle is equal to the sum of the two opposite interior angles. $a + b = d$

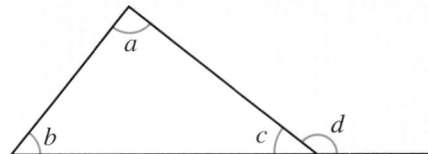

- Types of triangle:

Scalene	**Isosceles**	**Equilateral**
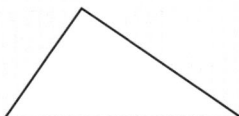	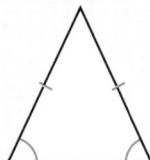	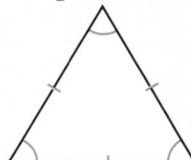

> A **sketch** is used when an accurate drawing is not required. Dashes across lines show sides that are equal in length. Equal angles are marked using arcs.

- A two-dimensional shape has **line symmetry** if the line divides the shape so that one side fits exactly over the other.
- A two-dimensional shape has **rotational symmetry** if it fits into a copy of its outline as it is rotated through 360°.
- A shape is only described as having rotational symmetry if the order of rotational symmetry is 2 or more.
- The number of times a shape fits into its outline in a single turn is the **order of rotational symmetry**.

Order of rotational symmetry 5

- A **quadrilateral** is a shape made by four straight lines.
- The sum of the angles in a quadrilateral is 360°.
- Facts about these special quadrilaterals:

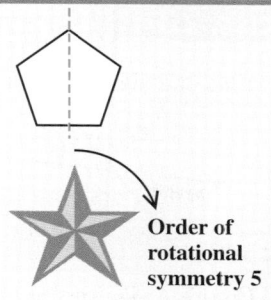

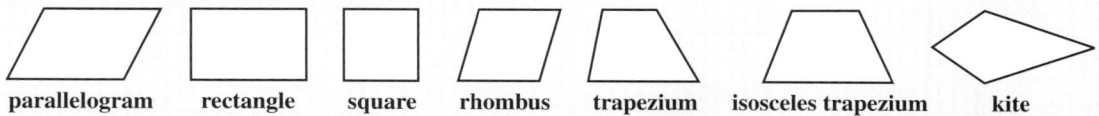

parallelogram   rectangle   square   rhombus   trapezium   isosceles trapezium   kite

Quadrilateral	Sides	Angles	Diagonals	Line symmetry	Order of rotational symmetry	Area formula
Parallelogram	Opposite sides equal and parallel	Opposite angles equal	Bisect each other	0	2	$A = bh$
Rectangle	Opposite sides equal and parallel	All 90°	Bisect each other	2	2	$A = bh$
Rhombus	4 equal sides, opposite sides parallel	Opposite angles equal	Bisect each other at 90°	2	2	$A = bh$
Square	4 equal sides, opposite sides parallel	All 90°	Bisect each other at 90°	4	4	$A = l^2$
Trapezium	1 pair of parallel sides					$A = \frac{1}{2}(a+b)h$
Isosceles trapezium	1 pair of parallel sides, non-parallel sides equal	2 pairs of equal angles	Equal in length	1	1*	$A = \frac{1}{2}(a+b)h$
Kite	2 pairs of adjacent sides equal	1 pair of opposite angles equal	One bisects the other at 90°	1	1*	

*A shape is only described as having rotational symmetry if the order of rotational symmetry is 2 or more.

- A **polygon** is a many-sided shape made by straight lines.
- A polygon with all sides equal and all angles equal is called a **regular polygon**.
- Shapes you need to know: A 5-sided polygon is called a **pentagon**.
                                  A 6-sided polygon is called a **hexagon**.
                                  An 8-sided polygon is called an **octagon**.
- The sum of the exterior angles of any polygon is 360°.
- At each vertex of a polygon: interior angle + exterior angle = 180°
- The sum of the interior angles of an *n*-sided polygon is given by:
$$(n-2) \times 180°$$
- For a regular *n*-sided polygon: exterior angle $= \dfrac{360°}{n}$
- A shape will **tessellate** if it covers a surface without overlapping and leaves no gaps.

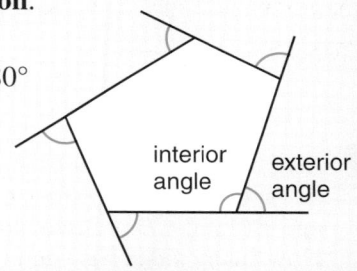

interior angle   exterior angle

The diagrams in this exercise have not been drawn accurately.

1 Find the size of the lettered angles. Give a reason for each answer.

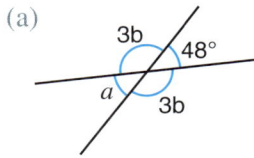

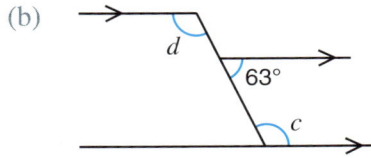

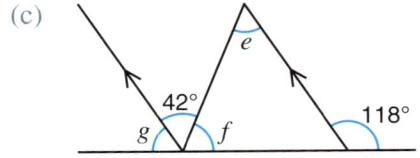

(a)

3b
48°
a
3b

(b)

d
63°
c

(c)

e
42°
g   f
118°

2 Find the size of the lettered angles.

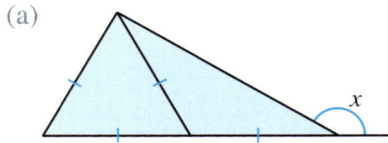

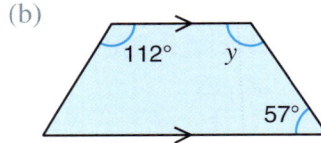

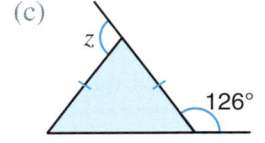

(a)

x

(b)

112°   y
57°

(c)

z
126°

3

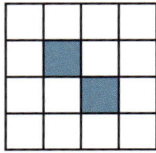

(a) Copy the diagram.
Shade two more squares so that the final diagram has line symmetry only.

(b) Make another copy of the diagram.
Shade two more squares so that the final diagram
has rotational symmetry only.

4

C
B
A   D

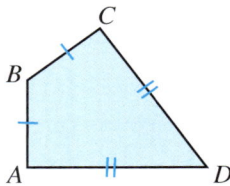

The diagram shows a quadrilateral *ABCD*.
AB = *BC* and   *CD* = *DA*.

Angle *ADC* = 36° and   angle *BCD* = 105°.
Work out the size of angle *ABC*.

5 In the figure,
  AB = *AD* and   *BD* = *BC*.
  AB is parallel to *DC*   and   angle *DBC* = 62°.

Explain why *BC* is not parallel to *AD*.

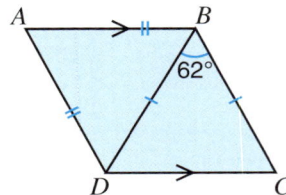

A   B
62°
D   C

AQA

6 (a) A regular polygon has 9 sides.
Find the size of an interior angle.

(b) A regular polygon has an exterior angle of 20°.
Show that the sum of the interior angles is 2880°.

7 (a) In the diagram the lines *PQ*, *XR* and *TS* are parallel.
Angle *QRS* = 65° and   angle *RST* = 156°.
Work out the size of angle *PQR*.

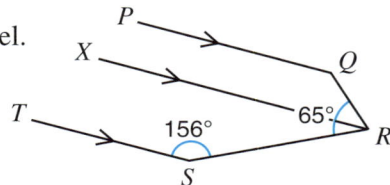

P
X   Q
T
156°   65°
S   R

(b)

L
M   30°   X
N

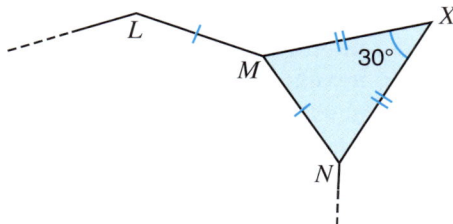

LM and *MN* are two sides of a regular
10-sided polygon.
MNX is an isosceles triangle with *MX* = *XN*.
Angle *MXN* = 30°.

Work out the size of the obtuse angle *LMX*.

AQA

8 *ABC* is an equilateral triangle.
AC and *CD* are two sides of a regular polygon
and *BC* and *CD* are two sides of an identical polygon.
How many sides has each of these polygons?

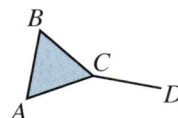

B
C
A   D

Circle Properties

What you need to know

- A **circle** is the shape drawn by keeping a pencil the same distance from a fixed point on a piece of paper.

- You should know the meaning of the words shown on the diagrams below.

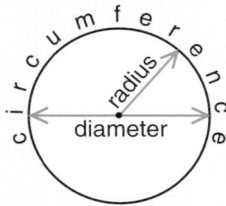

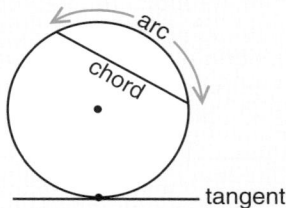

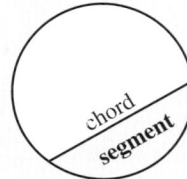

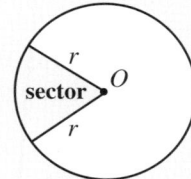

- The vertices of a **cyclic quadrilateral** lie on the circumference of a circle.

- **Circle properties**

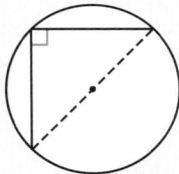

The angle in a semi-circle is a right angle.

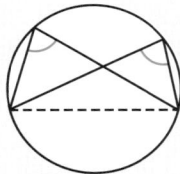

Angles in the same segment are equal.

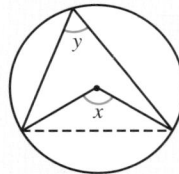

$x = 2y$
The angle at the centre is twice the angle at the circumference.

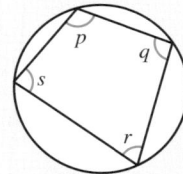

$p + r = 180°$ and $q + s = 180°$
Opposite angles of a cyclic quadrilateral are supplementary.

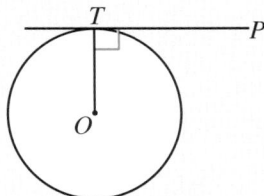

A tangent is perpendicular to the radius at the point of contact.

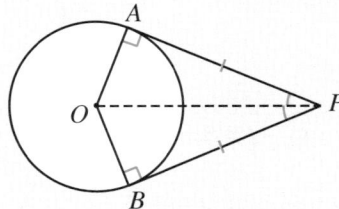

Tangents drawn to a circle from the same point are equal.

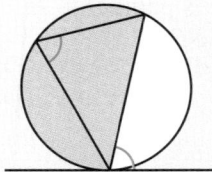

The angle between a tangent and a chord is equal to any angle in the alternate (opposite) segment.

- You should be able to use circle properties to solve problems.

Eg 1 O is the centre of the circle. Find the marked angles.
$a = 43°$ (angles in the same segment)
$b = 2 \times 43°$ ($\angle$ at centre = twice $\angle$ at circum.)
$b = 86°$
$c = 180° - 43°$ (opp. $\angle$s of a cyclic quad)
$c = 137°$

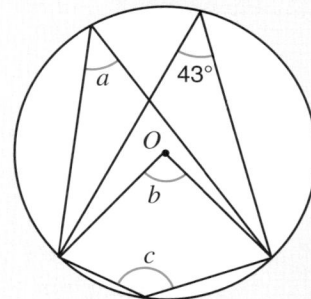

You should be able to prove that:

- the angle at the centre is twice the angle at the circumference,
- the angle in a semi-circle is a right angle,
- angles in the same segment are equal,
- opposite angles of a cyclic quadrilateral are supplementary,
- the angle between a tangent and a chord is equal to any angle in the alternate segment.

The diagrams in this exercise have not been drawn accurately.

1 O is the centre of the circle.
Work out the size of the lettered angles. Give a reason for each of your answers.

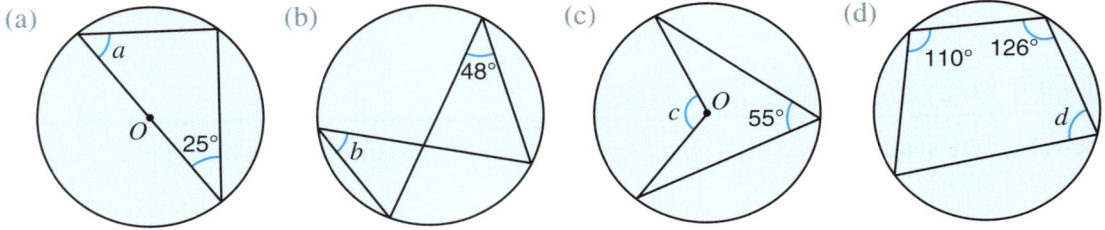

(a)

(b)

(c)

(d)

2 O is the centre of the circle.
Work out the size of angle x.

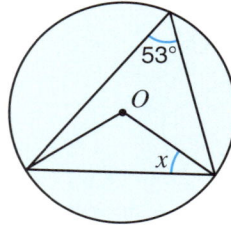

3 (a) AB is a tangent to the circle, centre O. Angle $OAB = 28°$.

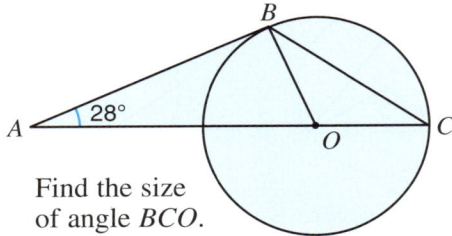

Find the size of angle BCO.

(b) AXB is a tangent to the circle, centre O.

Find the size of the angles marked a, b and c.

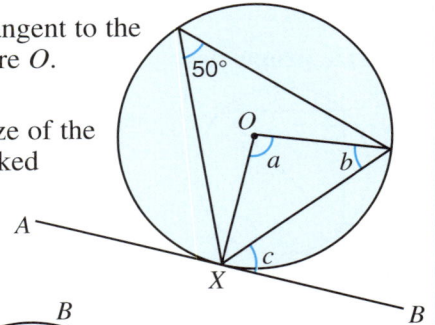

4 $ABCD$ is a cyclic quadrilateral.
AD is parallel to BC.
$\angle ABD = 32°$ and $\angle CBD = 53°$.
Find (a) angle ADB, (b) angle ACD,
(c) angle ADC, (d) angle BAD.

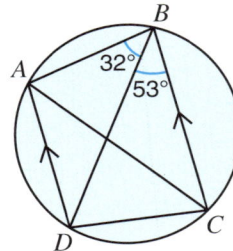

5 The diagram shows a semi-circle, centre O.
Angle $CAD = x°$ and BC is parallel to AD.
Find, in terms of x, angle ABC.

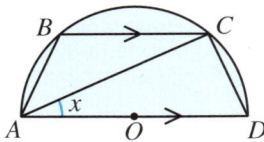

6 A, B and C are points on the circumference of a circle, centre O.
D is a point on BC such that AOD is a straight line.
PA is a tangent to the circle at A. Calculate angles x, y and z.

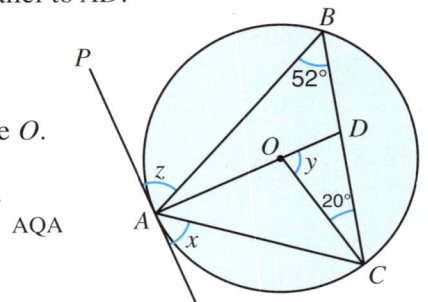

AQA

7 AT and BT are tangents to the circle, centre C.
P is a point on the circumference, as shown.
Angle $BAT = 65°$.

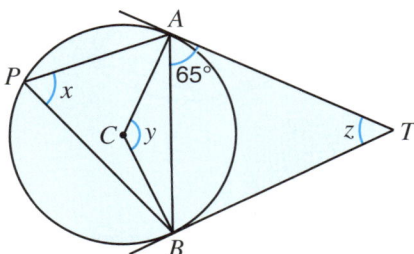

Calculate the size of (a) x, (b) y, (c) z.

AQA

Circles and Other Shapes

What you need to know

● You should be able to calculate **lengths** and **areas** associated with **circles**.

Circumference of a circle is given by: $C = \pi d$ or $C = 2\pi r$
Area of a circle is given by: $A = \pi r^2$

The **lengths of arcs** and the **areas of sectors** are proportional to the angle at the centre of the circle.

For a sector with angle $a°$

Length of arc $= \dfrac{a}{360} \times \pi d$

Area of sector $= \dfrac{a}{360} \times \pi r^2$

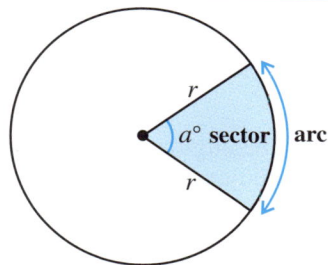

Eg 1 A circle has a circumference of 25.2 cm. Find the diameter of the circle.

$C = \pi d$ so $d = \dfrac{C}{\pi}$

$d = \dfrac{25.2}{\pi}$

$d = 8.021\ldots$

$d = 8.0$ cm, correct to 1 d.p.

Eg 2 A circle has an area of 154 cm². Find the radius of the circle.

$A = \pi r^2$ so $r^2 = \dfrac{A}{\pi}$

$r^2 = \dfrac{154}{\pi} = 49.019\ldots$

$r = \sqrt{49.019\ldots} = 7.001\ldots$

$r = 7$ cm, to the nearest cm.

Eg 3 *OAB* is a sector of a circle of radius 7.2 cm. Angle *AOB* = 50°.
Calculate   (a)   the length of arc *AB*,
              (b)   the area of sector *AOB*.

(a)   Length of arc $= \dfrac{a}{360} \times \pi d = \dfrac{50}{360} \times \pi \times 14.4$

$= 6.2831\ldots$
$= 6.28$ cm, correct to 3 s.f.

(b)   Area of sector $= \dfrac{a}{360} \times \pi r^2 = \dfrac{50}{360} \times \pi \times 7.2^2$

$= 22.619\ldots$
$= 22.6$ cm², correct to 3 s.f.

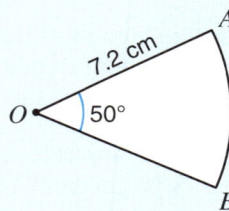

● Shapes formed by joining different shapes together are called **compound shapes**.
To find the area of a compound shape we must first divide the shape up into rectangles, triangles, circles, etc, and find the area of each part.

Exercise 25

Take π to be 3.14 or use the π key on your calculator.

1 (a)   Calculate the circumference of a circle of diameter 26 cm.
  (b)   Calculate the area of a circle of radius 2.5 cm.

AQA

2 Triangle *XYZ* has an area of 12 cm².
XZ = 5 cm.
Calculate *YP*.

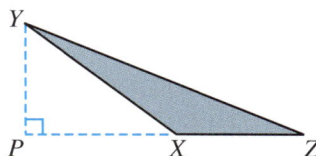

3 In the rectangle a triangular region has been shaded.
What percentage of the rectangle is shaded?
Give your answer to an appropriate degree of accuracy.

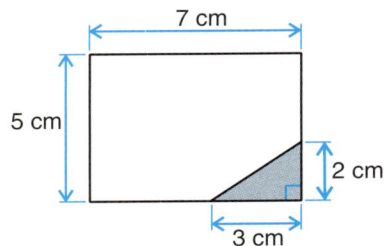

7 cm

5 cm

2 cm

3 cm

AQA

4

P   5.5 cm   Q

7 cm

S   9.5 cm   R

The diagram shows a trapezium *PQRS*.
Calculate the area of the trapezium.

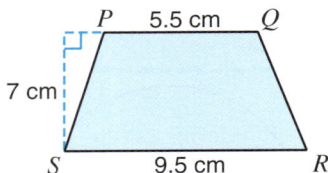

5 A rectangular carpet is twice as long as it is wide. The carpet covers an area of 24.5 m².
Calculate the length of the carpet.

6 The diagram shows the plan of a swimming pool.
The arc *QR* is a semi-circle.
PS = 12 m   and   *PQ* = *RS* = 20 m.
Calculate the area of the pool.

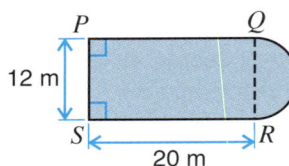

P   Q

12 m

S   R

20 m

7 Rashida has a hoop with a circumference of 300 cm. Calculate the radius of Rashida's hoop.

AQA

8 Three circles overlap, as shown.
The largest circle has a diameter of 12 cm.
The ratio of the diameters $x : y$ is 1 : 2.
Calculate the shaded area.
Give your answer in terms of π.

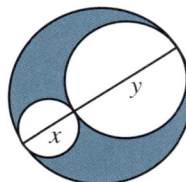

y

x

9 A circle has an area of 100 cm².
Calculate the circumference of the circle.
Give your answer correct to three significant figures.

10 Alfie says, "A semi-circle with a radius of 10 cm has a larger area than a whole circle with half the radius." Is he correct? You **must** show working to justify your answer.

11 *BAC* is a sector of a circle, radius 20 cm, whose centre is at *A*.
Angle *BAC* = 43°.

(a) Calculate the area of the sector *BAC*.

(b) The area of sector *QAR* is 450 cm².
Angle *QAR* is $x°$.
Calculate the value of x.

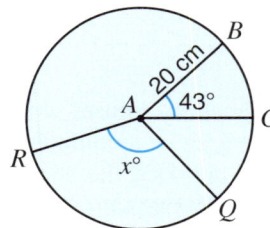

B

20 cm

A   43°

C

R

$x°$

Q

AQA

12 *OAB* is a minor sector of a circle of radius 6 cm.
Angle *AOB* = 120°.

(a) Calculate the area of the minor sector *OAB*.
Give your answer in terms of π.

(b) Calculate the perimeter of the minor sector *OAB*.
Give your answer in terms of π.

(c) The triangle *OAB* is reflected in the chord *AB* to form the quadrilateral *OAPB*.
Does point *P* lie inside the circle, outside the circle, or on the arc *AB*?
Explain your reasoning clearly.

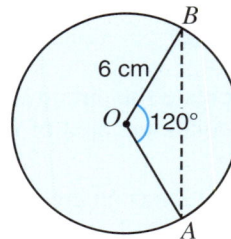

B

6 cm

O   120°

A

AQA

Loci and Constructions

What you need to know

- The path of a point which moves according to a rule is called a **locus**.

- The word **loci** is used when we talk about more than one locus.

- You should be able to draw the locus of a point which moves according to a given rule.

  Eg 1 A ball is rolled along this zig-zag.
  Draw the locus of *P*, the centre
  of the ball, as it is rolled along.

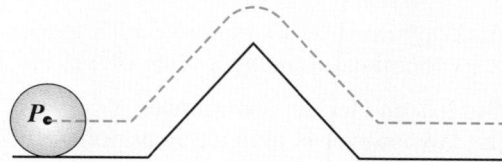

- Using a ruler and compasses you should be able to carry out the **constructions** below.

1 **The perpendicular bisector of a line.**

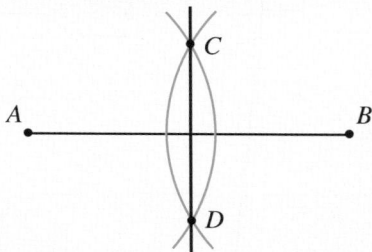

Points on the line *CD* are **equidistant**
from the points *A* and *B*.

2 **The bisector of an angle.**

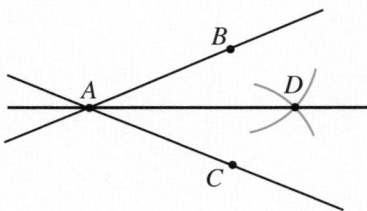

Points on the line *AD* are **equidistant**
from the lines *AB* and *AC*.

3 **The perpendicular from a point to a line.**

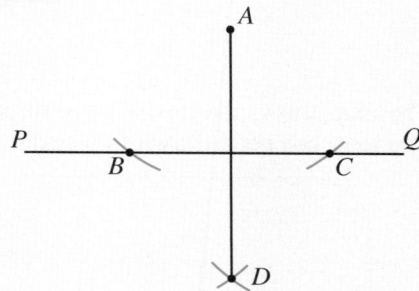

4 **The perpendicular from a point on a line.**

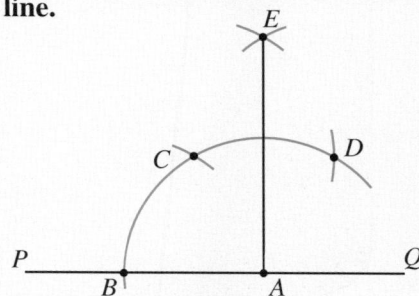

- You should be able to solve loci problems which involve using these constructions.

  Eg 2 *P* is a point inside triangle *ABC* such that:
  (i)   *P* is equidistant from points *A* and *B*,
  (ii) *P* is equidistant from lines *AB* and *BC*.
  Find the position of *P*.

  > To find point *P*:
  > (i) construct the perpendicular bisector of line *AB*,
  > (ii) construct the bisector of angle *ABC*.

  P is at the point where these lines intersect.

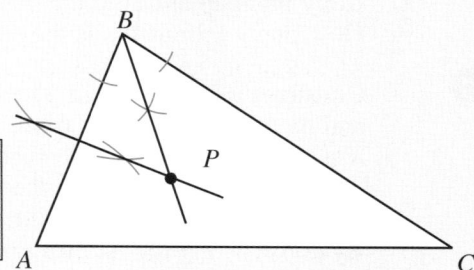

63

1 The ball is rolled along the zig-zag.
Copy the diagram and draw the locus of the centre of the ball as it is rolled from *X* to *Y*.

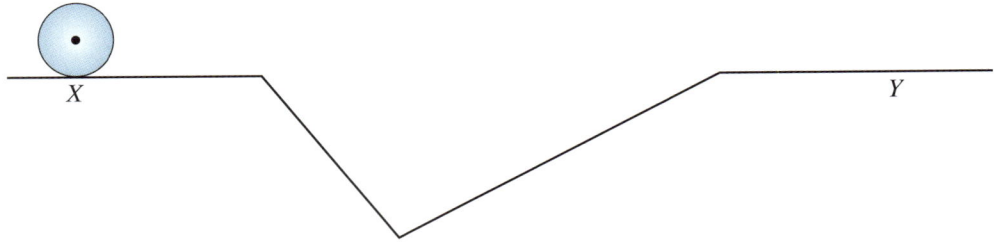

2 The diagram shows a plan of Paul's garden.
Draw the diagram using a scale of 1 cm to 1 m.

Paul has an electric lawnmower.
The lawnmower is plugged in at point *P*.

It can reach a maximum distance of 12 metres from *P*.
Using the same scale, show on your diagram the area
of the garden which the lawnmower can reach.

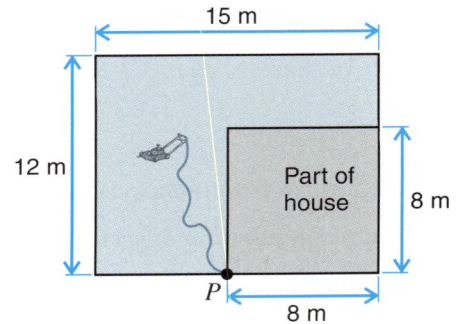

AQA

3 The map shows the positions of three villages *A*, *B* and *C*.
The map has been drawn to a scale of 1 cm to 2 km.

A supermarket is equidistant from villages *A*, *B* and *C*.
(a) Copy the map and find the position of the supermarket on your diagram.
(b) How many kilometres is the supermarket from village *A*?

4 (a) Construct a kite *PQRS* in which   *PQ* = *PS* = 7 cm,   *QR* = *RS* = 5 cm
and the diagonal   *QS* = 6 cm.
X is a point inside the kite such that:
(i) *X* is equidistant from *P* and *Q*,
(ii) *X* is equidistant from sides *PQ* and *PS*.
(b) By constructing the loci for (i) and (ii) find the position of *X*.
(c) Measure the distance *PX*.

Transformations

What you need to know

- The movement of a shape from one position to another is called a **transformation**.

- **Single transformations** can be described in terms of a reflection, a rotation, a translation or an enlargement.

- **Reflection**: The image of the shape is the same distance from the mirror line as the original.

- **Rotation**: All points are turned through the same angle about the same point, called a centre of rotation.

- **Translation**: All points are moved the same distance in the same direction without turning.

- **Enlargement**: All lengths are multiplied by a scale factor.

Scale factor $= \dfrac{\text{new length}}{\text{original length}}$ | New length = scale factor × original length |

The size of the original shape is:
    increased by using a scale factor greater than 1,
    reduced by using a scale factor which is a fraction, i.e. between 0 and 1.
When a shape is enlarged using a **negative scale factor** the image is **inverted**.

- You should be able to draw the transformation of a shape.

  Eg 1 Draw the image of triangle P after it has been translated with vector $\begin{pmatrix} -3 \\ 2 \end{pmatrix}$.

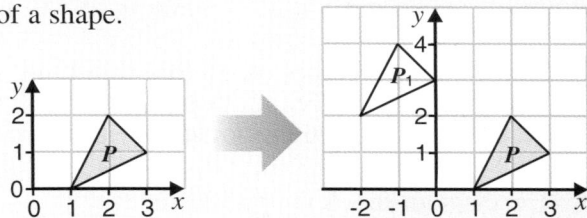

- You should be able to fully describe transformations.

Transformation	Image same shape and size?	Details needed to describe the transformation
Reflection	Yes	Mirror line, sometimes given as an equation.
Rotation	Yes	Centre of rotation, amount of turn, direction of turn.
Translation	Yes	Vector: top number = horizontal movement, bottom number = vertical movement.
Enlargement	No	Centre of enlargement, scale factor.

  Eg 2 Describe the single transformation which maps
    (a) A onto B,
    (b) A onto C,
    (c) A onto D,
    (d) D onto E,
    (e) E onto F.

    (a) **Reflection** in the line $x = 3$.
    (b) **Rotation** of $180°$ about $(2, 1)$.
    (c) **Translation** with vector $\begin{pmatrix} 2 \\ -3 \end{pmatrix}$.
    (d) **Enlargement** scale factor 2, centre $(2, 0)$.
    (e) **Enlargement** scale factor $-\frac{1}{2}$, centre $(6, -2)$.

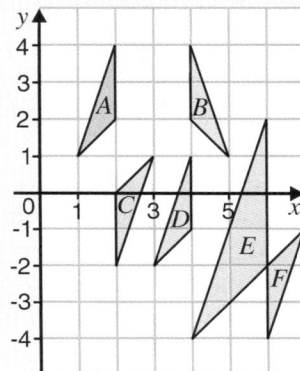

1 The diagram shows the positions of kites *P*, *Q*, *R* and *S*.

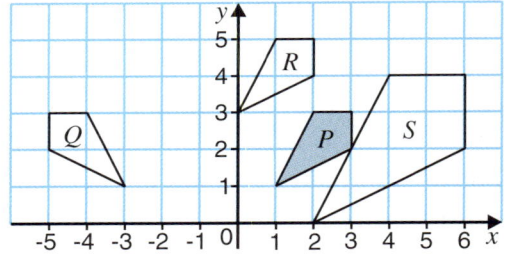

(a) (i) *P* is mapped onto *Q* by a reflection.
What is the equation of the
line of reflection?
(ii) *P* is mapped onto *R* by a translation.
What is the vector of the translation?
(iii) *P* is mapped onto *S* by an enlargement.
What is the centre and scale factor of
the enlargement?

(b) *P* is mapped onto *T* by a rotation through 90° clockwise about $(1, -2)$.
On squared paper, copy *P* and draw the position of *T*.

2 In each diagram, *A* is mapped onto *B* by a single transformation. Describe each transformation.

(a)

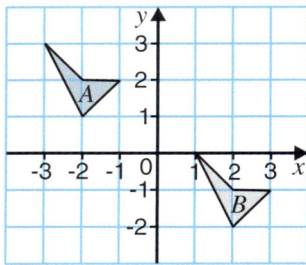

(b)

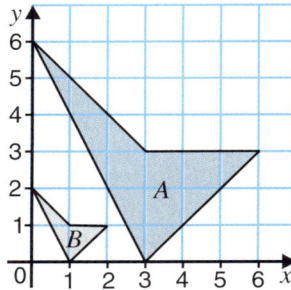

(c)

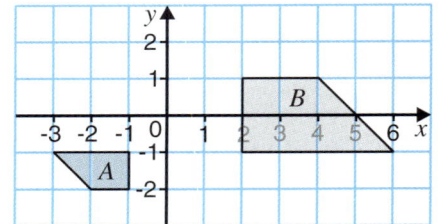

3 Triangle *X* has vertices $(1, 2)$, $(0, 3)$, $(-1, 1)$.
Triangle *Y* has vertices $(2, 1)$, $(3, 0)$, $(1, -1)$.
Describe the single transformation which maps *X* onto *Y*.

4 The diagram shows the position of *P*.
P has coordinates $(3, 1)$.

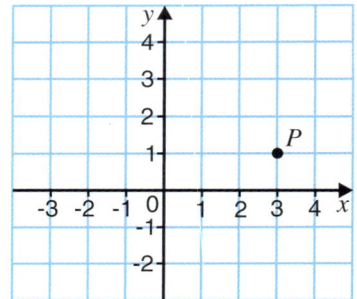

(a) *P* is mapped onto *Q* by a reflection in the line $y = x$.
What are the coordinates of *Q*?

The translation $\begin{pmatrix} -2 \\ 1 \end{pmatrix}$ maps *P* onto *R*.

The translation $\begin{pmatrix} 3 \\ -4 \end{pmatrix}$ maps *R* onto *S*.

(b) (i) What are the coordinates of *S*?
(ii) What is the translation which maps *S* onto *P*?

(c) *T* has coordinates $(-1, 1)$.
P is mapped onto *T* by a rotation through 90° anticlockwise about centre *X*.
What are the coordinates of *X*?

AQA

5 Triangle *PQR* has vertices $P(2, -3)$, $Q(-2, -5)$, $R(-4, -3)$.
On squared paper, draw and label triangle *PQR*.

(a) Enlarge triangle *PQR* by scale factor $\frac{1}{2}$ from the centre of enlargement $(4, -1)$.
Label the image *A*.
(b) Rotate triangle *PQR* through 180° about the point $(-2, -1)$.
Label the image *B*.
(c) Describe fully the single transformation which maps triangle *A* onto triangle *B*.

Pythagoras' Theorem

●●●●●

What you need to know

- The longest side in a right-angled triangle is called the **hypotenuse**.

- The **Theorem of Pythagoras** states:
  "In any right-angled triangle the square on the hypotenuse is equal to the sum of the squares on the other two sides."
  $$a^2 = b^2 + c^2$$

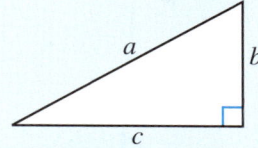

- When we know the lengths of two sides of a right-angled triangle, we can use the Theorem of Pythagoras to find the length of the third side.

> $a^2 = b^2 + c^2$
> Rearranging gives: $b^2 = a^2 - c^2$
> $c^2 = a^2 - b^2$

Eg 1 Calculate the length of side a, correct to 1 d.p.

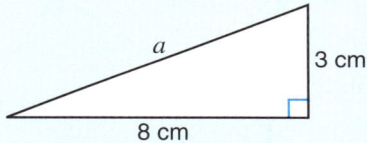

$a^2 = b^2 + c^2$
$a^2 = 8^2 + 3^2$
$a^2 = 64 + 9 = 73$
$a = \sqrt{73} = 8.544\ldots$
$a = 8.5\,\text{cm}$, correct to 1 d.p.

Eg 2 Calculate the length of side b, correct to 1 d.p.

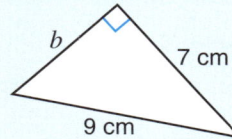

$b^2 = a^2 - c^2$
$b^2 = 9^2 - 7^2$
$b^2 = 81 - 49 = 32$
$b = \sqrt{32} = 5.656\ldots$
$b = 5.7\,\text{cm}$, correct to 1 d.p.

- When solving problems in three dimensions you often need to use more than one triangle to solve the problem.

Exercise 28

The diagrams in this exercise have not been drawn accurately.
Do not use a calculator for questions 1 and 2.

1 ABC is a right-angled triangle.
$AB = 5\,\text{cm}$ and $AC = 12\,\text{cm}$.
Calculate the length of BC.

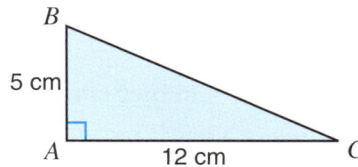

2 The positions of three villages, Oldacre (O), Adchester (A) and Byetoft (B), are shown on the diagram.
Angle $OAB = 90°$.
The distance from Oldacre to Adchester is 8 km.
The distance from Oldacre to Byetoft is 10 km.
Calculate the distance from Adchester to Byetoft.

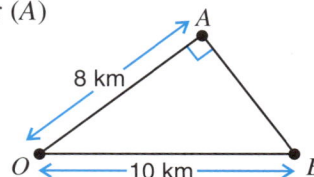

AQA

3 The diagram shows a rectangular sheet of paper.
The paper is 20 cm wide and the diagonal, d, is 35 cm.
Calculate the length of the sheet of paper.

4 Calculate the length of the line joining the points $A(-3, 2)$ and $B(6, -2)$.

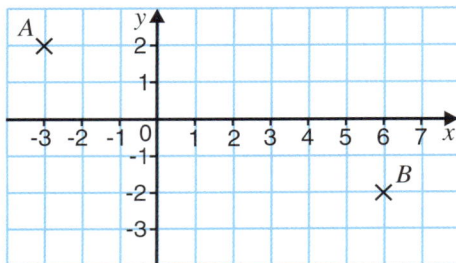

AQA

5

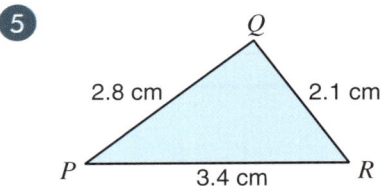

Is PQR: an acute-angled triangle,
an obtuse-angled triangle,
or a right-angled triangle?

Show your calculations and state your conclusions.

6 In the diagram, $BCDX$ is a square.
AXE is a straight line with $AX = 6.5$ cm and $XE = 3$ cm. $DE = 2$ cm.

(a) Calculate the area of $BCDX$.

(b) Calculate the length of AB, correct to one decimal place.

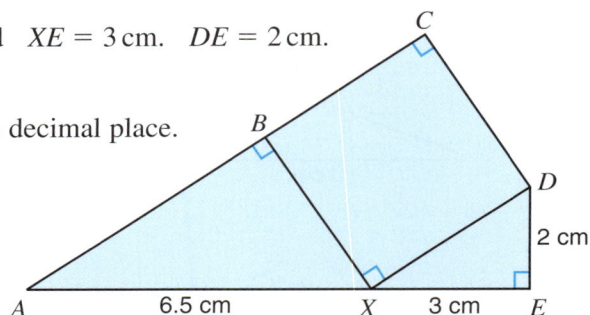

7

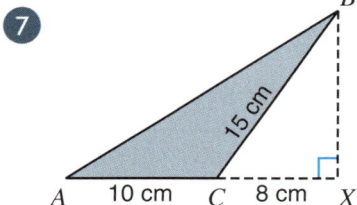

The diagram shows a triangle ABC.
Angle $BXA = 90°$, $BC = 15$ cm, $CX = 8$ cm and $AC = 10$ cm.

Calculate the area of triangle ABC.
Give your answer correct to 3 significant figures.

AQA

8 A cuboid has dimensions 20 cm by 10 cm by 5 cm.

Calculate the length of the diagonal AB.
Give your answer to a suitable degree of accuracy.

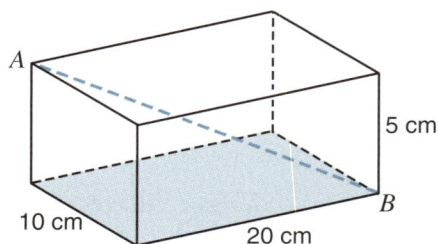

9

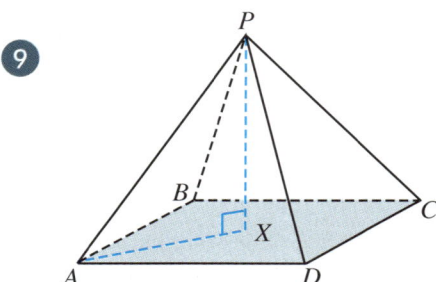

The diagram shows a square-based pyramid.
The edges $PA = PB = PC = PD = 9$ cm.
X is at the centre of the base $ABCD$.
$PX = 8$ cm.

Calculate the area of the base, $ABCD$.

Trigonometry

What you need to know

- **Trigonometry** is used to find the lengths of sides and the sizes of angles in right-angled triangles.

- You must learn the **sine**, **cosine** and **tangent** ratios.

$$\sin a = \frac{\text{opposite}}{\text{hypotenuse}} \quad \cos a = \frac{\text{adjacent}}{\text{hypotenuse}} \quad \tan a = \frac{\text{opposite}}{\text{adjacent}}$$

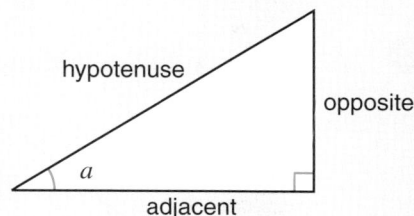

- Each ratio links the size of an angle with the lengths of two sides. If we are given the values for two of these we can find the value of the third.

- When we look **up** from the horizontal the angle we turn through is called the **angle of elevation**.

- When we look **down** from the horizontal the angle we turn through is called the **angle of depression**.

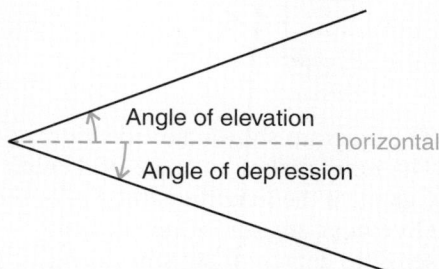

- **Three-figure bearings**
  Bearings are used to describe the direction in which you must travel to get from one place to another. They are measured from the North line in a clockwise direction. A bearing can be any angle from 0° to 360° and is written as a three-figure number.

- You should be able to use trigonometry to find the lengths of sides and the sizes of angles when solving problems involving right-angled triangles.

Eg 1 Find the length, d, giving the answer to 3 significant figures.

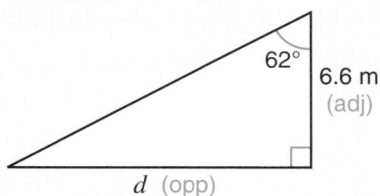

$$\tan a = \frac{\text{opp}}{\text{adj}}$$
$$\tan 62° = \frac{d}{6.6}$$
$$d = 6.6 \times \tan 62°$$
$$d = 12.412\ldots$$
$$d = 12.4 \,\text{m}, \text{ correct to 3 s.f.}$$

Eg 2 Find the size of angle a, correct to one decimal place.

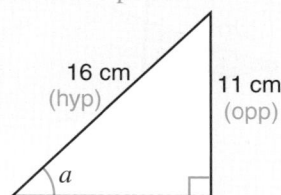

$$\sin a = \frac{\text{opp}}{\text{hyp}}$$
$$\sin a° = \frac{11}{16}$$
$$a = \sin^{-1}\frac{11}{16}$$
$$a = 43.432\ldots$$
$$a = 43.4°, \text{ correct to 1 d.p.}$$

- When working in three dimensions the first task is to identify the length, or angle, that you are trying to find. The length, or angle, will always form part of a triangle together with either:

  two other sides of known length, or
  one side of known length and an angle of known size.

  Sometimes, more than one triangle is needed to solve a problem.

- A straight line meets a plane at a **point**.
  The angle XPT is the **angle between the line and the plane**.
  The line XT is perpendicular to the plane.

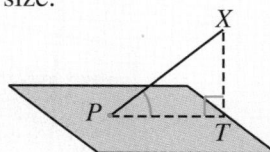

The diagrams in this exercise have not been drawn accurately.
Do not use a calculator for question 1.

1 LMN is a right-angled triangle.
$LN = 8$ cm.
$\sin x = 0.6$, $\cos x = 0.8$ and $\tan x = 0.75$.

Calculate the length of MN.

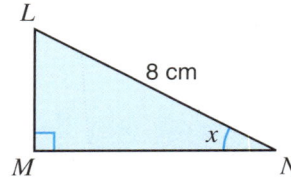

AQA

2 (a) Calculate angle x in triangle ABC.

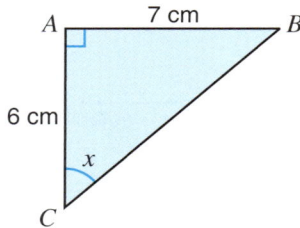

(b) Calculate length QR in triangle PQR.

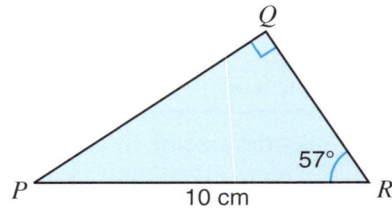

AQA

3 The diagram shows the side view of a wheelchair ramp.
The ramp makes an angle of 4° with the horizontal.
Calculate the length, marked x, of the ramp.
Give your answer in metres to a
sensible degree of accuracy.

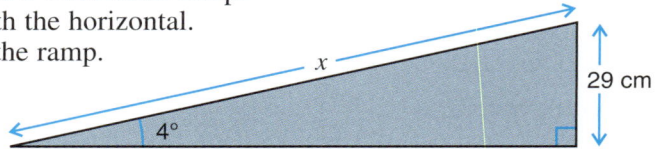

AQA

4 The diagram shows the path of a jet-ski from P to Q to R.

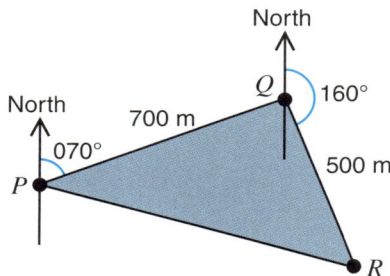

Q is 700 m from P on a bearing of 070°.
R is 500 m from Q on a bearing of 160°.

Calculate the bearing of P from R.

5 $VABCD$ is a pyramid on a square base of side 10 cm.
$VA = VB = VC = VD = 12$ cm.

(a) Calculate VO, the perpendicular height of the pyramid.

(b) Find the angle between VC and the base.

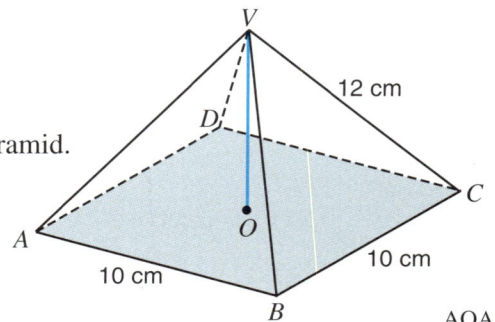

AQA

6

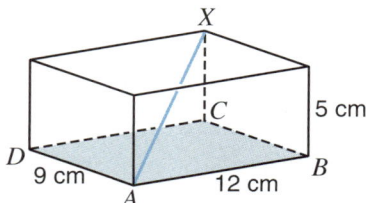

A cuboid has dimensions 12 cm by 9 cm by 5 cm.

Calculate the angle between the diagonal XA and the
base $ABCD$.

Volumes and Surface Areas

What you need to know

- You should be able to solve problems involving the volumes and surface areas of **cubes** and **cuboids**.

- **Prisms**
  If you make a cut at right angles to the length of a prism you will always get the same cross-section.

  cross-section ← → length

- Volume of a prism = area of cross-section × length

- A **cylinder** is a prism.
  Volume of a cylinder is: $V = \pi r^2 h$

  Surface area of a cylinder is:
  Surface area $= 2\pi r^2 + 2\pi rh$

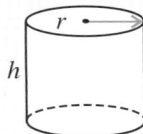

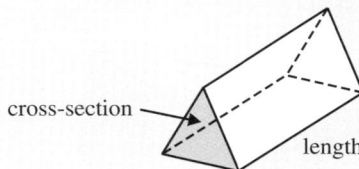

  Eg 1 A cylinder has a radius of 4 cm and a height of 6 cm.
  Calculate the volume of the cylinder.

  Volume $= \pi r^2 h$
  $= \pi \times 4 \times 4 \times 6$
  $= 301.592\ldots$
  $= 302\,\text{cm}^3$, correct to 3 s.f.

  Eg 2 A cylinder has a height of 7 cm.
  The volume of the cylinder is 550 cm³.
  Calculate the radius of the cylinder.

  Volume $= \pi r^2 h$
  $550 = \pi \times r^2 \times 7$
  $r^2 = \dfrac{550}{7\pi} = 25.01\ldots$
  $r = \sqrt{25.01\ldots} = 5\,\text{cm}$

- These formulae are used in calculations involving **cones**, **pyramids** and **spheres**.

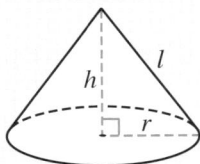

Cone

$V = \frac{1}{3} \times \text{base area} \times \text{height}$
$V = \frac{1}{3} \pi r^2 h$
Curved surface area $= \pi rl$

Pyramid

$V = \frac{1}{3} \times \text{base area} \times \text{height}$

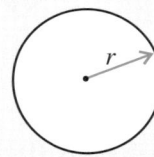

Sphere

Volume $= \frac{4}{3} \pi r^3$
Surface area $= 4\pi r^2$

Eg 3 A cone is 6.4 cm high and has a radius of 4.8 cm.
Calculate the curved surface area of the cone.

Slant height, $l = \sqrt{6.4^2 + 4.8^2}$
$= \sqrt{64} = 8\,\text{cm}$

Curved surface area is given by:
$\pi rl = \pi \times 4.8 \times 8 = 120.637\ldots$
$= 120.6\,\text{cm}^2$, correct to 1 d.p.

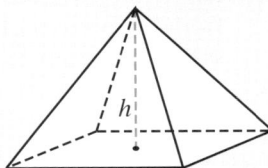

Eg 4 A steel ball has a radius of 4 cm.
Calculate (a) the volume,
(b) the surface area of the ball.

(a) Volume $= \frac{4}{3} \pi r^3 = \frac{4}{3} \times \pi \times 4^3$
$= 268.082\ldots$
$= 268\,\text{cm}^3$, correct to 3 s.f.

(b) Surface area $= 4\pi r^2 = 4 \times \pi \times 4^2$
$= 201.061\ldots$
$= 201\,\text{cm}^2$, correct to 3 s.f.

- A **frustum of a cone** is formed by removing the top of a cone with a cut parallel to its circular base.

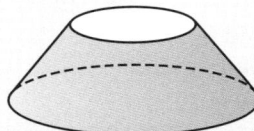

Do not use a calculator for question 1.

1 A cuboid has a volume of 100 cm³.
The cuboid is 8 cm long and 5 cm wide.
Calculate the surface area of the cuboid.

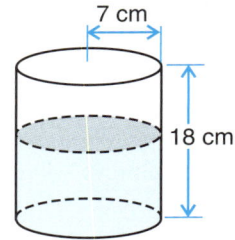
7 cm
18 cm

2 A cylinder of radius 7 cm and height 18 cm is half full of water.
One litre of water is added.
Will the water overflow?
You must show all your working.

AQA

3
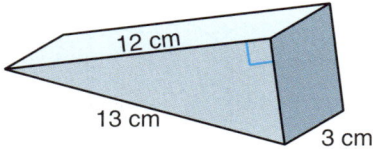
12 cm
13 cm
3 cm
Calculate the volume of this wedge.

4 A cylindrical water tank has radius 40 cm and height 90 cm.
(a)   Calculate the total surface area of the tank.

A full tank of water is used to fill a paddling pool.
(b)   The paddling pool is a cylinder with diameter 2.4 metres.
Calculate the depth of water in the pool.

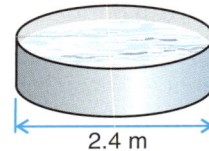
2.4 m

5
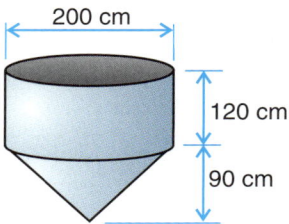
200 cm
120 cm
90 cm

A container consists of a cylinder on top of a cone.
The container is full of oil.
The diameter of the cylinder and cone is 200 cm.
The height of the cone is 90 cm and the height of the
cylinder is 120 cm.
(a)   Calculate the volume of oil in the container.

Oil flows from the container until it reaches a level 45 cm
from the bottom of the container.
(b)   What volume of oil has flowed from the container?

AQA

6 A cone is 10 cm high and has a base radius of 6 cm.
(a)   Calculate the curved surface area of the cone.

The top of the cone is cut off to leave a frustum 8 cm high.
(b)   Calculate the volume of the frustum.

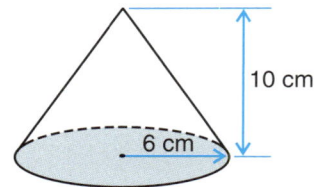
10 cm
6 cm

7
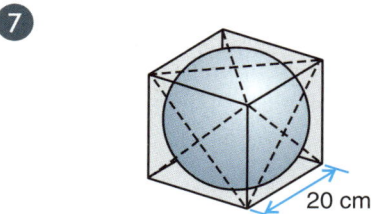
20 cm

Rachel buys a ball in a box.
The ball touches each side of the box.
The box is a cube with sides of length 20 cm.
(a)   Calculate the difference between the volume of the
box and the volume of the ball.
(b)   Calculate the difference between the surface area of
the box and the surface area of the ball.

8 The diagram shows a triangular pyramid.
Angle $ABC = 90°$, $AB = 5$ cm   and $BC = 3$ cm.
The volume of the pyramid is 28 cm³.
Calculate the height of the pyramid.

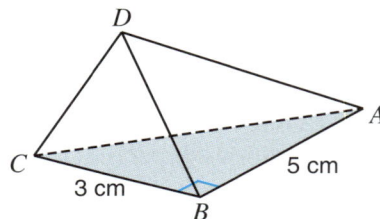
D
A
C
3 cm
5 cm
B

Understanding and Using Measures

What you need to know

- The common units − both **metric** and **imperial** − used to measure **length**, **mass** and **capacity**.

- How to convert from one unit to another. This includes knowing the connection between one metric unit and another and the approximate equivalents between metric and imperial units.

Metric Units	Imperial Units	Conversions
Length 1 kilometre (km) = 1000 metres (m) 1 m = 100 centimetres (cm) 1 cm = 10 millimetres (mm) **Mass** 1 tonne (t) = 1000 kilograms (kg) 1 kg = 1000 grams (g) **Capacity and volume** 1 litre = 1000 millilitres (ml) 1 cm³ = 1 ml	**Length** 1 foot = 12 inches 1 yard = 3 feet **Mass** 1 pound = 16 ounces 14 pounds = 1 stone **Capacity and volume** 1 gallon = 8 pints	**Length** 5 miles is about 8 km 1 inch is about 2.5 cm 1 foot is about 30 cm **Mass** 1 kg is about 2.2 pounds **Capacity and volume** 1 litre is about 1.75 pints 1 gallon is about 4.5 litres

- How to change between units of area.   For example $1 \, m^2 = 10\,000 \, cm^2$.

- How to change between units of volume.   For example $1 \, m^3 = 1\,000\,000 \, cm^3$.

- You should be able to recognise limitations on the accuracy of measurements.
  A **discrete measure** can only take a particular value and a **continuous measure** lies within a range of possible values which depends upon the degree of accuracy of the measurement.

> If a **continuous measure**, c, is recorded to the nearest x, then the limits of the possible values of c can be written as $c \pm \frac{1}{2} x$.

Eg 1   A log is 12 m in length. The length is correct to the nearest metre.
What is the minimum length of the log?   Minimum length = 12 − 0.5 = 11.5 m

Eg 2   A road is 400 m long, to the nearest 10 m.
Between what lengths is the actual length of the road?
Actual length = 400 m ± 5 m   395 m ≤ actual length < 405 m

Eg 3   A punnet of strawberries weighs 2.4 kg, correct to the nearest 100 g.
Between what limits must the weight of the strawberries lie?
Actual weight = 2.4 kg ± 0.05 kg
Lower limit   = 2.35 kg
Upper limit   = 2.45 kg
So,   2.35 kg ≤ actual weight < 2.45 kg.

- By analysing the **dimensions** of a formula it is possible to decide whether a given formula represents a **length** (dimension 1), an **area** (dimension 2) or a **volume** (dimension 3).

Eg 4 p, q, r and s represent lengths.
By using dimensions, decide whether the expression $pq + qr + rs$
could represent a perimeter, an area or a volume.
Writing $pq + qr + rs$ using dimensions:
$$L \times L + L \times L + L \times L = L^2 + L^2 + L^2 = 3L^2$$
So, $pq + qr + rs$ has dimension 2 and could represent an area.

1 On a map the distance between two hospitals is 14.5 cm.
The map has been drawn to a scale of 1 to 250 000.
Calculate the actual distance between the hospitals in kilometres.

2 Mum's Traditional Jam is sold in two sizes.
A 1 lb pot of jam costs 71 pence. A 1 kg pot of jam costs £1.50.
Which pot of jam is better value for money? You must show all your working.

3 Debbie is 5 feet 4 inches tall and weighs 9 stone 2 lb. Joyce is 155 cm tall and weighs 60 kg.
Who is taller? Who is heavier? You must show your working.

4 Last year Felicity drove 2760 miles on business.
Her car does 38 miles per gallon. Petrol costs 69 pence per litre.
She is given a car allowance of 25 pence per kilometre.
How much of her car allowance is left after paying for her petrol?
Give your answer to the nearest £.

5 Vicky measures her handspan and writes down the result as:

> **18 cm, correct to the nearest centimetre.**

(a) Write down the greatest length her handspan could be.

Chris has measured his handspan as 17.5 cm, correct to the nearest half centimetre.
(b) Write down the smallest length his handspan could be.

Paul says that Chris should write his answer down as 17.50 cm.
(c) Give a reason why this is not appropriate.   AQA

6 Bags of potatoes each weigh 25 kg correct to the nearest kg.
What is the minimum weight of 9 bags of potatoes?   AQA

7 The dimensions of a triangular prism are shown.
The following formulae represent certain quantities
connected with the prism.

$$d(a + b + c) \qquad \frac{abd}{2} \qquad \sqrt{(a^2 + b^2)} \qquad cd \qquad \tfrac{1}{2}\,ab$$

(a) Which of these formulae represents a length?
(b) Which of these formulae represents a volume?   AQA

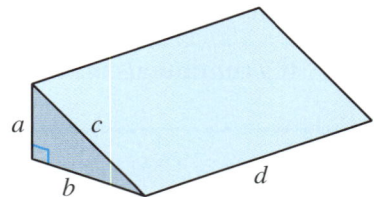

8 The measurements of a rectangular ticket are given as 5 cm by 3 cm,
correct to the nearest centimetre.
(a) Between what limits must the width of the ticket lie?
(b) Between what limits must the area of the ticket lie?
(c) The area of the ticket is given as $(15 \pm x)\,\text{cm}^2$.
    Suggest a suitable value for x.

9 Michael rides his bicycle to work.
The diameter of each wheel is 65 cm, correct to the nearest centimetre.
The distance he cycles to work is 2.4 km, correct to one decimal place.
Calculate the least number of turns each wheel makes when Michael cycles to work.

10 p, q and r are three continuous measures.
$p = 5.3$ to an accuracy of two significant figures.
$q = 0.64$ and $r = 0.64$,   each to an accuracy of two decimal places.
(a) Calculate   (i)   the lower bound of $p - q$,   (ii)   the upper bound of $\frac{p + q}{r}$.

(b) T is an integer where $T = 50$ to the nearest 5. Calculate the largest possible value of Tp.
                                                                    AQA

Congruent Triangles and Similar Figures

What you need to know

- When two shapes are the same shape and size they are said to be **congruent**.

- There are four ways to show that a pair of triangles are congruent.

SSS	3 corresponding sides.	**ASA**	2 angles and a corresponding side.
SAS	2 sides and the included angle.	**RHS**	Right angle, hypotenuse and one other side.

Eg 1 Show that triangles ABC and XYZ are congruent.

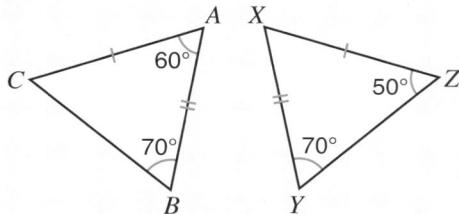

$$AC = XZ \quad \text{(given)}$$
$$AB = XY \quad \text{(given)}$$
$$\angle BAC = \angle YXZ = 60° \quad \text{(sum of angles in } \Delta = 180°)$$

So, triangles ABC and XYZ are congruent (SAS).

- When two figures are **similar**:
  their **shapes** are the same, their **angles** are the same,
  corresponding **lengths** are in the same ratio,
  this ratio is the **scale factor** of the enlargement.

$$\text{Scale factor} = \frac{\text{new length}}{\text{original length}}$$

- For **similar triangles**:
  corresponding lengths are opposite equal angles,
  the scale factor is the ratio of the corresponding sides.

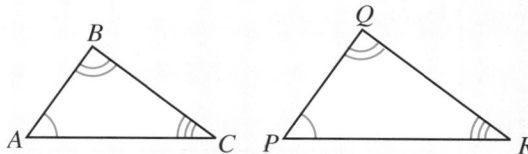

$$\frac{AB}{PQ} = \frac{BC}{QR} = \frac{CA}{RP} = \text{scale factor}$$

- You should be able to find corresponding lengths in similar triangles.

Eg 2 These two triangles are similar.
Find the lengths of the sides marked x and y.

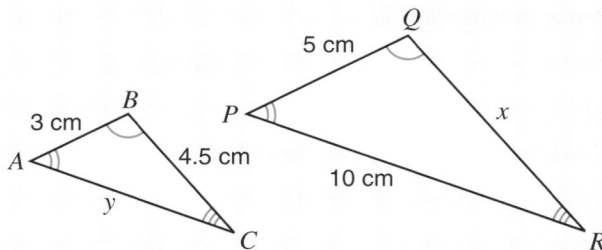

AB and PQ are corresponding sides.
Scale factor $= \frac{PQ}{AB} = \frac{5}{3}$

$$x = 4.5 \times \frac{5}{3} = 7.5 \text{ cm}$$
$$y = 10 \div \frac{5}{3} = 6 \text{ cm}$$

- You should be able to find corresponding lengths, areas and volumes in similar figures.

When the **length** scale factor $= k$, the **area** scale factor $= k^2$, the **volume** scale factor $= k^3$.

Eg 3 Two fish tanks are similar. The smaller tank is 12 cm high and holds 4 litres of water. The larger tank is 18 cm high. How many litres of water does the larger tank hold?

Ratio of heights is $12 : 18 = 2 : 3$.
Ratio of volumes is $2^3 : 3^3 = 8 : 27$.

Water in larger tank $= 4 \times \frac{27}{8} = 13.5$ litres

To find the ratio of volumes, cube the ratio of lengths.

The diagrams in this exercise have not been drawn accurately.

1 Which two of these triangles are congruent to each other?
Give a reason for your answer.

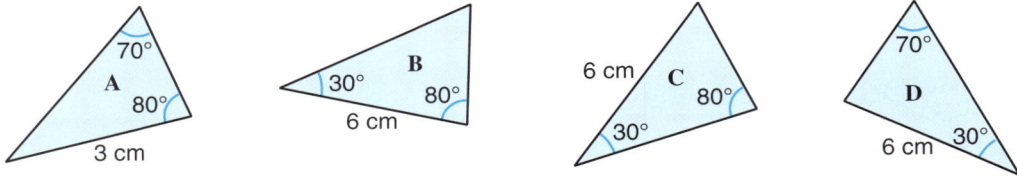

70°
A
80°
3 cm

B
30°
80°
6 cm

6 cm
C
80°
30°

70°
D
6 cm
30°

2 The diagram shows two regular hexagons.
(a) Name a triangle which is similar but **not** congruent to triangle *BCD*.

(b) *AB* : *PQ* is 2 : 3.
(i) Angle *AEF* = 30°.
What is the size of angle *PTU*?
(ii) *AF* = 2.4 cm.
Calculate the perimeter of the hexagon *PQRSTU*.

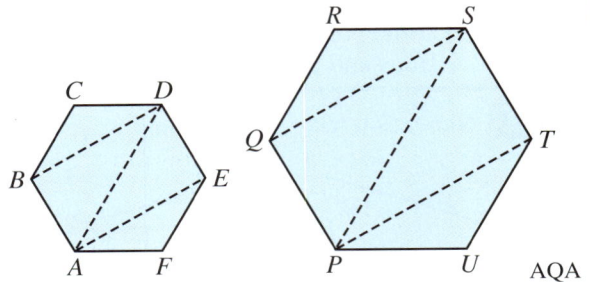

C   D
B   E
A   F

R   S
Q   T
P   U

AQA

3 Noel (*N*) can just see the top of the church tower (*C*)
appearing over the tree (*T*).

Noel is 20 metres from the tree.
The tree is 30 metres from the tower.
The tower is 44 metres high.
Calculate the height of the tree.

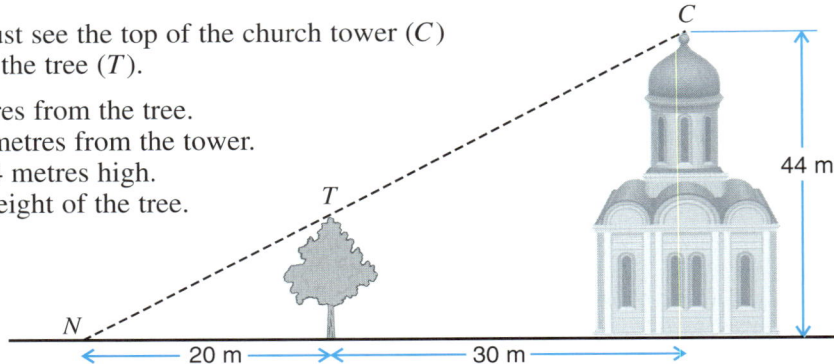

C

44 m

T

N

←— 20 m —→←——— 30 m ———→

AQA

4 In the diagram, *AB* is parallel to *DE*.
AB = 4.5 cm, *AC* = 2.7 cm and *CE* = 2.4 cm.

(a) Explain why triangle *ABC* is similar to triangle *EDC*.
(b) Calculate the length of *DE*.

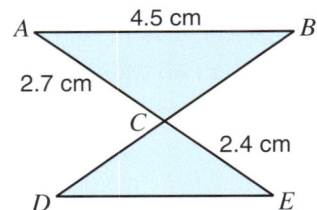

A   4.5 cm   B
2.7 cm
C
2.4 cm
D   E

5 (a) Two bottles of perfume are similar to each other.
The heights of the bottles are 4 cm and 6 cm.
The smaller bottle has a volume of 24 cm³.
Calculate the volume of the larger bottle.

(b) Two bottles of aftershave are similar to each other.
The areas of the bases of these bottles are 4.8 cm² and 10.8 cm².
The height of the smaller bottle is 3 cm.
Calculate the height of the larger bottle.

AQA

6 *A* and *B* are two similar cylinders.
The height of cylinder *A* is 10 cm and its volume is 625 cm³.
The volume of cylinder *B* is 5000 cm³.
Calculate the height of cylinder *B*.

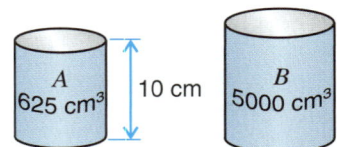

A
625 cm³

10 cm

B
5000 cm³

AQA

What you need to know

- **Vector quantities**
  Quantities which have both **size** and **direction** are called **vectors**.
  Examples of vector quantities are:

  Displacement – A combination of distance and direction.

  Velocity – A combination of speed and direction.

- **Vector notation**
  Vectors can be represented by **column vectors** or by **directed line segments**.
  Vectors can be labelled using:
  capital letters to indicate the start and finish of a vector,
  bold lower case letters.

  In a **column vector:**
  The top number describes the **horizontal** part of the movement:
  $+$ = to the right $-$ = to the left

  The bottom number describes the **vertical** part of the movement:
  $+$ = upwards $-$ = downwards

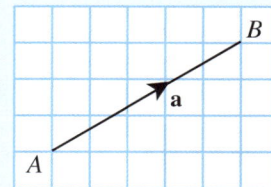

  $$\overrightarrow{AB} = \mathbf{a} = \begin{pmatrix} 5 \\ 3 \end{pmatrix}$$

- Vectors are **equal** if they have the same length **and** they are in the same direction.
  Vectors $\mathbf{a}$ and $-\mathbf{a}$ have the same length **but** are in **opposite directions**.
  The vector $n\mathbf{a}$ is parallel to the vector $\mathbf{a}$.
  The length of vector $n\mathbf{a} = n \times$ the length of vector $\mathbf{a}$.

- **Vector addition**
  The combination of the displacement from A to B followed by the displacement from B to C is equivalent to a total displacement from A to C.

  This can be written using vectors as $\overrightarrow{AB} + \overrightarrow{BC} = \overrightarrow{AC}$

  $\overrightarrow{AC}$ is called the **resultant vector**.

- Combinations of vectors can be shown on **vector diagrams**.

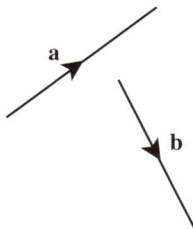

  With the arrow, +a
  With the arrow, +b
  Resultant vector, a + b

  With the arrow = +
  Against the arrow = −

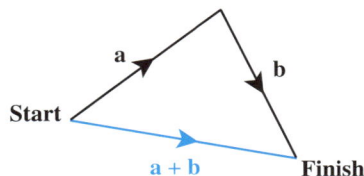

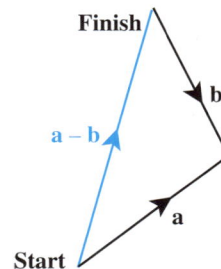

  With the arrow, +a
  Against the arrow, −b
  Resultant vector, a − b

33 ● You should be able to use **vector geometry** to solve simple geometrical problems, which can often involve parallel lines.

Eg 1 *OAXB* is a quadrilateral.

$\overrightarrow{OA} = \mathbf{a}$, $\overrightarrow{OB} = \mathbf{b}$ and $\overrightarrow{AX} = 2\overrightarrow{OB}$.

(a) Find, in terms of **a** and **b**,

    (i) $\overrightarrow{AX}$,   (ii) $\overrightarrow{BX}$.

(b) *M* and *N* are the midpoints of *OA* and *BX* respectively.

    (i) Find $\overrightarrow{MN}$, in terms of **a** and **b**.
    (ii) What can you say about the lines *OB* and *MN*?
    (iii) What type of quadrilateral is *OMNB*?

(a) (i) $\overrightarrow{AX} = 2\mathbf{b}$ (ii) $\overrightarrow{BX} = \mathbf{a} + \mathbf{b}$

(b) (i) $\overrightarrow{MN} = 1\frac{1}{2}\mathbf{b}$ (ii) $2\overrightarrow{MN} = 3\overrightarrow{OB}$ (iii) Trapezium
                           MN is parallel to *OB*.

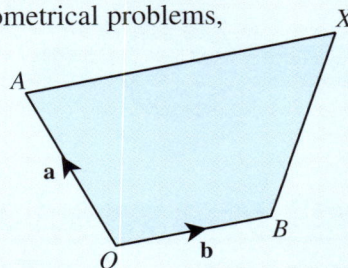

Exercise 33   The diagrams in this exercise have not been drawn accurately.

1 Vectors representing **a** and **b** are drawn, as shown.
On squared paper, draw and label a vector to represent

  (a) $\mathbf{a} + \mathbf{b}$,

  (b) $\mathbf{a} - \mathbf{b}$,

  (c) $2\mathbf{a} + \mathbf{b}$.

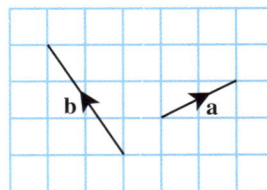

2 In the diagram, $\overrightarrow{OX} = \mathbf{x}$ and $\overrightarrow{OY} = \mathbf{y}$.

  (a)   Write, in terms of **x** and **y**, the vector $\overrightarrow{XY}$.

  (b)   *P* and *Q* are the midpoints of *OX* and *OY* respectively.

       Find, in terms of **x** and **y**, the vector $\overrightarrow{QP}$.

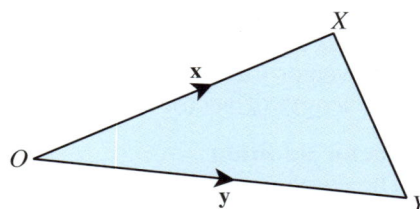

3 *A* is the point $(-3, 5)$ and *B* is the point $(3, 1)$.

  (a)   Find $\overrightarrow{AB}$ as a column vector.

   C and *D* are points such that $\overrightarrow{CB} = \begin{pmatrix} -2 \\ -3 \end{pmatrix}$, and *ABCD* is a trapezium with $\overrightarrow{AB} = 2\overrightarrow{DC}$.
  (b)   Find the coordinates of *D*.

4 The vectors **a** and **b** and the points *P* and *Q* are shown.

  (a)   Write $\overrightarrow{PQ}$ in terms of **a** and **b**.

   Copy *P* and *Q* onto squared paper.

  (b) $\overrightarrow{QR} = 4\mathbf{a} - 2\mathbf{b}$.
      (i)   Show the position of *R* on your diagram.
      (ii)   Write $\overrightarrow{RP}$ in terms of **a** and **b**.
  (c) $\overrightarrow{RS} = -\overrightarrow{PQ}$
      (i)   What can you say about the lines *QR* and *PS*?
      (ii)   What type of quadrilateral is *PQRS*?

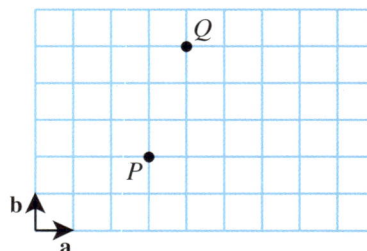

5 In the diagram, $\overrightarrow{OP} = 3\mathbf{a}$, $\overrightarrow{PA} = \mathbf{a}$, $\overrightarrow{OB} = 4\mathbf{b}$ and $\overrightarrow{BR} = 2\mathbf{b}$.
Q is the midpoint of AB.

(a) Find, in terms of $\mathbf{a}$ and $\mathbf{b}$, the vectors

    (i) $\overrightarrow{AB}$,   (ii) $\overrightarrow{PQ}$.

(b) Explain clearly why the points PQR lie on a straight line.

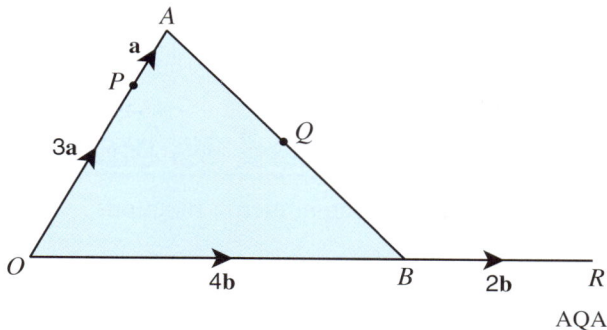

AQA

6 $\overrightarrow{OP} = -2\mathbf{a} + 4\mathbf{b}$ and $\overrightarrow{OQ} = 4\mathbf{a} - 2\mathbf{b}$.

(a) Express $\overrightarrow{PQ}$ in terms of $\mathbf{a}$ and $\mathbf{b}$.

R is the midpoint of PQ.

(b) Express $\overrightarrow{OR}$ in terms of $\mathbf{a}$ and $\mathbf{b}$.

$\overrightarrow{PS} = 7\mathbf{a} + \mathbf{b}$.

(c) Express $\overrightarrow{OS}$ in terms of $\mathbf{a}$ and $\mathbf{b}$.

(d) What **two** facts do $\overrightarrow{OR}$ and $\overrightarrow{OS}$ indicate about the points O, R and S?

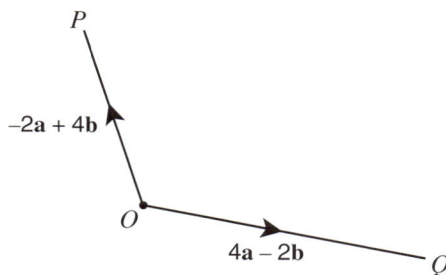

AQA

7 $OABC$ is a quadrilateral.

$\overrightarrow{OA} = \mathbf{a}$, $\overrightarrow{OB} = \mathbf{b}$, $\overrightarrow{OC} = \mathbf{c}$.
The midpoints of OC, CB, BA, AO are
P, Q, R and S, respectively.

(a) Find, in terms of $\mathbf{a}$, $\mathbf{b}$ and $\mathbf{c}$, the vectors representing

    (i) $\overrightarrow{PS}$,   (ii) $\overrightarrow{QB}$,   (iii) $\overrightarrow{BR}$.

(b) What type of quadrilateral is $PQRS$?
Give a reason for your answer.

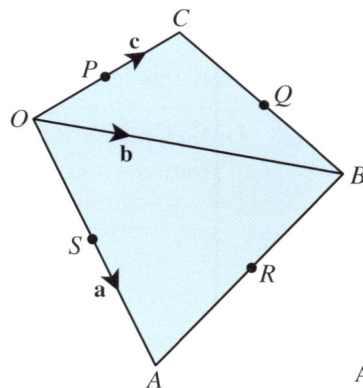

AQA

8 $OPQR$ is a parallelogram.
A and B are points on OP and OR respectively.

$\overrightarrow{OA} = \mathbf{a}$ and $\overrightarrow{OB} = \mathbf{b}$.
$\overrightarrow{OP} = 4\overrightarrow{OA}$ and $\overrightarrow{OR} = 3\overrightarrow{OB}$.

(a) Find, in terms of $\mathbf{a}$ and $\mathbf{b}$,

    (i) $\overrightarrow{AB}$,   (ii) $\overrightarrow{RA}$,   (iii) $\overrightarrow{BQ}$.

(b) S is a point on PQ such that BQ is parallel to AS.

Find $\overrightarrow{AS}$ in terms of $\mathbf{a}$ and $\mathbf{b}$.

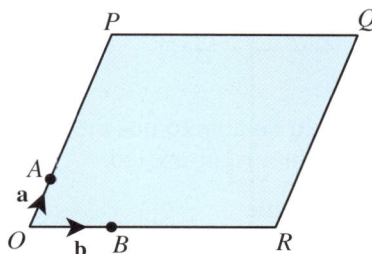

AQA

Further Trigonometry

What you need to know

- The graphs of the trigonometric functions.

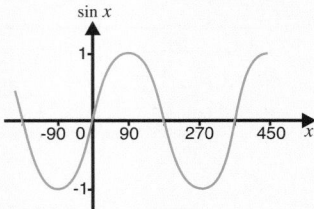

sin x

cos x

tan x

The **sine function** is a periodic function with period 360°.
$-1 \leqslant \sin x \leqslant 1$

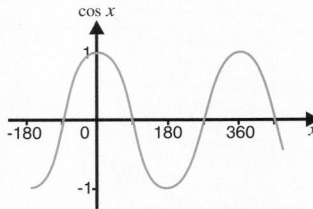

The **cosine function** is a periodic function with period 360°.
$-1 \leqslant \cos x \leqslant 1$

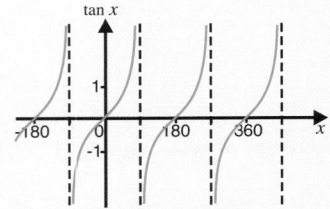

The **tangent function** is a periodic function with period 180°.
Tan x is undefined at 90°, 270°, ...

- For every angle $x°$, the signs of $\sin x°$, $\cos x°$ and $\tan x°$ can be shown on a diagram.

  Positive angles are measured **anticlockwise**.
  Negative angles are measured **clockwise**.

  For angles greater than 360°: subtract 360°, or multiples of 360°, to get the equivalent angle between 0° and 360°.

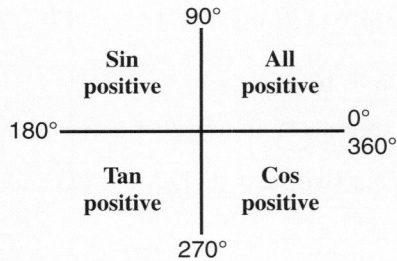

	90°	
Sin positive		**All** positive
180°		0° 360°
Tan positive		**Cos** positive
	270°	

  Eg 1 Sin 53.1° = 0.8, correct to 1 d.p.
  (a) Write down the other value of x for which $\sin x = 0.8$ for $0° \leqslant x \leqslant 360°$.
  (b) Solve the equation $\sin x = -0.8$ for $0° \leqslant x \leqslant 360°$.

  (a) | Always work from 0° or 180° or 360°. When sin x is positive: $\sin x = \sin(180° - x)$ |

  $x = 180° - 53.1° = 126.9°$

  (b) | Sin x is negative, so values of x lie between 180° and 360° |

  $x = 180° + 53.1° = 233.1°$
  $x = 360° - 53.1° = 306.9°$
  So, $x = 233.1°$ or 306.9°

- The **exact values** of the trigonometric ratios for the angles 30°, 45° and 60° can be found from the triangles below.

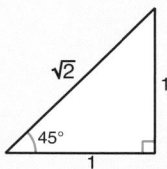

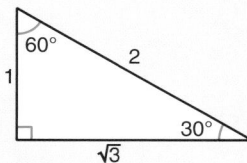

	30°	45°	60°
sin	$\frac{1}{2}$	$\frac{1}{\sqrt{2}}$	$\frac{\sqrt{3}}{2}$
cos	$\frac{\sqrt{3}}{2}$	$\frac{1}{\sqrt{2}}$	$\frac{1}{2}$
tan	$\frac{1}{\sqrt{3}}$	1	$\sqrt{3}$

- You should be able to use the **sine rule** and the **cosine rule** to solve problems involving triangles which are not right-angled.

- **The Sine Rule**

$$\frac{a}{\sin A} = \frac{b}{\sin B} = \frac{c}{\sin C}$$

This can be also written as: $\dfrac{\sin A}{a} = \dfrac{\sin B}{b} = \dfrac{\sin C}{c}$

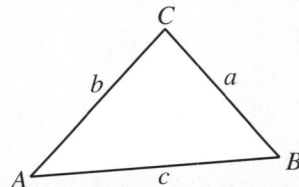

Eg 2 Calculate the length of side a, correct to 1 d.p.

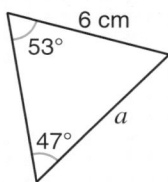

$\dfrac{a}{\sin 53°} = \dfrac{6}{\sin 47°}$

$a = \dfrac{6 \times \sin 53°}{\sin 47°}$

$a = 6.551...$

$a = 6.6\,\text{cm}$, to 1 d.p.

> To find a **side** you need:
> two angles of known size, **and** the length of a side which is opposite one of the known angles.

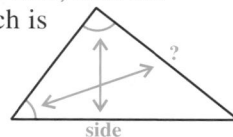

Eg 3 Calculate the size of angle P.

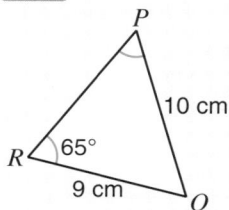

$\dfrac{\sin P}{9} = \dfrac{\sin 65°}{10}$

$\sin P = \dfrac{9 \times \sin 65°}{10}$

$\sin P = 0.8156...$

$P = 54.7°$, to 1 d.p.

> To find an **angle** you need:
> the length of the side opposite the angle you are trying to find, **and** the length of a side opposite an angle of known size.

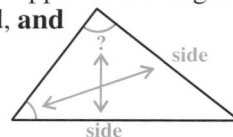

- **The Cosine Rule**

$$a^2 = b^2 + c^2 - 2bc \cos A$$

When using the Cosine Rule to find the size of an angle it is sometimes easier to rearrange the above formula as:

$$\cos A = \dfrac{b^2 + c^2 - a^2}{2bc}$$

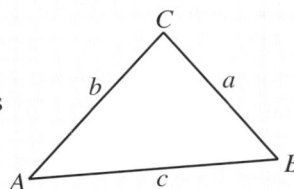

Eg 4 Calculate the length of side x.

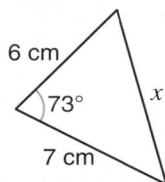

$x^2 = 6^2 + 7^2 - 2 \times 6 \times 7 \times \cos 73°$

$x^2 = 36 + 49 - 24.55...$

$x^2 = 60.44...$

$x = 7.8\,\text{cm}$, to 1 d.p.

> To find a **side** you need:
> two sides of known length, **and** the size of the angle between the known sides.

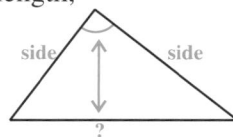

Eg 5 Calculate the size of angle A.

$\cos A = \dfrac{6^2 + 8^2 - 7^2}{2 \times 6 \times 8}$

$\cos A = 0.53125$

$A = 57.9°$, to 1 d.p.

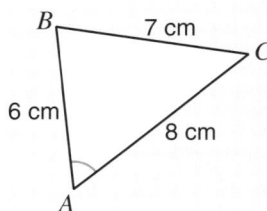

> To find an **angle** you need:
> three sides of known length.

- You should be able to find the area of a triangle which is not right-angled.

Eg 6 Calculate the area of triangle PQR, correct to 1 decimal place.

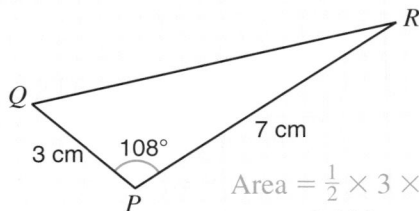

Area $= \frac{1}{2} \times 3 \times 7 \times \sin 108°$

$= 9.986...$

$= 10.0\,\text{cm}^2$, to 1 d.p.

> To find the **area of a triangle** you need:
> two sides of known length, **and** the size of the angle between the known sides.
> Area $= \frac{1}{2}\,ab \sin C$.

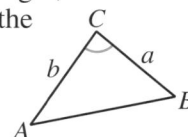

- You should be able to solve problems involving triangles.

For **right-angled triangles** use: the **trigonometric ratios** (sin, cos and tan), **Pythagoras' Theorem**.

For **triangles which are not right-angled** use: the **Sine Rule** or the **Cosine Rule**.

The diagrams in this exercise have not been drawn accurately.
Do not use a calculator for questions 1 and 2.

1 (a) Cos 60° = 0.5
  (i) Write down the other value of x for which $\cos x = 0.5$ for $0° \leqslant x \leqslant 360°$.
  (ii) Solve the equation $\cos x = -0.5$ for $0° \leqslant x \leqslant 360°$.

  (b) (i) On the same diagram, sketch the graphs of $y = \cos x$ and $y = \sin x$
      for $0° \leqslant x \leqslant 360°$.
  (ii) Hence, solve the equation $\cos x = \sin x$ for $0° \leqslant x \leqslant 360°$.

2 (a) Draw a sketch of the graph of $y = \sin x$ for $-180° \leqslant x \leqslant 180°$.
  (b) One solution of the equation $\sin x = 0.9$ is 64°, to the nearest degree.
      Find the other solution of the equation $\sin x = 0.9$ for $-180° \leqslant x \leqslant 180°$.
  (c) Find all the solutions of the equation $\sin x = -0.9$ for $-180° \leqslant x \leqslant 180°$.   AQA

3 In the triangle, $\sin x = \frac{2}{3}$.

  (a) Copy the diagram and mark the possible values of the
      lengths of the sides of the triangle.
  (b) Write the value of $\cos x$ as an irrational number.
  (c) An angle y is such that $\sin y = \sin x$, and $0° < y < 360°$, and y is not equal to x.
      Calculate the size of y.   AQA

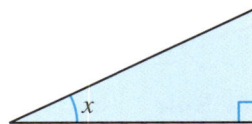

4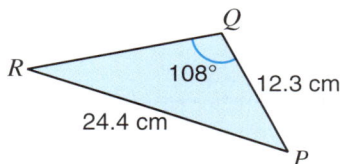

In the triangle PQR, angle $PQR = 108°$.
$PQ = 12.3$ cm and $PR = 24.4$ cm.

  (a) Calculate angle QRP.

  (b) Calculate the area of triangle PQR.

5 A gardener pegs out a rope, 19 metres long, to form a flower bed.
Calculate:

  (a) the size of the angle BAC,

  (b) the area of the triangular flower bed.

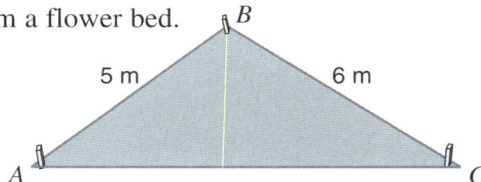

AQA

6 A, B and C are three points which lie in a straight line on horizontal ground.
BT is a vertical tower.
The angle of elevation of T from A is 21.5°.
The angle of elevation of T from C is 13.3°.
$AC = 1200$ m.

Calculate the height of the tower.

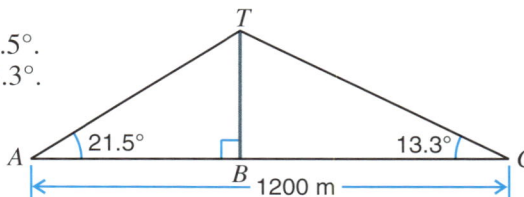

AQA

7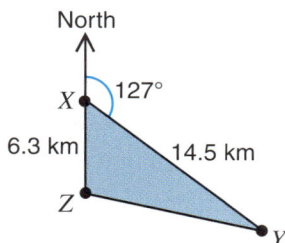

The diagram shows the positions of ships X, Y and Z.
X is 6.3 km due North of Z.
Y is 14.5 km from X on a bearing of 127°.

Calculate the distance and bearing of Z from Y.

8 In the triangle ABC, $AB = 6$ cm and $AC = 9$ cm.
The area of triangle ABC is 24 cm².

  (a) Calculate the two possible values of angle BAC.
  (b) Calculate the length of BC, when angle BAC is obtuse.

Section Review - Shape, Space and Measures

The diagrams in this exercise have not been drawn accurately.
Do not use a calculator for questions 1 to 13.

1 Find the size of the angles marked *a*, *b*, *c* and *d*.

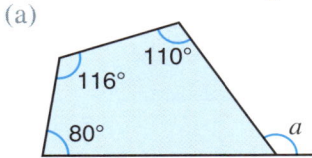

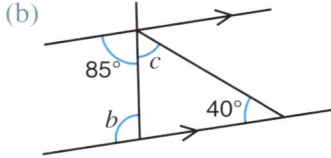

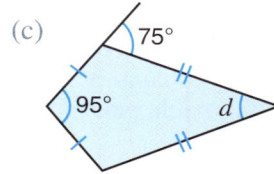

(a)

110°
116°
80° a

(b)

85° c
b 40°

(c)

75°
95° d

2 Colin is 5 feet 10 inches tall and weighs 11 stones.
On a medical form he is asked to give his height in centimetres and his weight in kilograms.
What values should he give?

3 The diagram shows a cuboid.
By rounding each of the measurements to
one significant figure, estimate the volume of the cuboid.
You must show all your working.

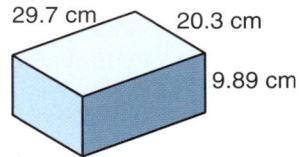

29.7 cm   20.3 cm
9.89 cm

AQA

4 Use only the information given to find two triangles which are congruent to each other.
Give a reason for your answer.

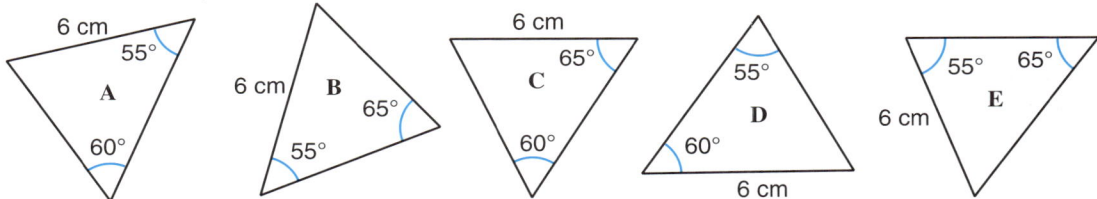

6 cm
55°
A
60°

6 cm   **B**
65°
55°

6 cm
65°
C
60°

55°
D
60°
6 cm

55°   65°
E
6 cm

5 The diagram shows the angle formed when three regular polygons
are placed together, as shown.

(a) Explain why angle *a* is 120°.

(b) Work out the size of the angle marked *b*.

b
a

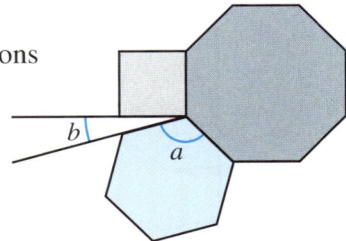

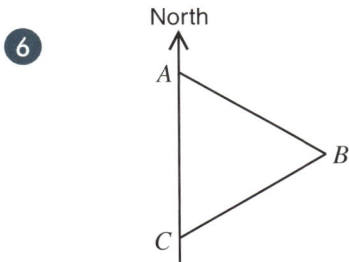

6 The sketch shows the positions of
three footpaths which meet at *A*, *B* and *C*.
A is due north of *C*.
Triangle *ABC* is equilateral.

North
A
B
C

(a) Write down the three-figure bearing of *B* from *C*.

(b) Write down the three-figure bearing of *A* from *B*.

AQA

7 Mr Jones weighs his case on his bathroom scales which weigh to the nearest kilogram.
He finds that his case weighs 20 kg.
(a) What are the greatest and least weights of the case?
(b) On the way to the airport he removes a sweater from this case.
At the airport the scales give the weight of his case as 19.4 kg to the nearest tenth of a
kilogram. What is the heaviest weight that the sweater could be?

AQA

8 (a) Construct triangle ABC, in which $AB = 9.5\,\text{cm}$, $BC = 8\,\text{cm}$ and $CA = 6\,\text{cm}$.

(b) Using ruler and compasses only,
(i) bisect angle BAC,
(ii) draw the locus of points that are equidistant from A and C.

(c) Shade the region inside the triangle where all the points are less than $7.5\,\text{cm}$ from B, nearer to A than to C and nearer to AC than to AB.

9 The area of the trapezium is $20\,\text{m}^2$.
The parallel sides a and b are different lengths.
The perpendicular height, h, is $4\,\text{m}$.
Find a possible pair of values for a and b.

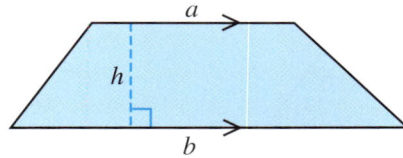

AQA

10 (a) Calculate the sum of the interior angles of a regular 10-sided polygon.

(b) The diagram shows a square and a regular hexagon which meet at M.
LM and MN are two sides of another regular polygon.
How many sides has this polygon?

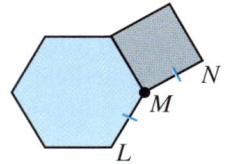

11 A circle has an area of $49\,\pi\,\text{cm}^2$.
Calculate the circumference of the circle, in terms of π.

12 Tan $XYZ = \frac{4}{3}$.

(a) Find (i) sin XYZ, (ii) cos XYZ.

(b) When $XZ = 10\,\text{cm}$, what are the lengths of XY and YZ?

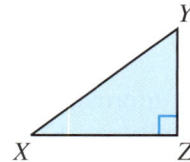

13 In these diagrams O is the centre of the circle.
Find the size of the angles a, b, c and x.
Give a reason for each of your answers.

(a)   (b)   (c)

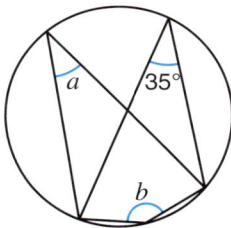 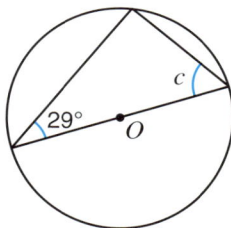 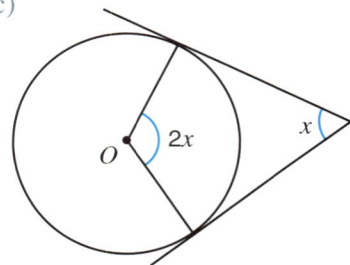

14 The diagram shows Fay's house, H, and her school, S.
To get to school Fay has a choice of two routes.
She can either walk along Waverly Crescent or
along the footpaths HX and XS.
Waverly Crescent is a semi-circle with diameter $650\,\text{m}$.
The footpath HX is $250\,\text{m}$ and meets the footpath XS
at right-angles.
Which of these routes is shorter? By how much?

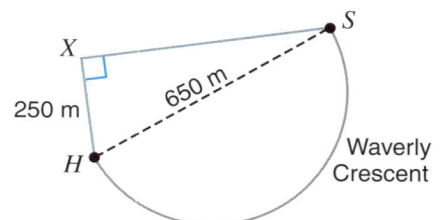

15 The diagram shows a bale of straw.
The bale is a cylinder with radius $70\,\text{cm}$ and height $50\,\text{cm}$.
Calculate the volume of the bale.

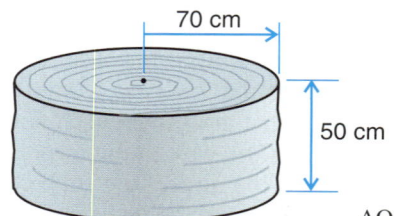

AQA

16 Copy the diagram onto squared paper.

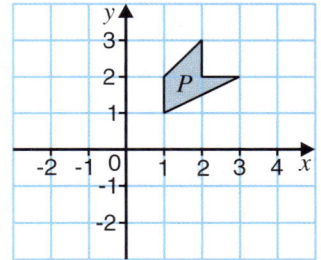

(a) P is mapped onto Q by an enlargement, scale factor 2, centre $(-1, 3)$. Draw and label Q.

(b) P is mapped onto R by a translation with vector $\begin{pmatrix} -3 \\ 2 \end{pmatrix}$. Draw and label R.

(c) Describe the single transformation which maps Q onto R.

17 Triangle ABC is similar to triangle APQ.

$AB = 4.5\,\text{cm}$, $BC = 3\,\text{cm}$, $PQ = 5\,\text{cm}$ and $CQ = 1.6\,\text{cm}$.

(a) Calculate the length of AP.

(b) Calculate the length of AC.

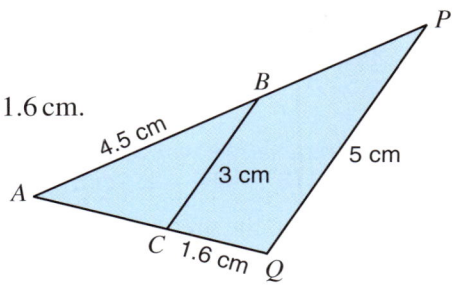

18 (a)

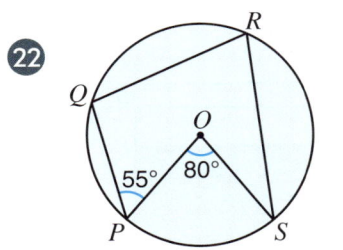

A letter L is drawn, as shown.
Draw the letter L accurately.
A point P is 2 cm from the letter L.
Draw the locus of all the possible positions of P.

(b) A letter Z is drawn in a rectangle measuring 7 cm by 9 cm, as shown. Calculate the size of the angle marked x.

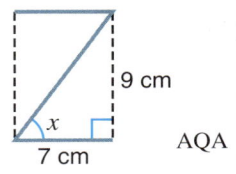

AQA

19 The following formulae represent certain quantities connected with containers, where a, b and c are dimensions.

$$\pi a \qquad abc \qquad \sqrt{a^2 - c^2} \qquad \pi a^2 b \qquad 2(a + b + c)$$

(a) Explain why abc represents a volume.

(b) Which of these formulae represent lengths?

20 When Jessie is standing 12 m from the bottom of a flag pole she finds the angle of elevation to the top of the pole is $37°$.
Calculate the height of the flag pole.

21 A rectangular painting which measures 40 cm by 25 cm fits into a rectangular frame which measures 50 cm by 35 cm.

Show that the two rectangles are not similar.

22

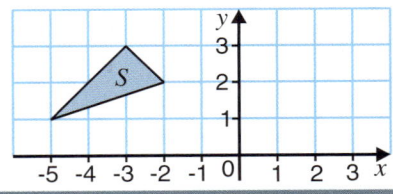

O is the centre of a circle through P, Q, R and S.

(a) Work out the size of angle QRS.

(b) X is a point on the minor arc PS. Explain why angle $PXS = 140°$.

23 Copy the diagram.

(a) Enlarge shape S, centre $(-1, 2)$, scale factor -2. Label the image T.

(b) Describe the single transformation which maps T onto S.

24 The diagram shows the roof of a building.
The base *ABCD* is a horizontal rectangle 10 m by 5 m.
The ends are equilateral triangles.
EFCB is an isosceles trapezium.
The length of the ridge of the roof, *EF*, is 7 m.
M is the midpoint of *AB*.
N is the midpoint of *CD*.

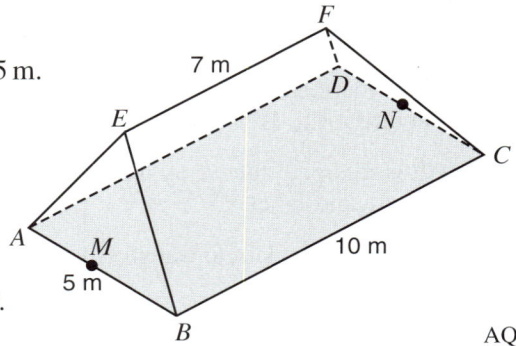

    (a)   Find the perpendicular distance between
           EF and *CB*, and hence find the area of *EFCB*.

    (b)   Find the size of the angle *EMN*?   AQA

25 The diagram shows two concentric circles with centre *O*.
$\angle XOY = 118°$. $OX = 8.5$ cm.

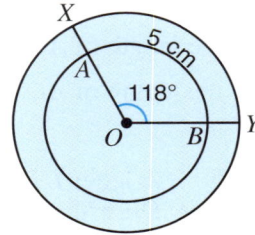

    (a)   Calculate the area of the sector *XOY*.

    (b)   The arc $AB = 5$ cm.
           Calculate *OA*.

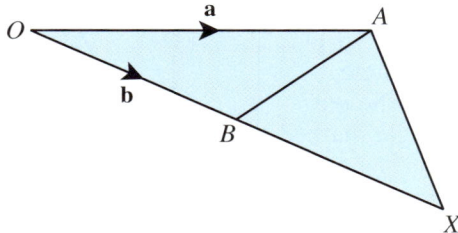

26   In the diagram $\overrightarrow{OA} = \mathbf{a}$ and $\overrightarrow{OB} = \mathbf{b}$.
    B is the midpoint of *OX*.

    (a)   Find, in terms of **a** and **b**, the vectors $\overrightarrow{OX}$ and $\overrightarrow{AX}$.

    (b)   *M* is the midpoint of *AX*.
           Prove that *BM* is parallel to *OA*.

27 A hemispherical bowl has a diameter of 18 cm.

    (a)   Calculate the volume of the bowl.
           Give your answer in terms of π.

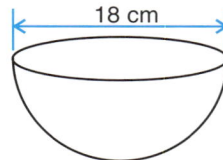

    Water is poured into the bowl to a depth of 6 cm,
    correct to the nearest centimetre.

    (b)   Calculate the minimum surface area of the water.

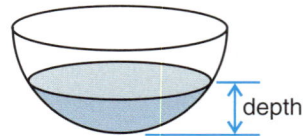

28 Find the two values of *x* between 0° and 360° which satisfy the equation $4 \sin x = -1$.
                                     AQA

29 The diagram shows a rectangular garden, *ABCD*.
A lawn, *CDEF*, is shaded.
The unshaded area, *ABFE*,
is a rectangular flower bed.

    $AB = 19.6$ m, $AD = 7.2$ m and $BF = 1.4$ m,
    all correct to 1 decimal place.

    Calculate the upper bound of the area of the lawn.   AQA

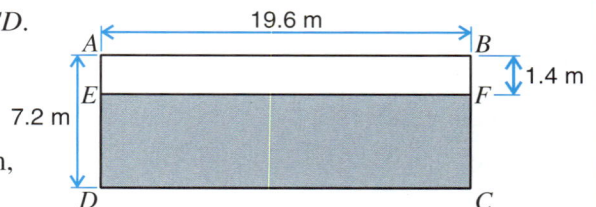

30 Draw the graphs of $y = \cos x°$ and $y = \sin 2x°$ for $0 \leqslant x \leqslant 360$.
    Use the graph to find all the solutions of the equation $\cos x° = \sin 2x°$ for $0 \leqslant x \leqslant 360$.
                                          AQA

31 (a) Calculate the area of triangle *ABD*.

(b) Calculate the length of *BD*.

(c) Calculate the size of angle *BCD*.

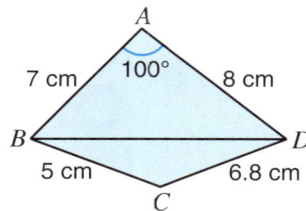

AQA

32

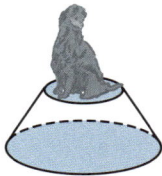

The stand on which the dog is sitting is the frustum of a cone.
The top of the stand has a radius of 0.5 m.
The bottom of the stand has a radius of 1 m.
The height of the stand is 0.6 m.

(a) Calculate the volume of the stand.
(b) The height of a similar stand is 0.4 m.
Calculate the volume of this stand.

33 The diagram shows a triangular piece of card.
Angle *BAC* is obtuse, $AB = 5.8$ cm and $AC = 7.4$ cm.
The area of the card is 20 cm².
Calculate the length of *BC*.
Give your answer to a suitable degree of accuracy.

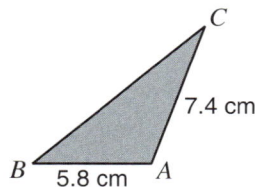

34 The volume of a cylinder is given as 680 cm³, correct to two significant figures.
The height is 9.6 cm to the nearest millimetre.
Calculate the upper and lower bounds of the radius.

35

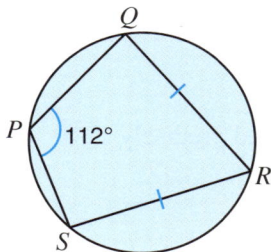

PQRS is a cyclic quadrilateral in which:
$QR = RS$, $PS = 5.2$ cm and $PQ = 6.8$ cm.
$\angle SPQ = 112°$.

Calculate the length of *QR*.

36 *OAXB* is a parallelogram.

$\overrightarrow{OA} = \mathbf{a}$ and $\overrightarrow{OB} = \mathbf{b}$

M is a point on *OA* such that $\overrightarrow{OM} = \frac{1}{3}\mathbf{a}$.

N is a point on *OB* such that $\overrightarrow{ON} = \frac{2}{3}\mathbf{b}$.

Find, in terms of **a** and **b**, $\overrightarrow{AB}$, $\overrightarrow{OX}$ and $\overrightarrow{MN}$.

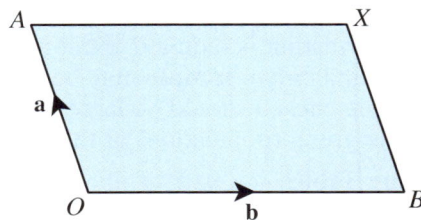

37 In triangle *ABC*, $AC = 7.6$ cm, angle $BAC = 35°$, angle $ACB = 65°$.
The length of *AB* is x cm. The size of angle *ABC* is $\theta°$.
(a) Calculate the value of x.

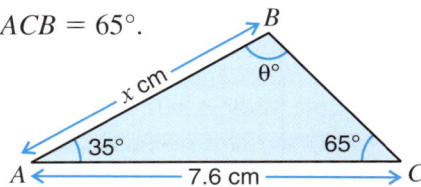

Alison constructs this triangle by first drawing the side *AC*.
She then uses a protractor to draw the angles at *A* and *C*.
In constructing the triangle, the length of *AC* is measured correct to the nearest mm.
The angles at *A* and *C* are measured correct to the nearest degree.
(b) (i) Write down the minimum value θ can take.
(ii) Hence, calculate the maximum and minimum values x can take.

AQA

Collection and Organisation of Data

What you need to know

- **Primary data** is data collected by an individual or organisation to use for a particular purpose. Primary data is obtained from experiments, investigations, surveys and by using questionnaires.

- **Secondary data** is data which is already available or has been collected by someone else for a different purpose. Sources of secondary data include the Annual Abstract of Statistics, Social Trends and the Internet.

- **Qualitative** data – Data which can only be described in words.

- **Quantitative** data – Data that has a numerical value. Quantitative data is either **discrete** or **continuous**. **Discrete** data can only take certain values. **Continuous** data has no exact value and is measurable.

- **Data Collection Sheets** – Used to record data during a survey.

- **Tally** – A way of recording each item of data on a data collection sheet.
  A group of five is recorded as ⳽⳽⳽.

- **Frequency Table** – A way of collating the information recorded on a data collection sheet.

- **Grouped Frequency Table** – Used for continuous data or for discrete data when a lot of data has to be recorded.

- **Database** – A collection of data.

- **Class Interval** – The width of the groups used in a grouped frequency distribution.

- **Questionnaire** – A set of questions used to collect data for a survey.
  Questionnaires should: (1) use simple language,
                          (2) ask short questions which can be answered precisely,
                          (3) provide tick boxes,
                          (4) avoid open-ended questions,
                          (5) avoid leading questions,
                          (6) ask questions in a logical order.

- **Hypothesis** – A hypothesis is a statement which may or may not be true.

- When information is required about a large group of people it is not always possible to survey everyone and only a **sample** may be asked.
  The sample chosen should be large enough to make the results meaningful and representative of the whole group (population) or the results may be **biased**.

- **Two-way Tables** – A way of illustrating two features of a survey.

- In a **simple random sample** everyone has an equal chance of being selected.

- In a **systematic random sample** people are selected according to some rule.

- In a **stratified random sample** the original group is divided up into separate categories or strata, such as male/female, age group, etc, before a random sample is taken.
  A simple random sample is then taken from each category in proportion to the size of the category.

Exercise 35

1 To find out how long students spend on homework each night, Pat asks a class of Year 7 students how much time they spent on their homework last night.
Give two reasons why his results may not be typical of all students.

2 This sample was used to investigate the claim: **"Women do more exercise than men."**

	Age (years)			
	16 to 21	22 to 45	46 to 65	Over 65
Male	5	5	13	7
Female	25	35	0	0

Give three reasons why the sample is biased.

3 Jamie is investigating the use made of his college library. Here is part of his questionnaire:

Library Questionnaire
1. How old are you? ....

(a) (i) Give a reason why this question is unsuitable.
    (ii) Rewrite the question so that it could be included.
(b) Jamie asks the librarian to give the questionnaires to students when they borrow books.
    (i) Give reasons why this sample may be biased.
    (ii) Suggest a better way of giving out the questionnaires.

4 The table shows the results of a survey of 500 people.

A newspaper headline states:

Survey shows that more women can drive than men.

	Can drive	Cannot drive
Men	180	20
Women	240	60

Do the results of the survey support this headline?
Give a reason for your answer.

5 A mobile phone company wants to build a transmitter mast on land belonging to a school.
The company offers the school £50 000 for the land.
The local paper receives 20 letters objecting to the proposal and 5 letters in favour.
One of the paper's reporters writes an article in which he claims:

'Objectors outnumber those in favour by 4 to 1'

(a) Give **two** reasons why the newspaper reporter's claim may **not** be correct.
(b) The school decides to take a stratified sample of the views of local people about the proposal.
    Give **two** factors that should be taken into account when selecting the sample.   AQA

6 At Paul's school there are 200 pupils in each of Years 7 to 11.
There are approximately equal numbers of girls and boys.
Describe how Paul could select a 10% stratified sample which is representative of all the pupils at the school.   AQA

7 Explain briefly in what circumstances a stratified random sample might be taken rather than a simple random sample.

8 A company has 24 managers, 35 secretaries and 65 other staff in work on a particular day.
A stratified sample of 18 of these 124 employees is to be chosen.
How many employees of each type should be chosen?   AQA

9 The table shows the number of employees at each of two factories.

Factory	A	B
Number of employees	733	467

A stratified random sample of 200 employees is to be taken from these factories.
(a) Calculate the number of employees which should be sampled from each factory.

There were 300 male employees at factory A.
(b) Calculate how many female employees should be part of the sample from factory A.   AQA

Averages and Range

What you need to know

- There are three types of **average**: the **mode**, the **median** and the **mean**.

  Eg 1 The number of text messages received by 7 students on Saturday is shown.

  2   4   3   4   4   3   2

  Find   (a) the mode,   (b) the median,   (c) the mean,   (d) the range.

  > The **mode** is the most common amount.
  >
  > The **median** is found by arranging the data in order of size and taking the middle amount (or the mean of the two middle amounts).
  >
  > The **mean** is found by dividing the total of all the data by the number of data values.
  >
  > The **range** is a measure of **spread**.
  > Range = highest amount − lowest amount

  (a) The mode is 4.

  (b) 2   2   3   ③   4   4   4
  The median is 3.

  (c) The mean $= \dfrac{2 + 4 + 3 + 4 + 4 + 3 + 2}{7}$
  $= \dfrac{22}{7} = 3.14\ldots$
  $= 3.1$, correct to 1 d.p.

  (d) The range $= 4 - 2 = 2$

- To find the mean of a **frequency distribution** use:

  $$\text{Mean} = \frac{\text{Total of all amounts}}{\text{Number of amounts}} = \frac{\Sigma fx}{\Sigma f}$$

  Eg 2 The table shows the number of stamps on some parcels.

Number of stamps	1	2	3	4
Number of parcels	5	6	9	4

  Find the mean number of stamps per parcel.

  $\text{Mean} = \dfrac{\Sigma fx}{\Sigma f}$

  $= \dfrac{1 \times 5 + 2 \times 6 + 3 \times 9 + 4 \times 4}{5 + 6 + 9 + 4}$

  $= \dfrac{60}{24} = 2.5$

- To find the mean of a **grouped frequency distribution**, first find the value of the midpoint of each class.

  Then use: $\text{Estimated mean} = \dfrac{\Sigma\,(\text{frequency} \times \text{midpoint})}{\text{Total frequency}} = \dfrac{\Sigma fx}{\Sigma f}$

  Eg 3 The table shows the weights of some parcels.

Weight (w grams)	Frequency
$100 \leqslant w < 200$	7
$200 \leqslant w < 300$	11
$300 \leqslant w < 400$	19
$400 \leqslant w < 500$	3

  Calculate an estimate of the mean weight of these parcels.

  $\text{Mean} = \dfrac{\Sigma fx}{\Sigma f}$

  $= \dfrac{150 \times 7 + 250 \times 11 + 350 \times 19 + 450 \times 3}{7 + 11 + 19 + 3}$

  $= \dfrac{11\,800}{40} = 295$ grams

- Choosing the best average to use:
  When the most **popular** value is wanted use the **mode**.
  When **half** of the values have to be above the average use the **median**.
  When a **typical** value is wanted use either the **mode** or the **median**.
  When all the **actual** values have to be taken into account use the **mean**.
  When the average should not be distorted by a few very small or very large values do **not** use the mean.

Do not use a calculator for questions 1 to 3.

1 The prices paid for eight different meals at a restaurant are:

£10   £9   £9.50   £12   £20   £11.50   £11   £9

(a) Which price is the mode?   (b) Find the median price.   (c) Calculate the mean price.

(d) Which of these averages best describes the average price paid for a meal?
    Give a reason for your answer.

2 (a) Calculate the mean of   13.9,   15.3,   11.7   and   16.2

(b) Using your result from part (a), explain how to find quickly the mean of
    14.9,   16.3,   12.7   and   17.2

(c) Calculate the median of the numbers in part (a).

(d) If the number 16.2 in part (a) was changed to 27.2, explain, without doing a calculation,
    whether the mean or the median would be more affected.   AQA

3 The graph shows the distribution of goals scored by a football team in home and away matches.

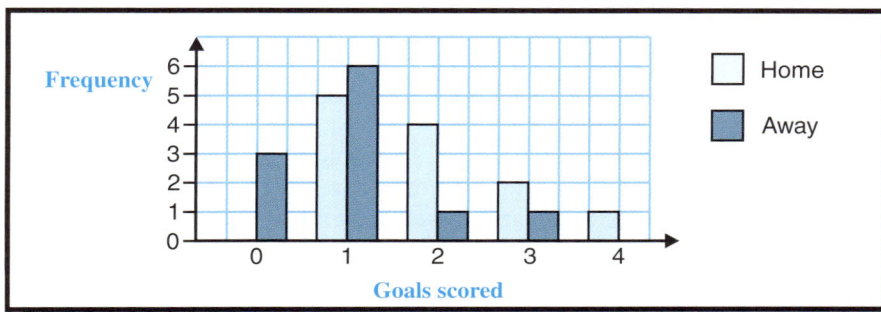

(a) What is the range of the number of goals scored at home matches?

(b) Calculate the mean number of goals per match for home matches.

(c) A supporter says, "The average number of goals per match is the same for both away
    matches and home matches." Which average is being used?   AQA

4 Four taxi drivers recorded how many passengers they carried on each journey during one
evening. The table shows the numbers of journeys they made with different numbers of
passengers.

		Number of passengers carried			
		1	2	3	4
Taxi	**A**	6	6	4	0
	B	7	7	3	1
	C	5	7	2	0
	D	4	4	3	1

(a) Which taxi completed the most journeys that evening?

(b) Calculate the total number of journeys in which exactly 3 passengers were carried.

(c) There were 60 journeys made altogether.
    Calculate the mean number of passengers per taxi journey.   AQA

5 Fred records the time taken by 30 pupils to
complete a cross-country run.

(a) Calculate an estimate of the mean time
    taken to complete the run.

(b) Which time interval contains the median
    time taken to complete the run?

Time (t minutes)	Number of pupils
$20 \leq t < 25$	9
$25 \leq t < 30$	8
$30 \leq t < 35$	5
$35 \leq t < 40$	2
$40 \leq t < 45$	6

AQA

Presentation of Data 1

What you need to know

- **Bar chart**. Used for data which can be counted.
  Often used to compare quantities of data in a distribution.
  The length of each bar represents frequency.

  > Bars can be drawn horizontally or vertically.

- **Bar-line graph**. Instead of drawing bars, horizontal or vertical lines are drawn to show frequency.

- **Pie chart**. Used for data which can be counted.
  Often used to compare proportions of data, usually with the total.
  The whole circle represents all the data.
  The size of each sector represents the frequency of data in that sector.

- **Stem and leaf diagrams**. Used to represent data in its original form. Data is split into two parts.
  The part with the higher place value is the stem.   e.g.   15 = stem 1, leaf 5.
  A key is given to show the value of the data.   e.g.   3|4 means 3.4 etc.
  The data is shown in numerical order on the diagram.   e.g.   2|3 5 9 represents 23, 25, 29.
  Back to back stem and leaf diagrams can be used to compare two sets of data.

- A **scatter graph** can be used to show the relationship between two sets of data.

- The relationship between two sets of data is referred to as **correlation**.

- You should be able to recognise **positive** and **negative** correlation.

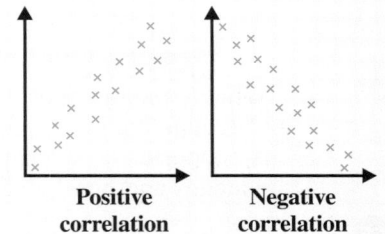

Positive correlation   Negative correlation

- When there is a relationship between two sets of data a **line of best fit** can be drawn on the scatter graph.
  The correlation is stronger as points get closer to a straight line.
  Perfect correlation is when all the points lie on a straight line.

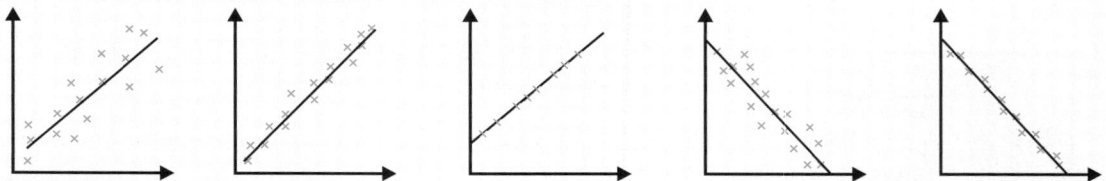

- The line of best fit can be used to **estimate** the value from one set of the data when the corresponding value of the other set is known.

Exercise 37

1 Twenty children were asked to estimate the length of a leaf.
Their estimates, in centimetres, are:

Boys				
4.5	5.0	4.0	3.5	4.0
4.5	5.0	4.5	3.5	4.5

Girls				
4.5	5.0	3.5	4.0	5.5
3.5	4.5	3.5	3.0	2.5

(a)   Construct a back to back stem and leaf diagram to represent this information.
(b)   Compare and comment on the estimates of these boys and girls.

2 The bar chart shows information about the injuries of drivers involved in road accidents at a busy junction.

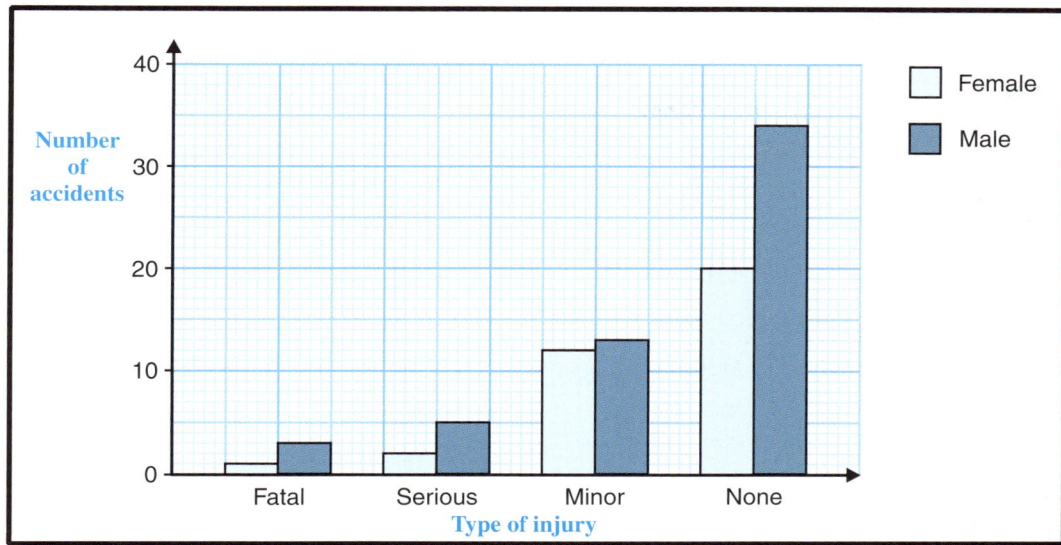

(a) What percentage of drivers had no injuries?
(b) What is the ratio of female to male drivers involved in these accidents?
Give your answer in its simplest form.
(c) Draw a pie chart to illustrate the proportion of drivers with each type of injury.

3

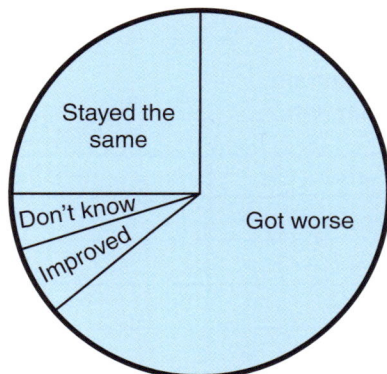

In a survey, parents were asked:

> *'Do you think the behaviour of children has improved in the last ten years?'*

The results of the survey are shown in the pie chart.

(a) Estimate the fraction of parents who think that the behaviour of children has got worse.

(b) 75 parents in the survey said, 'Don't know'.
This was 5% of all the parents.
Calculate the number of parents that took part in the survey.

AQA

4 The scatter graphs below show the results of a questionnaire given to pupils who have jobs.
(a) Which scatter graph shows the number of hours worked plotted against:
(i) the earnings of pupils,
(ii) the time taken by pupils to travel to work?
(b) State which one of the graphs shows a negative correlation.

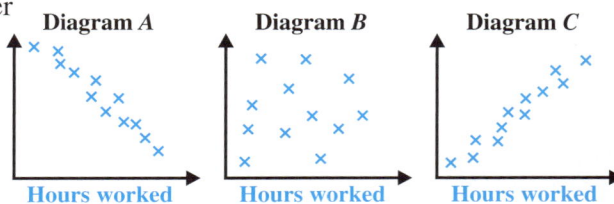

Diagram A   **Diagram B**   **Diagram C**

Hours worked   Hours worked   Hours worked

AQA

5 The table shows the ages and heights of trees in a wood.
(a) Draw a scatter graph for the data.
(b) Draw a line of best fit.
(c) Use the graph to estimate the height of a tree which is
(i) 8 years old, (ii) 13 years old.
(d) Which of your answers in (c) is more likely to be reliable?
Give a reason for your answer.

Age (years)	1	3	4	5	7	9	10
Height (m)	0.5	1.2	1.7	2.5	3.3	4.5	4.8

AQA

Presentation of Data 1

Presentation of Data 2

What you need to know

- A **time series** is a set of readings taken at time intervals.

> Only the plotted points represent actual values.
> Points are joined by lines to show the **trend**.

- A **line graph** is used to show a time series.

- Variations in a time series which recur with the seasons of the year are called **seasonal variations**.

- **Moving averages** are used to smooth out variations in a time series so that the trend can be seen.

  Eg 1 The graph shows the amount of gas used by a householder each quarter over a period of 3 years.

  The blue crosses show the 4-quarterly moving average values.

  A line of best fit, drawn for the moving averages, shows the general **trend**.

  The trend shows a slight increase in the amount of gas used.

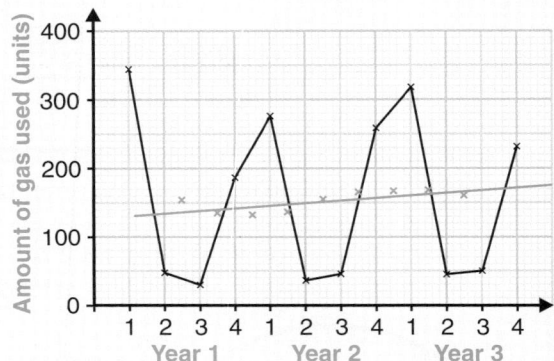

- **Frequency polygon**. Used to illustrate grouped frequency distributions.
  Often used to compare two or more distributions on the same diagram.

  Eg 2 The frequency distribution of the heights of some boys is shown.

  Draw a frequency polygon to illustrate the data.

Height (h cm)	Frequency
$130 \leqslant h < 140$	1
$140 \leqslant h < 150$	7
$150 \leqslant h < 160$	12
$160 \leqslant h < 170$	9
$170 \leqslant h < 180$	3

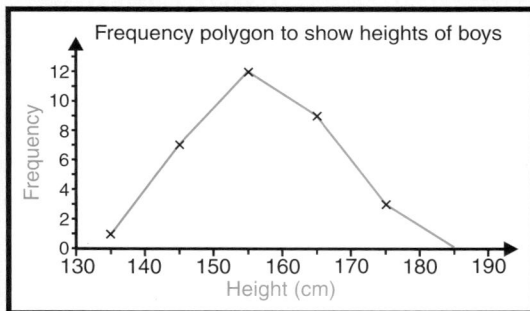

Frequency polygon to show heights of boys

> Frequencies are plotted at the midpoints of the class intervals and joined with straight lines.
> The horizontal axis is a continuous scale.

- **Histograms**. Used to illustrate grouped frequency distributions.
  The horizontal axis is a continuous scale.
  Bars are drawn between the lower and upper class boundaries for each class interval.
  When the classes have gaps between them the upper class boundary is halfway between the end of one class and the beginning of the next.

- Histograms can have equal or unequal class width intervals.
  With **equal** class width intervals: **frequency** is proportional to the **heights** of the bars.
  With **unequal** class width intervals: **frequency** is proportional to the **areas** of the bars.

  > frequency = frequency density × class width interval

Eg 3 The times taken by 40 pupils to solve a puzzle are:

Time (t seconds)	$10 \leqslant t < 20$	$20 \leqslant t < 25$	$25 \leqslant t < 30$	$30 \leqslant t < 45$
Frequency	6	12	10	12

Draw a histogram to represent the data.

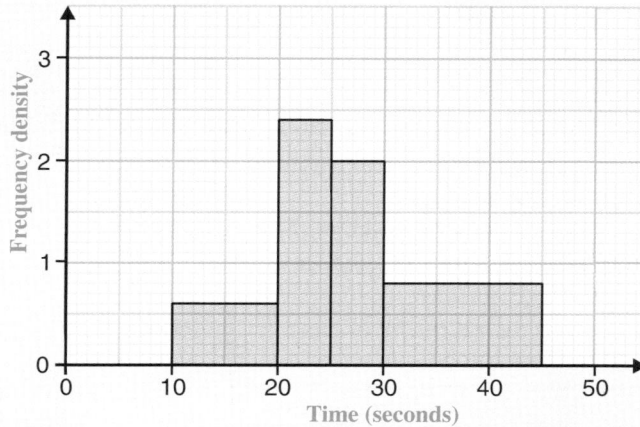

To find the height of each bar:
The height of each bar is given by the **frequency density** for each group, where:

$$\text{frequency density} = \frac{\text{frequency}}{\text{class width interval}}$$

E.g. For the group $10 \leqslant t < 20$: Frequency density $\frac{6}{10} = 0.6$
Draw the bar to a height of 0.6

Exercise 38

1 The number of words in the first 100 sentences of a book are shown in the table.

Number of words	1 to 10	11 to 20	21 to 30	31 to 40	41 to 50
Frequency	45	38	12	4	1

(a) Draw a frequency polygon for these data.
(b) Write down the class which contains the median.

AQA

2 The graph shows the age distribution of people in a nursing home.

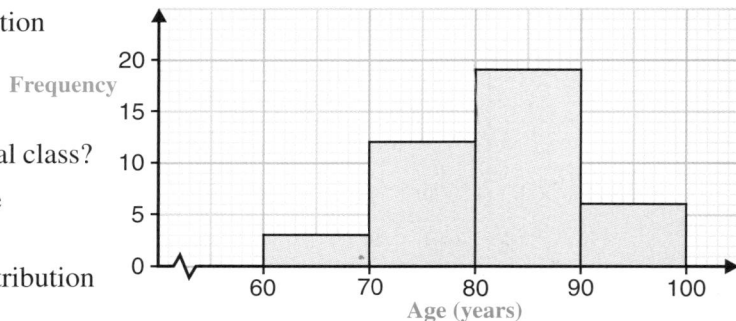

(a) Which age group is the modal class?

(b) How many people are in the nursing home?

(c) The table shows the age distribution of men in the home.

Age (a years)	$60 \leqslant a < 70$	$70 \leqslant a < 80$	$80 \leqslant a < 90$	$90 \leqslant a < 100$
Frequency	2	7	6	0

(i) Draw a frequency polygon to represent this information.
(ii) On the same diagram draw a frequency polygon to represent the age distribution of women in the home.
(iii) Compare and comment on the ages of men and women in the home.

3 Calculate the second average in a 3-point moving average for these values.

15   23   19   12   17   22   28   20   16

4 The table shows the number of units of electricity used each quarter by a householder over a period of 3 years.

Year	1999				2000				2001			
Quarter	1	2	3	4	1	2	3	4	1	2	3	4
Units used	680	810	470	740	640	850	420	750	970	880	490	760

(a)   Plot these values on graph paper.
(b)   Calculate a 4-point moving average.
(c)   Plot the moving average values on your graph.
(d)   Comment on the trend in the units of electricity used.

5 A London taxi driver keeps a record of the distance travelled for each of 50 journeys.
The data is summarised in the table below.

Distance travelled (d km)	Number of journeys
$0 < d \leqslant 2$	12
$2 < d \leqslant 3$	11
$3 < d \leqslant 4$	10
$4 < d \leqslant 6$	10
$6 < d \leqslant 10$	6
$10 < d \leqslant 15$	1

(a)   (i)   Draw a histogram to illustrate this data.
      (ii) Use your histogram to estimate the median distance.

(b)   The mean distance is 3.7 km. Should the taxi driver use the mean or the median to represent the average distance for a journey? Give a reason for your answer.

AQA

6 The heights of a randomly selected group of 100 boys in a school are shown in this table.

Height (h cm)	$125 \leqslant h < 140$	$140 \leqslant h < 145$	$145 \leqslant h < 150$	$150 \leqslant h < 160$	$160 \leqslant h < 175$
Frequency	9	21	24	31	15

(a)   Draw a histogram to show this information.

The heights of a randomly selected group of 100 girls in the school are shown in this histogram.

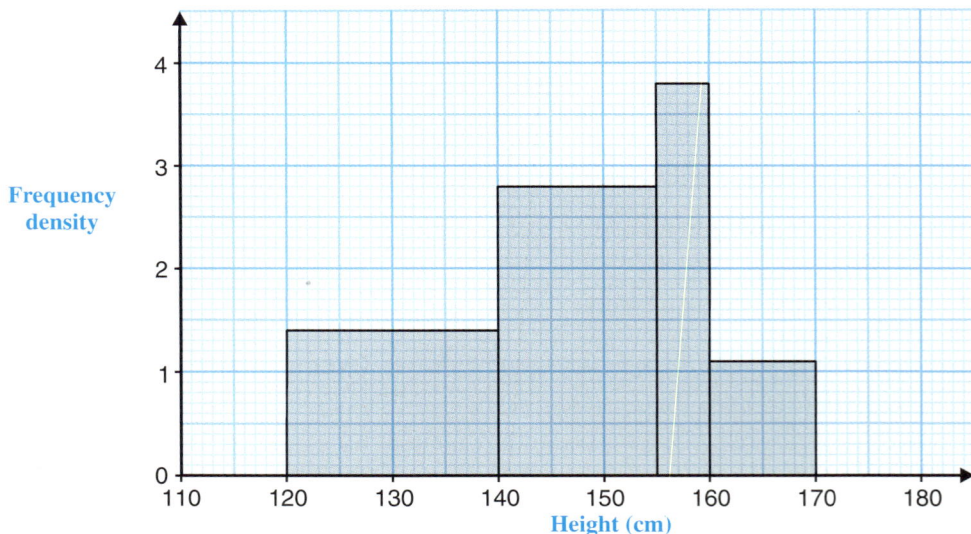

(b)   Calculate an estimate of how many girls have a height of less than 145 cm.

AQA

Cumulative Frequency ●●●●●

What you need to know

- The information given in a frequency table can be used to make a **cumulative frequency table**.

- You should be able to **draw cumulative frequency graphs**.

To draw a cumulative frequency graph:
1. Draw and label: the variable on the horizontal axis, cumulative frequency on the vertical axis. 2. Plot the cumulative frequency against the upper class boundary of each class. 3. Join the points with a smooth curve.

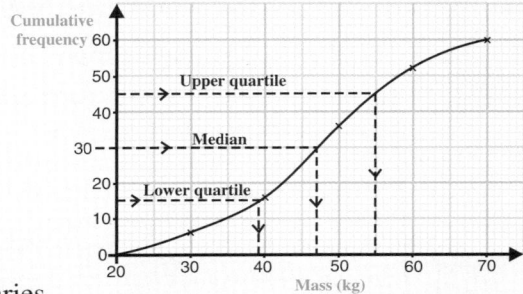

- If the question does not give the upper class boundaries,
  then the upper class boundary of each class is equal to the lower class boundary of the next class.

- When the classes have gaps between them then the upper class boundary is halfway between the
  end of one class and the beginning of the next.

- You should be able to **interpret cumulative frequency graphs**.

The **median** is the value of the middle number. The **lower quartile** is the value located at $\frac{1}{4}$ of the total frequency. The **upper quartile** is the value located at $\frac{3}{4}$ of the total frequency. The **interquartile range** measures the spread of the middle 50% of the data. Interquartile range = Upper Quartile − Lower Quartile

Eg 1 The times spent by students on the Internet one day are shown.

Time (t minutes)	$0 \leqslant t < 20$	$20 \leqslant t < 40$	$40 \leqslant t < 60$	$60 \leqslant t < 80$
Frequency	55	25	15	5

(a) Draw a cumulative frequency graph.
(b) Use your graph to find:
   (i) the median, (ii) the interquartile range.

(a) | Make a cumulative frequency table
that can be used to draw the graph. |

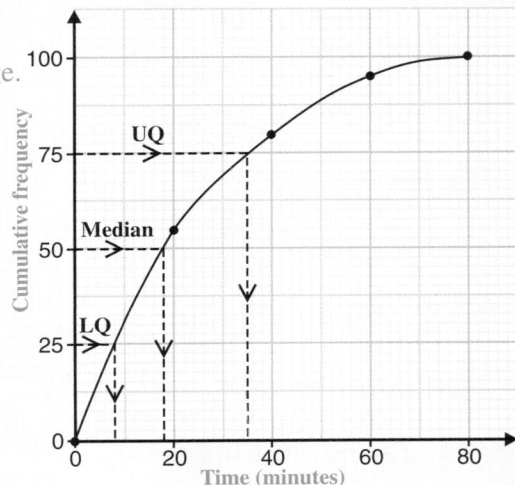

Time (mins) less than	0	20	40	60	80
Cumulative frequency	0	55	80	95	100

(b) Reading from the graph:
   (i) Median = 18 minutes
   (ii) Lower quartile (LQ) = 8 minutes
       Upper quartile (UQ) = 35 minutes
       Interquartile range = UQ − LQ = 35 − 8 = 27 minutes

39

- A **box plot** is used to represent the range, the median and the quartiles of a distribution.

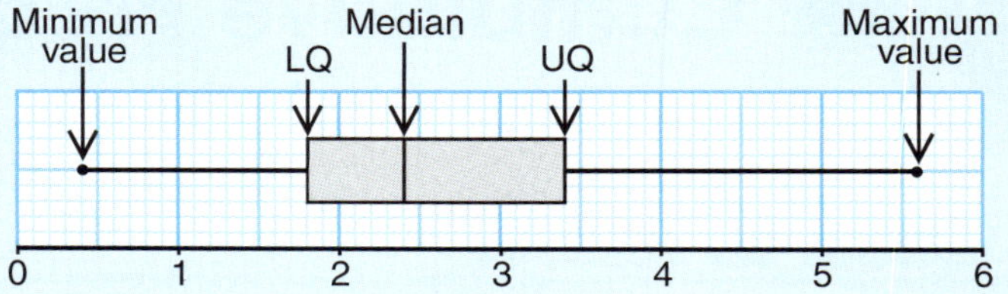

- The box plot shows how the data is spread out and how the middle 50% of data is clustered.

- Box plots can be used to compare two (or more) distributions.

- You should be able to draw and interpret box plots.

Eg 2 15 pupils were asked to estimate the size of an angle.
Their estimates, in degrees, are shown.

40 20 38 30 32 45 35 36 40 35 30 40 45 42 25

Draw a box plot to illustrate the data.

> Put the data in order and locate the median, lower quartile and upper quartile.
> Then use these values to draw the box plot.

20 25 30 (30) 32 35 35 (36) 38 40 40 (40) 42 45 45

LQ   Median   UQ

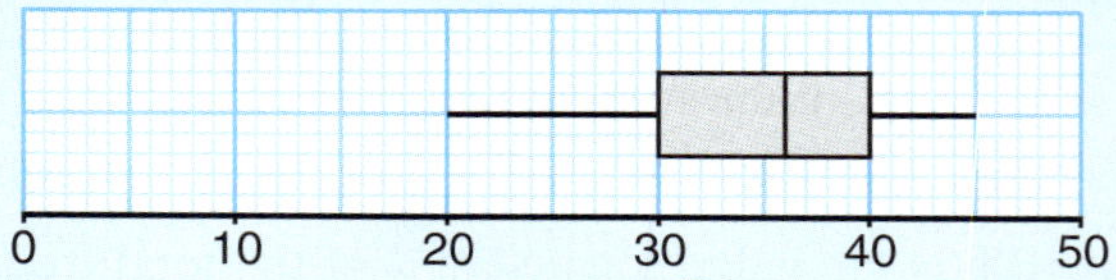

Exercise 39

1 As part of a lifesaving course a group of students were asked to swim as far as possible wearing shoes and clothes.
The cumulative frequency graph shows the distances swum.

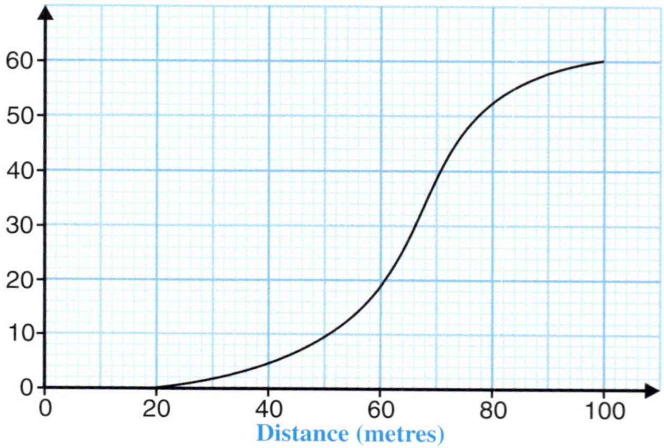

(a) Use the graph to find:
  (i) the median distance, (ii) the interquartile range.
(b) Draw a box plot to illustrate the distances swum.

2 A group of children were asked to estimate the weight of a bucket of water.
Their estimates, in kilograms, are shown.

| 10 | 9 | 17.5 | 8 | 7.5 | 5 | 10 | 15 | 12.5 | 20 | 8 | 10 | 14 | 18 | 11 |

(a) Find   (i)   the median estimate,   (ii)   the interquartile range of these estimates.
(b) Draw a box plot to represent these estimates.

3 An English examination was taken by two groups of students.
The cumulative frequency graphs show information about the marks scored by each group.

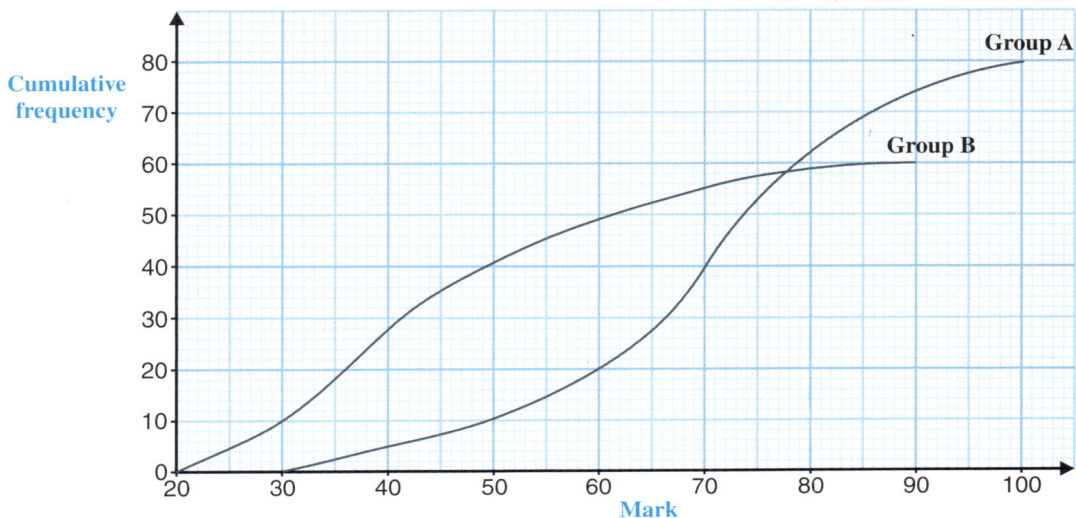

(a) Find the difference in the median marks of the two groups.
(b) (i)   Which group had the larger interquartile range?
    (ii) Find the interquartile range for this group.

AQA

4 The box plots illustrate the distribution of weights for a sample of eating apples and a sample of cooking apples.

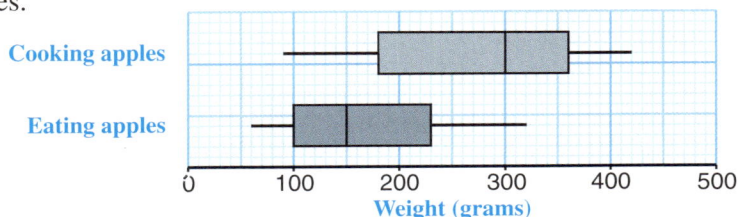

(a) What is the range in the weights of the eating apples?
(b) Which type of apple has the higher median weight?
(c) What is the interquartile range for cooking apples?
(d) Compare and comment on these distributions.

5 Laura and Joy played 80 games of golf together. The table below shows Laura's scores.

Scores x	$70 < x \leqslant 80$	$80 < x \leqslant 90$	$90 < x \leqslant 100$	$100 < x \leqslant 110$	$110 < x \leqslant 120$
Frequency	2	8	30	34	6

(a) Draw a cumulative frequency diagram to show Laura's scores.
(b) Use your graph to find: (i)   Laura's median score,
                              (ii) the interquartile range of her scores.
(c) Joy's median score was 103. The interquartile range of her scores was 6.
    (i)   Who was the more consistent player? Give a reason for your choice.
    (ii) The winner of a game of golf is the one with the lowest score.
          Who won most of these 80 games? Give a reason for your choice.

AQA

Probability

What you need to know

- **Probability** describes how likely or unlikely it is that an event will occur.
  Probabilities can be shown on a probability scale.

  > Probability **must** be written as a **fraction**, a **decimal** or a **percentage**.

- How to work out probabilities using **equally likely outcomes**.

  > The probability of an event $= \dfrac{\text{Number of outcomes in the event}}{\text{Total number of possible outcomes}}$

  Eg 1 A box contains 7 red pens and 4 blue pens. A pen is taken from the box at random.
  What is the probability that the pen is blue?

  > P(blue) stands for the probability that the pen is blue.

  $P(\text{blue}) = \dfrac{\text{Number of blue pens}}{\text{Total number of pens}} = \dfrac{4}{11}$

- How to estimate probabilities using **relative frequency**.

  > Relative frequency $= \dfrac{\text{Number of times the event happens in an experiment (or in a survey)}}{\text{Total number of trials in the experiment (or observations in the survey)}}$

  Eg 2 A spinner is spun 20 times. The results are shown.

  4   1   3   1   4   2   2   4   3   3   4   1   4   4   3   2   2   1   3   2

  What is the relative frequency of getting a 4?

  $\text{Relative frequency} = \dfrac{\text{Number of 4's}}{\text{Number of spins}} = \dfrac{6}{20} = 0.3$

  > Relative frequency gives a better estimate of probability the larger the number of trials.

- How to use probabilities to **estimate** the number of times an event occurs in an **experiment** or **observation**.

  > Estimate = total number of trials (or observations) $\times$ probability of event

  Eg 3 1000 raffle tickets are sold. Alan buys some tickets.
  The probability that Alan wins first prize is $\frac{1}{50}$.

  How many tickets did Alan buy?   Number of tickets $= 1000 \times \frac{1}{50} = 20$

- **Mutually exclusive events** cannot occur at the same time.

  > When A and B are mutually exclusive events: $P(A \text{ or } B) = P(A) + P(B)$

  Eg 4 A box contains red, green, blue and yellow counters.
  The table shows the probability of getting each colour.

Colour	Red	Green	Blue	Yellow
Probability	0.4	0.25	0.25	0.1

  A counter is taken from the box at random.
  What is the probability of getting a red or blue counter?

  $P(\text{Red or Blue}) = P(\text{Red}) + P(\text{Blue}) = 0.4 + 0.25 = 0.65$

- > The probability of an event, A, **not happening** is: $P(\text{not A}) = 1 - P(A)$

- How to find all the possible outcomes when two events are combined.
  By **listing** the outcomes systematically.
  By using a **possibility space diagram**.
  By using a **tree diagram**.

- The outcomes of **independent events** do not influence each other.

  > When A and B are independent events: $P(A \text{ and } B) = P(A) \times P(B)$

Eg 5 Box A contains 3 white cubes (W) and 1 blue cube (B).
Box B contains 2 white cubes (W) and 3 blue cubes (B).
A cube is drawn from each box at random.
(a) Draw a tree diagram to show all the possible outcomes.
(b) Calculate the probability of getting two white cubes.

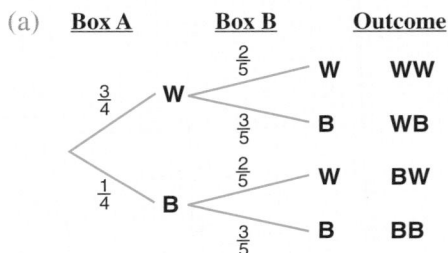

(a)

Box A	Box B	Outcome

W $\frac{3}{4}$

$\frac{2}{5}$ W   WW
$\frac{3}{5}$ B   WB

B $\frac{1}{4}$

$\frac{2}{5}$ W   BW
$\frac{3}{5}$ B   BB

(b) To calculate P(WW), multiply the probabilities along the branches of the tree diagram.

$P(WW) = \frac{3}{4} \times \frac{2}{5}$

$= \frac{6}{20}$

$= \frac{3}{10}$

- **Conditional probabilities** arise when the probabilities of particular events occurring are affected by other events.

Eg 6 In a drawer there are 4 black socks and 2 green socks. Two socks are taken at random.
What is the probability that they are both the same colour?

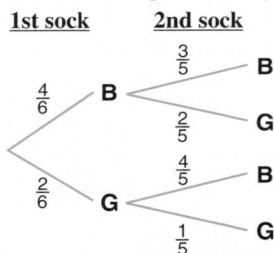

1st sock **2nd sock**

$\frac{4}{6}$ B
$\frac{3}{5}$ B
$\frac{2}{5}$ G

$\frac{2}{6}$ G
$\frac{4}{5}$ B
$\frac{1}{5}$ G

$P(\text{same colour}) = P(BB) + P(GG)$

$= \left(\frac{4}{6} \times \frac{3}{5}\right) + \left(\frac{2}{6} \times \frac{1}{5}\right)$

$= \frac{12}{30} + \frac{2}{30}$

$= \frac{14}{30} = \frac{7}{15}$

$P(\text{same colour}) = \frac{7}{15}$

The probabilities for the second sock are **dependent** on the colour of the first sock.

Exercise 40

1 A box contains counters. The counters are numbered 1, 2, 3, 4 or 5.
A counter is taken from the box at random.
(a) Copy and complete the table to show the probability of each number being chosen.
(b) Is the number on the counter chosen more likely to be odd or even?
You must show your working.

Number on counter	1	2	3	4	5
Probability	0.20	0.30	0.15		0.10

AQA

2 Petra has 5 numbered cards.
She uses the cards to do this experiment:
She repeats the experiment 20 times and gets these results.

> Shuffle the cards and then record the number on the top card.

3 3 2 3 4 3 5 2 3 4 3 5 3 3 4 2 5 3 4 2
(a) What is the relative frequency of getting a 3?
(b) What numbers do you think are on the five cards? Give a reason for your answer.
(c) She repeats the experiment 500 times.
Estimate the number of times she will get a 5. Give a reason for your answer.

Probability . . . . Probability . . . . Probability . . . .

3 Jeff tosses a coin three times. What is the probability that he gets one head and two tails?

4 The table shows information about the colour and type of symbol printed on some cards.

Colour of symbol

		Red	Yellow	Blue
Type of symbol	**O**	9	4	5
	X	2	7	3

(a) A card is taken at random.
  (i) What is the probability that it has a red symbol?
  (ii) What is the probability that it has a blue symbol **or** an X?
(b) A yellow card is taken at random.
  What is the probability that it has the symbol X?

AQA

5 On Tuesday Jim has to catch a bus and a train to get to work.
The probability that the train is late is 0.4. The probability that the bus is late is 0.7.
(a) Copy and complete the tree diagram.

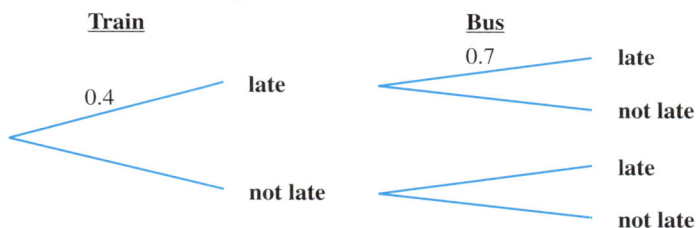

Train   **Bus**

        0.4   late   0.7   late

                                                  not late

                       not late   late

                                                  not late

(b) What is the probability that both the bus and the train are late?
(c) What is the probability that either the train or the bus is late but not both?

6 (a) A box contains 2 red (R) counters and 3 green (G) counters.
    Two counters are taken at random from the box.
    Calculate the probability that the two counters are a different colour.

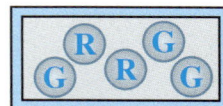

(b) Box A and Box B contain the following counters.

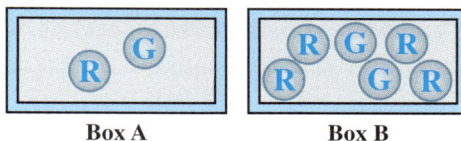

Box A   Box B

One counter is taken at random form Box A and put in Box B.
One counter is then taken at random from Box B and put in Box A.

What is the probability that Box A now contains counters of the same colour?

AQA

7 Each month a restaurant offers two special meals.
Each special meal includes a bottle of either red or white wine.
In May the special meals are Chicken Kiev and Fish Casserole.

The probability that a customer chooses a special meal is 0.4.
If a special meal is chosen the probability of it being Chicken Kiev is 0.35.
If the chosen special meal is Chicken Kiev then the probability of red wine being chosen is 0.9.
If the chosen special meal is Fish Casserole then the probability of red wine being chosen is 0.2.

The restaurant expects 2500 customers in May.
How many bottles of **white** wine is the restaurant likely to need for the special meals in May?

AQA

Section Review - Handling Data

1 Winston has designed a data collection sheet to record the number of bottles that each person puts into a bottle bank.

(a) Give **three** criticisms of the class intervals that Winston has chosen.

Number of bottles	Tally	Frequency
0 to 2		
3 to 6		
6 to 8		

Anna and Patrick watch people using the bottle bank.
Anna watches 60 people and calculates the mean to be 8.5 bottles per person.
Patrick watches 15 people and calculates the mean to be 9.2 bottles per person.

(b) Which of the two means would you expect to give the more reliable estimate of the mean number of bottles per person? Give a reason for your answer.

AQA

2 Corrin throws a dice 40 times. Her results are shown.

(a) Which score is the mode?
(b) Calculate the mean score.
(c) What is the median score?

Score	1	2	3	4	5	6
Frequency	7	6	7	6	6	8

3 A teacher asked the pupils in his maths class how long they had spent revising for a maths test.
He drew a scatter graph to compare their test results and the time they had spent revising.

(a) State which point A, B, C or D represents the statement:
   (i) Keith, "Even though I spent a long time revising, I still got a poor test result."
   (ii) Val, "I got a good test result despite not doing much revision."
   (iii) Jane, "I revised for ages and got a good test result."

(b) Make up a statement which matches the point you have **not** used in your answer to part (a).

(c) What does the scatter graph tell you about the relationship between the time the pupils spent revising and their test results?

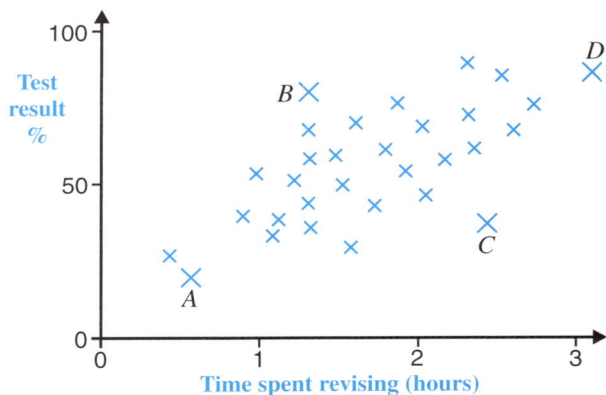

AQA

4 The table shows the weight distribution of the fish caught in a fishing competition.

(a) Calculate an estimate of the mean weight of a fish.

(b) Draw a frequency polygon to represent this distribution.

Weight (g grams)	Frequency
$0 \leqslant g < 100$	0
$100 \leqslant g < 200$	16
$200 \leqslant g < 300$	36
$300 \leqslant g < 400$	20
$400 \leqslant g < 500$	8
$500 \leqslant g < 600$	0

AQA

5 To collect data for a survey on the amount of milk bought each week by families, Grant stands outside his local supermarket and asks 10 people as they leave the shop how much milk they have just bought. He repeats this each day for a week.
Write down two reasons why his results may be biased.

6 The table shows information about a group of students.

	Can speak French	Cannot speak French
Male	5	20
Female	12	38

(a) One of these students is chosen at random.
What is the probability that the student can speak French?

(b) Pru says, "If a female student is chosen at random she is more likely to be able to speak French than if a male student is chosen at random."
Is she correct? Explain your answer.

7 One person is to be chosen at random from four men and two women.

Jack   Trevor   Eric   Jeff   Joan   Jill

Four events are defined as   Event *J*: Someone with a name beginning with J is chosen.
Event *M*: A man is chosen.
Event *N*: Someone reading a newspaper is chosen.
Event *W*: A woman is chosen.

What is the probability that, if **one person** is chosen at random:
(a) both *J* and *M* are true,   (b) both *J* and *N* are true,   (c) either *N* or *W* is true?

AQA

8 The table shows the rainfall (cm) and the number of hours of sunshine for various towns in August one year.

Rainfall (cm)	0.1	0.1	0.2	0.5	0.8	1	1	1.5	1.5	1.9
Sunshine (hours)	200	240	210	190	170	160	130	100	120	90

(a) Use this information to draw a scatter graph.
(b) Draw a line of best fit on your diagram.
(c) Use your line of best fit to estimate the number of hours of sunshine for a town that had:
(i) 1.4 cm of rain in August that year,
(ii) 2.5 cm of rain in August that year.
(d) Which of the answers from part (c) would you expect to be the more reliable?
Give a reason for your answer.

AQA

9 The graph shows the distribution of the best height jumped by each girl in a high jump competition.

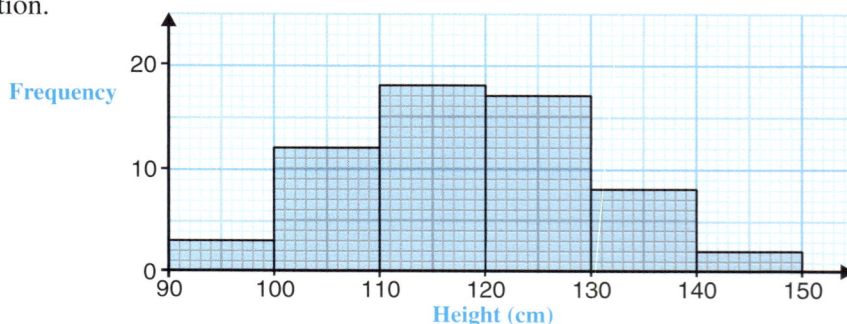

(a) Which class interval contains the median height?
(b) Calculate an estimate of the mean of these heights.

10 A bag contains a number of counters.
Each counter is coloured red, white or blue. Each counter is numbered 1, 2 or 3.
The table shows the probability of colour and number for these counters.

Colour of counter

		Red	White	Blue
	1	0.2	0.1	0
Number on counter	2	0.1	0.3	0.1
	3	0.1	0	0.1

(a) A counter is taken from the bag at random.
    (i) What is the probability that the counter is red or white?
    (ii) What is the probability that the counter is white or numbered 2?
(b) There are 10 blue counters in the bag.
    How many counters are in the bag altogether?

A counter is taken from the bag at random.
The colour is noted and the counter is then **returned** to the bag.
Another counter is then taken from the bag at random.
(c) What is the probability that both counters are the same colour?

AQA

11 (a) Part of a cumulative frequency graph for a set of data is shown.
    The lower quartile is 15.
    How many values are in the set of data?
(b) **Without** doing any calculations, state which of
    the three averages, mean, mode or median,
    would best describe the following data.
    Give reasons why the other two are **not** as suitable.
      5, 6, 6, 6, 7, 8, 12, 12, 14, 15,
    17, 18, 22, 22, 24, 26, 37, 49, 158, 196.

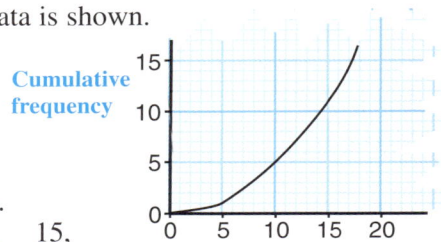

Cumulative frequency

AQA

12 A sack contains a number of gold and silver discs.
An experiment consists of taking a disc from the sack at random, recording its colour and then replacing it.
The experiment is repeated 10, 50, 100, 150 and 200 times. The table shows the results.

Number of experiments	10	50	100	150	200
Number of gold discs	3	8	23	30	38

(a) Draw a graph to show how the relative frequency of a gold disc changes as the number of experiments increases.
(b) The sack contains 1000 discs. Estimate the number of gold discs in the sack.
    Explain how you estimated your answer.

AQA

13 Here is a list of the last 8 quarterly gas bills for a householder.

Month	Jan.	Apr.	Jul.	Oct.	Jan.	Apr.	Jul.	Oct.
Amount	£67	£188	£27	£18	£139	£103	£23	£27

Calculate the first two 4-point moving averages for this data.

14 John is taking part in a spelling test.
Words are chosen at random.
The probability that he spells a word correctly is $\frac{7}{10}$.
John is given two words to spell.
(a) What is the probability that he spells both words correctly?
(b) What is the probability that he spells only one of the words correctly?

AQA

15 Students in Year 11 were asked to write an essay on "Popstars".

(a) The table shows the distribution of the times taken by male students to complete the essay.

Time (t minutes)	$10 \leqslant t < 20$	$20 \leqslant t < 30$	$30 \leqslant t < 40$	$40 \leqslant t < 50$
Frequency	8	27	19	6

    (i) Draw a cumulative frequency graph for the data.

    (ii) Use your graph to estimate the median and the interquartile range.

(b) The box plot illustrates the distribution of the times taken by female students to complete the essay.

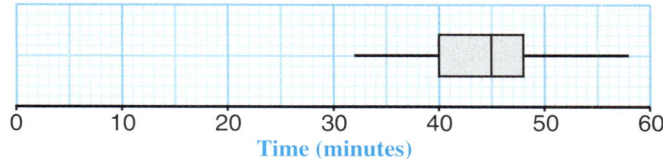

Time (minutes)

    Estimate the median and the interquartile range.

(c) Compare and comment on the times taken by male students and the times taken by female students to complete the essay.

16 Giles has two chickens.

The probability that a chicken will lay an egg on any day is 0.8.

(a) What is the probability that both chickens will lay an egg on Sunday?

(b) What is the probability that only one chicken will lay an egg on Monday?

17 Ruben is doing a survey of the use of mobile phones among students at his school.

(a) Give reasons why a sample of the sixth form only, may be biased.

(b) Ruben decides to take a stratified random sample of 10% of all the students in the school.

    (i) Describe how he chooses his sample.

    (ii) Give one advantage this method has over a simple random sample.

18 The table shows the distribution of the times, in minutes, that people had to wait for their meals at a restaurant.

Time (t minutes)	$0 \leqslant t < 10$	$10 \leqslant t < 15$	$15 \leqslant t < 25$	$25 \leqslant t < 40$
Frequency	25	21	24	9

(a) Draw a histogram to represent these waiting times.

(b) Estimate the median waiting time.

(c) Estimate how many people had to wait more than 30 minutes for their meal.

19 In Kim's purse there are two 20 pence coins and one 10 pence coin.

In Sally's purse there are three 20 pence coins and one 10 pence coin.

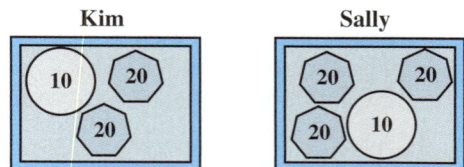

Kim takes one coin at random from her purse and gives it to her friend Tiaz.

Sally takes two coins at random from her purse and gives them both to Tiaz.

(a) Calculate the probability that Kim and Sally give Tiaz a total of 60 pence.

(b) Calculate the probability that Kim and Sally have the same coins as each other left in their purses.

AQA

20 A bag contains 5 lemon, 4 orange and 3 cherry flavoured sweets.

Ivan eats three sweets at random.

Calculate the probability that he has eaten

(a) one lemon and two orange flavoured sweets,

(b) at least one cherry flavoured sweet.

21 A bag contains two black discs and three white discs.
Three children play a game in which each draws a disc from the bag.
Parveen goes first, then Seema, and Jane is last.
Each time a disc is withdrawn it is not replaced.
The first child to draw a white disc wins the game.

(a) In a game, calculate the probability that
   (i) Parveen wins,
   (ii) Seema wins.

They replace the discs and play the game a second time.
(b) Calculate the probability that
   (i) Parveen wins neither the first nor the second game,
   (ii) Jane wins both games.

AQA

22 A school has 670 students.
The school carries out a survey on the time that the students spend doing homework over one weekend.
(a) This table shows the number of students in each year group in the school.

Year	8	9	10	11
Number	153	172	181	164

In the survey the school uses a stratified random sample of size 100.
How many students in each year group will be included in the sample?

This histogram shows the results of the survey.

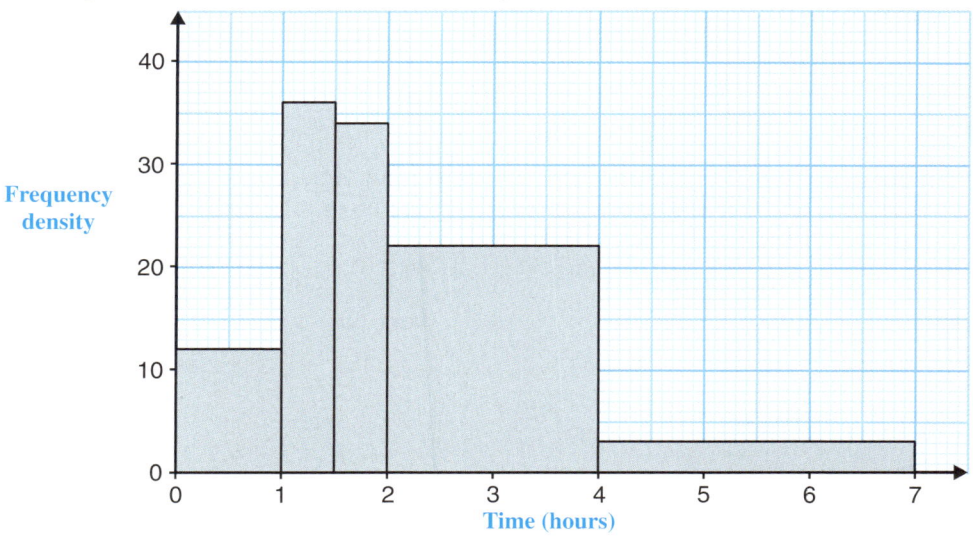

Frequency density vs Time (hours)

(b) Calculate the number of students in the survey who do homework for between 1 and 2 hours.

In the survey, 64% of the students who do homework for between 3 and 5 hours are girls.
(c) Use the histogram to estimate the number of girls in the survey who do homework for between 3 and 5 hours.

AQA

23 Whether or not Jonathan gets up in time for school depends on whether he remembers to set his alarm clock the evening before.
For 85% of the time he remembers to set the clock; the other 15% of the time he forgets.
If the clock is set, he gets up in time for school on 90% of the occasions.
If the clock is not set, he does not get up in time for school on 60% of the occasions.

On what proportion of the occasions does he get up in time for school?

AQA

Exam Practice - Non-calculator Paper ● ● ●

Do not use a calculator for this exercise.

1 Use these numbers to answer the following questions.

  3   7   11   15   19   23   27

  (a) Which number in the list is a factor of another number in the list?
  (b) Which number is a cube number?
  (c) (i) Which numbers are not prime numbers? Give a reason for your answer.
    (ii) The numbers are part of a sequence.
      What is the next number in the sequence which is not a prime number?

2 Karina is playing a game with these cards. $\boxed{X}$ $\boxed{Y}$ $\boxed{1}$ $\boxed{1}$ $\boxed{3}$

  One card is taken at random from the letters.
  One card is taken at random from the numbers.
  (a) List all the possible outcomes.

  (b) Explain why the probability of getting $\boxed{X}$ $\boxed{1}$ is not $\frac{1}{4}$.

3 A plank of wood is 225 cm in length. It is cut into two pieces.
  One piece is 37 cm longer than the other.
  What is the length of the shorter piece of wood?   AQA

4 A is the point $(-4, -1)$. B is the point $(2, 3)$.   What is the midpoint of AB?

5 A cuboid has a volume of 50 cm³. The base of the cuboid measures 4 cm by 5 cm.
  Calculate the height of the cuboid.

6 A concrete block weighs 11 kg, correct to the nearest kilogram.
  Write down the greatest and least possible weight of the block.

7 Solve the equations   (a) $3a - 2 = -5$,   (b) $5m + 3 = 7 - m$,   (c) $3(a - 2) = 6$.

8 (a) What is the reciprocal of $1\frac{1}{4}$?   (b) Work out. (i) $1\frac{1}{4} + \frac{2}{3}$ (ii) $1\frac{1}{4} \times \frac{2}{3}$

9 OBC is a straight line.
  AOB is an isosceles triangle with $OB = AB$.
  Angle $AOB = x°$.
  (a) Write down, in terms of x,   (i) angle OAB,
        (ii) angle ABC.
  (b) Angle OBA is $(x - 12)$ degrees.
    Find the value of x.   AQA

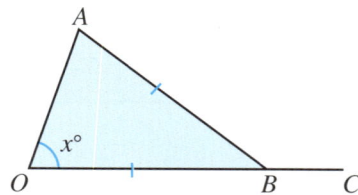

10 Each term in a sequence of numbers is obtained by multiplying the previous terms by -2.
  The first three terms are: 1, -2,   4,   …
  (a) Write down the next two terms in the sequence.
  (b) Will the 50th term of the sequence be positive or negative? Explain your reasoning.
  (c) The n th term of this sequence is $(-2)^{n-1}$.
    Write down the values of the first three terms of a different sequence whose n th term
    is $(-2)^{1-n}$.   AQA

11 Draw a rectangle 4 cm by 5 cm.
  Construct, on the outside of the rectangle, the locus of points that are 2 cm from the edges of
  the rectangle.

12 A sequence begins: -1, 2, 5, 8, 11, …
Write in terms of n, the nth term of the sequence.

13 Copy shape A onto squared paper.

(a) A is mapped onto B by a translation with vector $\begin{pmatrix} 0 \\ -4 \end{pmatrix}$.
Draw the position of B on your diagram.

(b) A is mapped onto C by a rotation through $180°$ about $(3, 1)$.
Draw the position of C on your diagram.

(c) Describe the single transformation which maps B onto C.

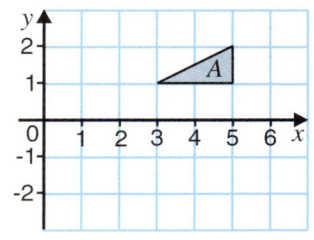

14 A youth club organises a skiing holiday for 45 children.
The ratio of boys to girls is $5 : 4$.
40% of the boys have skied before.
How many boys have skied before?

15 (a) Write 48 as a product of its prime factors.
(b) Write 108 as a product of its prime factors.
(c) Hence find the least common multiple of 48 and 108.

16 (a) Copy and complete the table of values for $y = x^2 - 3x + 1$.

x	-1	0	1	2	3	4
y		1	-1			5

(b) Draw the graph of $y = x^2 - 3x + 1$ for values of x from -1 to 4.
(c) Use your graph to find the value of y when $x = 1.5$.
(d) Use your graph to solve the equation $x^2 - 3x + 1 = 0$.

17 (a) Estimate the value of $\sqrt{\dfrac{(9.8)^3}{0.39}}$

(b) Cocoa is sold in cylindrical tins.
The height of a tin is 7.9 cm. The radius of a tin is 4.1 cm.
Use approximations to estimate the volume of a tin.
Show all your working.

18 Solve the equation $\frac{1}{3}(2x - 1) = \frac{1}{5}(3x + 2)$.

19 Sixty cyclists were asked how many kilometres they had cycled last week.
The cumulative frequency graph shows the results.

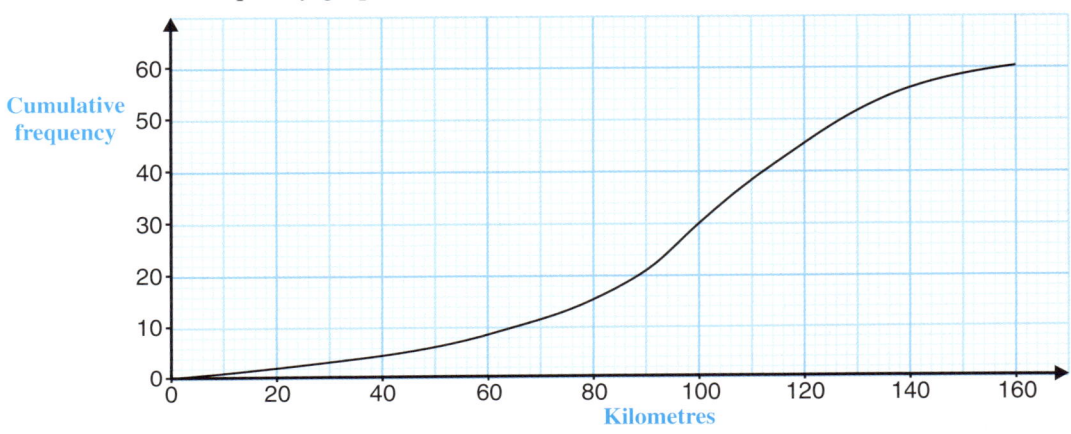

(a) How many of the cyclists had cycled less than 50 kilometres last week?
(b) Estimate the median and interquartile range for the distances.

AQA

20 (a) List the values of n, where n is an integer, such that $3 \leqslant 3n < 18$.
(b) Solve the simultaneous equations $2x + y = 9$,
$$x - 2y = 7.$$
(c) Factorise the expression $n^2 - n$.
(d) Simplify $3a^2b \times 2a^3b$. AQA

21 Work out. (a) $2\frac{1}{2} - 1\frac{2}{3}$ (b) $2\frac{1}{2} \div 1\frac{2}{3}$

22 The diagram shows a quadrilateral $ABCD$.
$AB = 9\,\text{cm}$ and $AC = 15\,\text{cm}$.

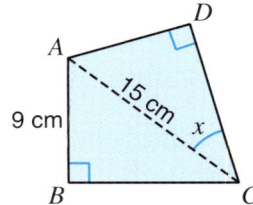

(a) Calculate the length of BC.

(b) Given that $\cos x = 0.7$,
calculate the length of CD. AQA

23 (a) What is the value of n in each of the following?
(i) $y^6 \div y^n = y^3$ (ii) $y^4 \times y^2 = y^n$
(b) Calculate 3×10^5 times 4×10^{-3}.
Give your answer in standard form.

24 It takes 15 minutes to fill a paddling pool at the rate of 12 litres per minute.
How many minutes less would it take to fill the pool at the rate of 20 litres per minute?

25 At a fete Jessie has one go on the hoopla and one go on the darts.
The probability she wins a prize on the hoopla is 0.3.
The probability she wins a prize on the darts is 0.4.
(a) Copy and complete the tree diagram for these two events.

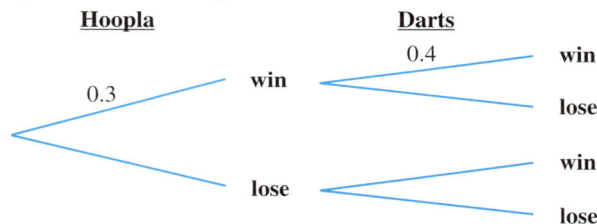

Hoopla   **Darts**

0.4   **win**
0.3   **win**
    lose

    win
lose
    lose

(b) Calculate the probability that she does not win a prize.
(c) Calculate the probability that she wins only one prize.

26 These formulae represent quantities connected with containers, where a, b and c are dimensions.
$$2(ab + bc + cd) \qquad abc \qquad \sqrt{a^2 + b^2} \qquad 4(a + b + c)$$
Which of these formulae represent lengths? Explain how you know.

27 (a) Factorise completely. $3x^2 - 6x$
(b) Expand and simplify. $(3x + 2)(x - 4)$
(c) Make t the subject of the formula. $W = \dfrac{5t + 3}{4}$ AQA

28 Hugh buys a box of fireworks. After lighting 40% of the fireworks he has 24 fireworks left.
How many fireworks did he buy?

29 You are given the formula $a = bc^2$.
(a) Calculate the value of a when $b = 100$ and $c = -\frac{3}{5}$.
(b) Rearrange the formula to give c in terms of a and b.

30 (a) Simplify (i) $2a^3 \times 3a^2$, (ii) $4a^6 \div 2a^3$.
(b) Solve the quadratic equation $x^2 + 3x - 10 = 0$.
(c) Solve the inequality $3 < 2x + 1 < 5$. AQA

31 The sum of two numbers is 8.
The product of these numbers is 15.
If one of the numbers is x, show that $x^2 - 8x + 15 = 0$.

AQA

32 The diagram shows the positions of shapes P, Q and R.

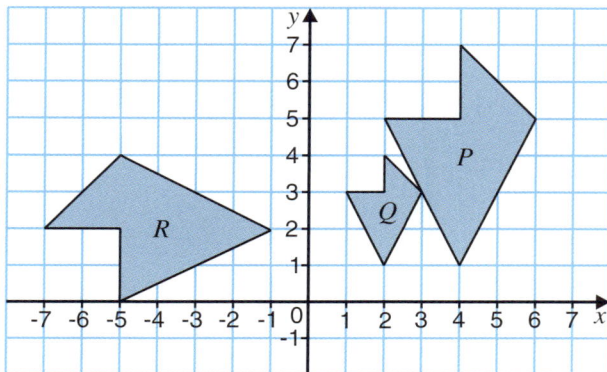

(a) Describe fully the single transformation which takes P onto Q.

(b) Describe fully the single transformation which takes P onto R.

(c) Copy shape Q onto squared paper and draw an enlargement of the shape with scale factor -2, centre $(0, 3)$.

33 (a) The diagram shows the line $4y = x + 5$.
(i) What are the coordinates of the point marked P?
(ii) What is the gradient of the line?

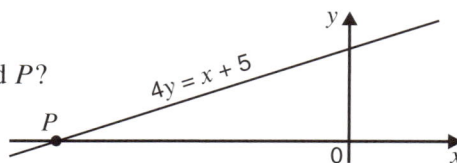

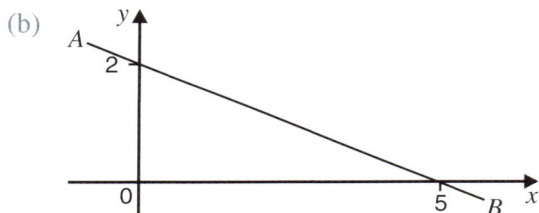

(b)

(i) Find the equation of the straight line, AB, shown in the diagram.

(ii) The line CD is perpendicular to AB and goes through $(0, 0)$.
Find the equation of the line CD.

34 These kites are similar.

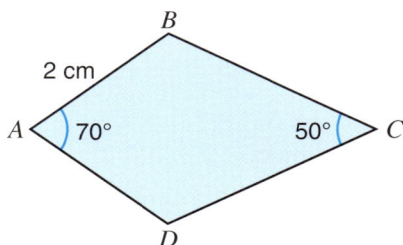

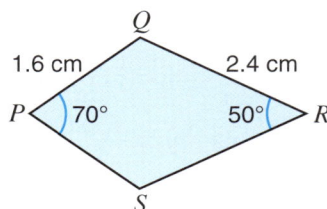

Not drawn accurately

(a) Work out the size of angle PQR.
(b) Calculate the length of BC.
(c) Express the area of $ABCD$ to the area of $PQRS$ as a ratio in the form $1 : n$.

35 After plans for a by-pass to a large town were announced, the local newspaper received twelve letters on the subject. Eleven were opposed to it.

The newspaper claimed: 'OVER 90% ARE AGAINST NEW BY-PASS'

(a) Give **two** reasons why the newspaper could be criticised for making this claim.
(b) The local council is to carry out a survey to find the true nature of local opinion.
Give **two** factors that should be taken into account when selecting the sample.

AQA

36 Show that $(n - 3)^2 - 2(n - 3) = (n - 3)(n - 5)$.

Practice Exam Questions

EP

37 (a) Write down the inequalities which describe the shaded region.

(b) On another diagram, shade the region which satisfies these inequalities:

$$1 \leqslant y \leqslant 3, \quad 2y \geqslant x \quad \text{and} \quad 2x \geqslant y + 1.$$

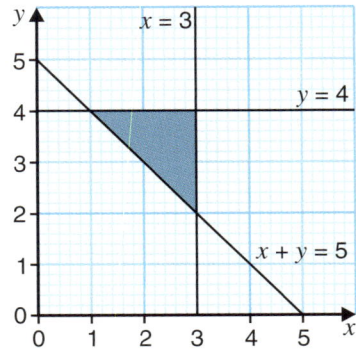

38 The sketches show the graphs of four equations. Write down the equation for each graph.

(a) 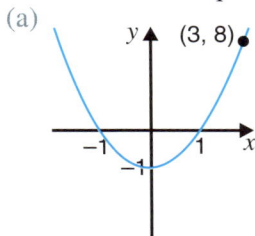   (b) 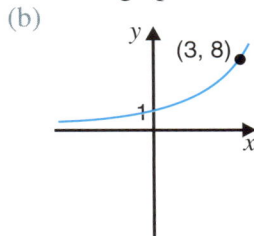   (c) 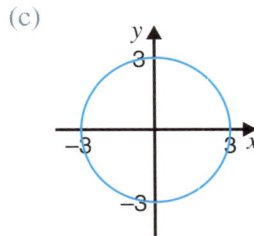   (d)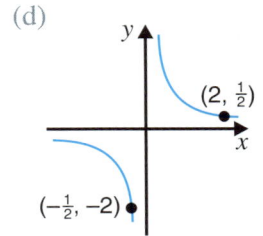

39 T is directly proportional to the positive square root of M and $T = 32$, when $M = 16$.

(a) Calculate T when M is 100.   (b) Calculate M when T is 9.6.

AQA

40 Alex does a triple jump, i.e. a hop, step and jump.
The step is 5.14 metres and the jump is 6.75 metres.
The total triple jump is 15.74 metres.
All these measurements are to the nearest centimetre.
What is the maximum length of Alex's hop?

AQA

41 (a) Evaluate (i) $16^{\frac{3}{4}}$, (ii) $27^{-\frac{2}{3}}$.   (b) Show that $\dfrac{2}{\sqrt{3}} - \dfrac{\sqrt{3}}{2} = \dfrac{\sqrt{3}}{6}$.

42 (a) Simplify $(3a^3)^2$.

(b) Solve $\dfrac{2}{x + 1} + \dfrac{1}{x - 1} = 1$.

(c) Rearrange the formula $m = \dfrac{3(n + 1)}{2 - n}$ to make n the subject.

43 $OABC$ is a trapezium.

$\overrightarrow{OA} = 2\mathbf{a}, \quad \overrightarrow{OC} = 8\mathbf{b}$ and $\overrightarrow{AB} = \frac{1}{4}\overrightarrow{OC}$.

Find, in terms of $\mathbf{a}$ and $\mathbf{b}$, (a) $\overrightarrow{BA}$, (b) $\overrightarrow{BC}$.

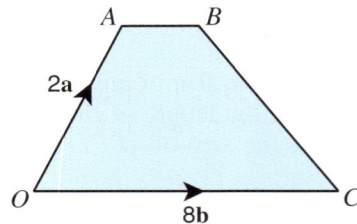

AQA

44

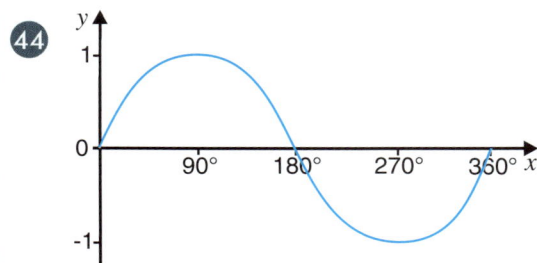

A sketch of $y = f(x)$ for $0° \leqslant x \leqslant 360°$ is shown. Draw sketches to show each of these transformations of $y = f(x)$.

(a) $y = f(x) + 2$
(b) $y = 2f(x)$
(c) $y = f(2x)$

45 This solid is made from a cylinder and a hemisphere.
The height of the cylinder is y cm.
The radius of both the cylinder and the hemisphere is x cm.
(a) Calculate, in terms of π, the volume of the solid
when $x = 6$ and $y = 8$.

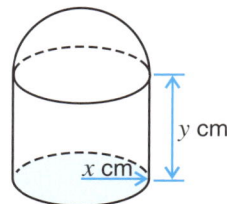

The total surface area, A, of the solid is given by the
expression $A = 3\pi x^2 + 2\pi xy$.
(b) Write down and solve an equation to find x when $A = 26\pi$ and $y = 3.5$.   AQA

46 You are given that $m = 1 + \sqrt{2}$ and $n = 1 - \sqrt{2}$.
(a) $m - n = \sqrt{a}$. Find the value of a.   (b) Find the value of $\dfrac{mn}{m + n}$.

47 In a class of 25 students, 5 are left-handed and the rest are right-handed.
Two students are chosen at random, one at a time.
Calculate the probability that:
(a) they are both left-handed,   (b) one is left-handed and one is right-handed.

48 A leisure company runs two sports clubs, A and B.
The age distribution of the members of club A is shown in this table.

Age (y years)	$15 \leqslant y < 20$	$20 \leqslant y < 25$	$25 \leqslant y < 35$	$35 \leqslant y < 50$	$50 \leqslant y < 60$
Frequency	13	30	50	45	12

(a) (i) Show the distribution for club A on a histogram.
(ii) Estimate the number of members of club A in the age group $40 \leqslant y < 55$.
(b) Club B has a total of 250 members.
The distribution of the ages of the male and female members are shown in this table.

Age (y years)	$y < 20$	$20 \leqslant y < 50$	$\geqslant 50$
Male	20	120	30
Female	5	60	15

A survey of the club B membership is carried out using a stratified random sample of size 100.
(i) Find the number of male and female members of different ages included in the sample.
(ii) Give a reason why a stratified random sample should be used rather than a simple random sample.   AQA

49 Zarig took part in a 26-mile road race.
He ran the first 15 miles at an average speed of x mph.
He ran the last 11 miles at an average speed of $(x - 2)$ mph.
He took 4 hours to complete the race.
(a) Form an equation, in terms of x, and show that it can be written as $2x^2 - 17x + 15 = 0$.
(b) Solve this equation and obtain Zarig's average speed over the first 15 miles of the race.   AQA

50 (a) (i) Simplify $\left(3 + \sqrt{2}\right)^2$.
(ii) Is your answer to part (a)(i) a rational or an irrational number?
(b) A curve has the equation $y = x^2 - 6x + 7$.
(i) Find the value of y when $x = \left(3 + \sqrt{2}\right)$.
(ii) Explain what your answer tells you about the graph of $y = x^2 - 6x + 7$.   AQA

51 (a) Simplify the expression $\dfrac{2x^2 - 8x}{x^2 - 16}$.
(b) You are given the equation $\left(p + 2\right)^{\frac{1}{3}} = k \times 2^n$.
When $p = -1$, $n = -2$.
Calculate the value of n when $p = 6$.   AQA

Exam Practice - Calculator Paper

● ● ● ● ●

You may use a calculator for this exercise.

1   (a)   (i)   Work out $\sqrt{3}$.   Give your answer correct to two decimal places.
      (ii)   Work out $(0.6)^3$.
   (b)   What is the value of m, if $47.6 \div m = 0.\dot{3}$?

2   A pint of water weighs $1\frac{1}{4}$ lb. Calculate the weight of 5 litres of water in kilograms.

3   Cheri is paid a basic rate of £5.40 per hour for a 35-hour week.
Overtime is paid at $1\frac{1}{2}$ times the basic rate. Last week she was paid £221.40.
How many hours did Cheri work last week?

4   The annual rate of inflation is 2.4%.
In the budget the price of petrol is increased from 69.9p per litre to 72.3p per litre.
Megan says the price of petrol has increased by the rate of inflation.
Is she correct? Give a reason for your answer.

5   The mean weight of 7 netball players is 51.4 kg.
   (a)   Find the total weight of the players.

The mean weight of the 7 players and the reserve is 52.3 kg.
   (b)   Calculate the weight of the reserve.   AQA

6   Tom lives 2 kilometres from work. He walks to work at an average speed of 5 km/h.
He leaves home at 0845. At what time does he arrive at work?   AQA

7   A toilet roll has 240 single sheets per roll.
Each sheet is 139 millimetres long and 110 millimetres wide.

   (a)   Calculate the total area of paper on the roll.
      Give your answer in square metres.

   (b)   A shopkeeper buys a box of 48 toilet rolls for £18.
      He sells them for 52 pence each.
      Find his profit as a percentage of the cost price.

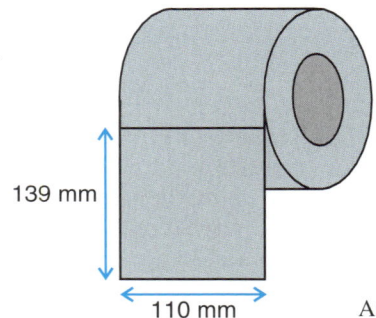

139 mm   110 mm   AQA

8   A hang glider flies 2.8 km on a bearing of 070° from P to Q and then 2 km on a bearing of
200° from Q to R.
   (a)   Make a scale drawing to show the flight of the hang glider from P to Q to R.
      Use a scale of 1 cm to 200 m.
   (b)   From R the hang glider flies directly back to P.
      Use your drawing to find the distance and bearing of P from R.

9   Some students took part in a sponsored silence.
The frequency diagram shows
the distribution of their times.

   (a)   How many students took part?
   (b)   Which time interval contains
      the median of their times?
   (c)   Calculate an estimate of the
      mean of their times.

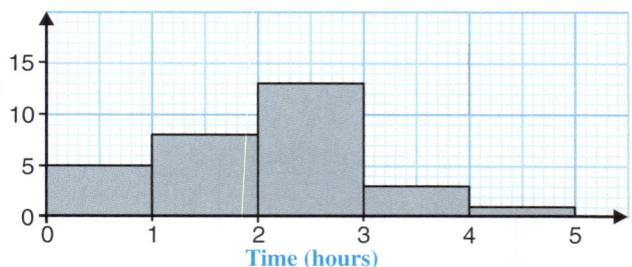

Frequency

Time (hours)

10 A hospital carries out a test to compare the reaction times of patients of different ages.
The results are shown.

Age in years	17	21	24	25	31	15	18	29	20	26
Time (hundredths of a second)	29	40	45	65	66	21	33	62	32	53

   (a)   Plot the results as a scatter graph.
   (b)   What does the scatter graph tell you about the reaction times of these patients?
   (c)   Draw a line of best fit on the scatter graph.
   (d)   The hospital is worried about the reaction time of one patient.
       (i)   How old is the patient?
       (ii)   Using the line of best fit, what should the reaction time be for this patient?   AQA

11 The sides of a six-sided spinner are numbered from 1 to 6.
The table shows the results for 100 spins.

Number on spinner	1	2	3	4	5	6
Frequency	27	18	17	15	16	7

   (a)   What is the relative frequency of getting a 1?
   (b)   Do you think the spinner is fair?
       Give a reason for your answer.
   (c)   The spinner is spun 3000 times.
       Estimate the number of times the result is 1 or 6.

12 (a)   Draw and label the lines $y = x + 1$ and $x + y = 3$ for values of x from -1 to 3.
   (b)   The region R is satisfied by all of these inequalities:
$$x > 0 \qquad y > x + 1 \qquad x + y < 3$$
       Label the region R on your diagram.

13 There are 52 cards in a pack. A dealer shares the pack between two players in the ratio 5 : 8.
How many cards does each player receive?   AQA

14 (a)   Gerald invests £4000 at 4.5% per annum compound interest.
       Calculate the interest on his investment at the end of 3 years.
   (b)   Steff invests her money at 5% per annum compound interest.
       Calculate the percentage increase in the value of her investment after 3 years.

15 (a)   Express the following numbers as products of their prime factors.
       (i)   72   (ii)   80
   (b)   Two cars go round a race track. The first car takes 1 minute 12 seconds to complete a
       circuit and the other car takes 1 minute 20 seconds.
       They start together on the starting line.
       Find the length of time, in minutes, before they are together again.   AQA

16 Use a trial and improvement method to find a solution to the equation $x^3 + x = 57$.
Show all your working and give your answer correct to one decimal place.

17 The diagram shows a semi-circle with diameter AB.
C is a point on the circumference.
$AC = 6\,\text{cm}$ and $CB = 8\,\text{cm}$.
Calculate the area of the shaded triangle as a
percentage of the area of the semi-circle.

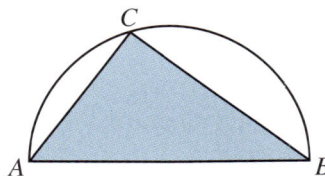

18 Use your calculator to find the value of $\dfrac{29.7 + 17.3}{1.54 \times 68.5}$.

Give your answer to a suitable degree of accuracy **and** give a reason for your choice.

19 The diagram shows a zig-zag path which joins the upper and lower gardens at a holiday resort.

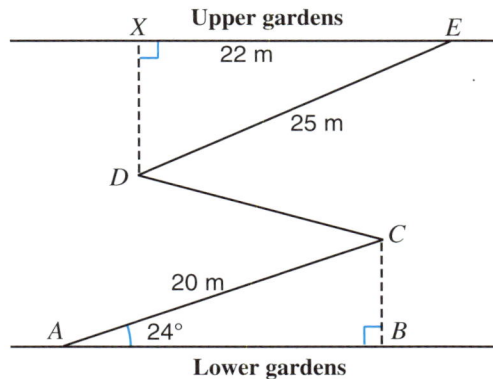

The path DE is 25 m long and $XE = 22$ m.
(a) Calculate XD.

The path AC is 20 m long and slopes at $24°$ to the horizontal.
(b) Calculate BC.

Upper gardens
X — 22 m — E
25 m
D
C
20 m
A — $24°$ ——— B
Lower gardens

AQA

20 (a) The frequency distribution table gives information about the distances travelled to school by pupils at a primary school.

Distance (k kilometres)	$0 \leqslant k < 1$	$1 \leqslant k < 2$	$2 \leqslant k < 3$	$3 \leqslant k < 4$	$4 \leqslant k < 5$
Frequency	36	76	28	12	8

   (i) Draw a cumulative frequency graph to illustrate the data.
   (ii) Use your graph to find the median and the interquartile range.
(b) A survey of the distances travelled to school by pupils at a secondary school gave the following information.

Shortest distance	0.2 km	Median	2.8 km
Longest distance	9.6 km	Lower quartile	2.0 km
		Upper quartile	3.4 km

   Draw a box plot to illustrate the data.
(c) Compare and comment on the distances travelled to school by pupils at these schools.

21 The volume of a cylinder is 75 400 cm³. The height of the cylinder is 60 cm.
Calculate the radius of the cylinder.

22 (a) Simplify (i) $36y^6 \div 9y^3$, (ii) $4m^2 \times 3m^3$.
(b) What is the value of $2^0 + 2^{-3}$?
(c) Work out $(6.5 \times 10^3) \div (9.2 \times 10^{-7})$.
   Give your answer in standard form correct to two significant figures.

23 You are given the equation $y = ax + 4$.
(a) Rearrange the equation to give x in terms of y.
(b) The line $y = ax + 4$ passes through the points $P(0, 4)$ and $Q(2, 0)$.
   Find the value of a.

24 (a) Write down the values of n, where n is an integer, which satisfies the inequality $-1 < x + 2 \leqslant 3$.
(b) Solve the inequality $2x + 3 < 4$.

25 (a) Solve the simultaneous equations $5x - 4y = -11$,
   $3x + 2y = 0$.
(b) Factorise fully (i) $3xy^2 + 6xy$, (ii) $ma - nb - mb + na$.
(c) Multiply out and simplify $(2x - 3)(x + 2)$.
(d) Solve the equation $x^2 - 7x + 12 = 0$.

26 Frank is investigating areas of rectangles. He tells Mandy,
"If you increase the length of a rectangle by $x\%$ and decrease the width of the rectangle by $x\%$ the area of the rectangle will stay the same." Is he correct? Explain your answer.

27 The diagram shows part of a roof structure.

$AB = 4\,m$, $DC = 5\,m$ and angle $BCD = 35°$.
BD is perpendicular to AC. Calculate angle BAD.

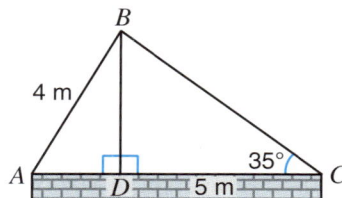

28

SALE PRICE £44.66

SALE "30% Off All Prices".
A suitcase costs £44.66 in the sale.
How much was the suitcase before the sale?

29 A pupil cycles to school. On her route, there is a set of traffic lights and a railway crossing.
She will be late for school if she has to stop at the traffic lights **and** at the railway crossing.
Otherwise she will be on time.
The probability that she does **not** have to stop at the traffic lights is 0.4.
The probability that she does **not** have to stop at the railway crossing is 0.9.
Calculate the probability that she is on time for school.   AQA

30 You are given the formula $p = \frac{2}{3}n^2$.

   (a) Find the value of p when $n = 5.7 \times 10^4$. Give your answer in standard form.

   (b) Rearrange the formula to give n in terms of p.   AQA

31 (a) Simplify $\dfrac{3x-6}{x^2-5x+6}$.

   (b) The diagram shows a rectangle which measures
       $(2x-4)\,cm$ by $(x+3)\,cm$.
       The rectangle has an area of $48\,cm^2$.
       Form an equation in x, and show that it can be
       simplified to $x^2 + x - 30 = 0$.

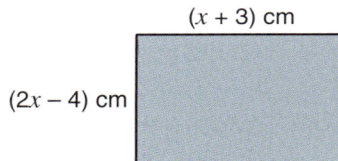

$(x + 3)$ cm

$(2x - 4)$ cm

32 A small tub of ice-cream weighs 50 g. The height of a small tub is 3 cm.
A large tub of ice-cream is a similar shaped tub that is 6 cm high.
What is the weight of a large tub of ice-cream?   AQA

33 y is inversely proportional to the square of x and $y = 2.4$ when $x = 2.5$
Find the value of x when $y = 60$.

34 The expression $4x^2 - 12x - 2$ can be written in the form $(ax + b)^2 - 11$.
Find the values of a and b.   AQA

35 $ABCDEF$ is a triangular prism, 16 cm long, as shown.
Calculate the size of the angle between AD and the base $BCDE$.

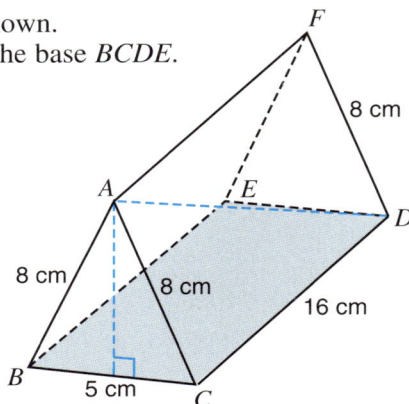

36 Solve the equation $3x^2 - x - 5 = 0$. Give your answers correct to two decimal places.

37 A solution of the equation $x = 3 - \dfrac{1}{2x}$

can be found by using the iterative formula $x_{n+1} = 3 - \dfrac{1}{2x_n}$.

Starting with $x_1 = 3$, find this solution, correct to two decimal places.
You **must** show all your working.

AQA

38

A party hat is made from card.
The hat is made in two parts: a cone on top of a ring.
The cone has a height of 20 cm and base radius of 7.5 cm.

The ring has an internal radius of 7.5 cm and an external
radius of 10 cm.
(a)   Calculate the area of the card used in making the
party hat.
Give your answer to an appropriate degree of accuracy.

A similar party hat is made in which the height of the
cone is 12 cm.
(b)   Calculate the area of card used to make this party hat.

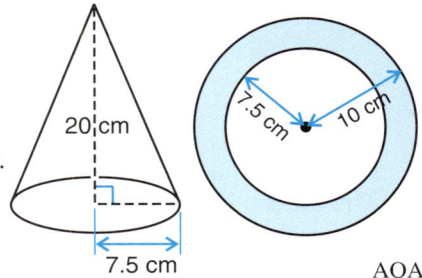

AQA

39 P, Q, R, and S are four points on the circumference of a circle.
PQ is a diameter and $PS = SR$. The lines PR and QS intersect at X.
Prove that angle $PXQ =$ angle SRQ.

40   (a)   (i)   Draw the graph of $y = \dfrac{5}{x}$ and $y = 11 - 2x$ for $0 \leqslant x \leqslant 8$.

(ii)   Use the graphs to solve the equation $\dfrac{5}{x} = 11 - 2x$.

(b)   (i)   Show that $\dfrac{5}{x} = 11 - 2x$ can be written as $2x^2 - 11x + 5 = 0$.

(ii)   Explain how your answer to part (a) can help you sketch the
graph of $y = 2x^2 - 11x + 5$.

(iii)   Sketch the graph of $y = 2x^2 - 11x + 5$.
Write down the coordinates of any points where the graph cuts the axes.

AQA

41   Solve the simultaneous equations $x = 2y + 4$ and $x^2 + y^2 = 5$.

42   A committee has 7 male members and 5 female members.
Two members of the committee are chosen at random to attend a conference.
What is the probability that both members are of the same sex?

43   (a)   Given that $\overrightarrow{OA} = 3\mathbf{p}$, $\overrightarrow{OB} = 3\mathbf{q}$ and $\overrightarrow{OC} = 4\overrightarrow{OB}$,

show that $\overrightarrow{AC} = 12\mathbf{q} - 3\mathbf{p}$.

(b)   Given that $\overrightarrow{AM} = \frac{2}{3}\overrightarrow{AB}$ and $\overrightarrow{AN} = \frac{1}{3}\overrightarrow{AC}$,

express $\overrightarrow{ON}$ in terms of $\mathbf{p}$ and $\mathbf{q}$.

(c)   Given that $\overrightarrow{OM} = \mathbf{p} + 2\mathbf{q}$
what can you say about the points O, M and N?

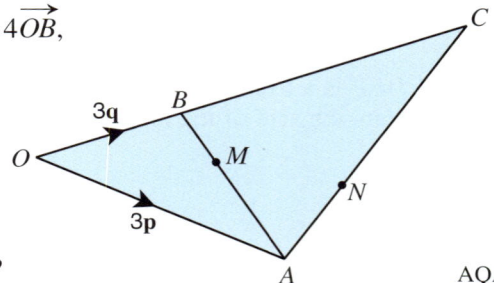

AQA

44   (a)   (i)   Show that $\sqrt{12} = 2\sqrt{3}$.

(ii)   Expand and simplify $\left(\sqrt{2} + \sqrt{6}\right)^2$.

(b)   Is triangle ABC right-angled?
Show your working clearly.

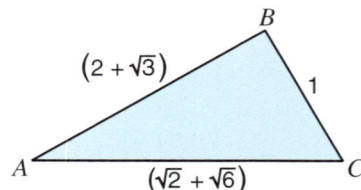

AQA

45 P, Q, R and S are points on the circumference of a circle, centre O.
POR is a straight line.
The tangent MN meets the circle at S.

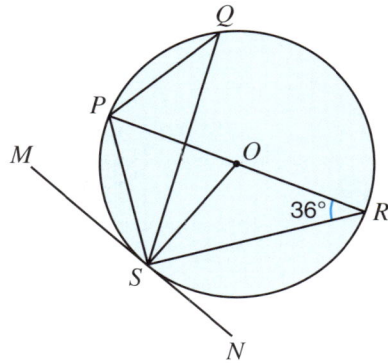

Given that $\angle PRS = 36°$, find
(a) $\angle PQS$, (b) $\angle POS$,
(c) $\angle PSR$, (d) $\angle PSM$.
Give a reason for each of your answers.

46 (a) Draw the graph of $y = 3 \sin x° + 2$ for $0° \leqslant x \leqslant 180°$.
(b) Use your graph to solve the equation $3 \sin x° + 2 = 4.1$. AQA

47 $p = 1.65 \times 10^7$ and $r = 6.17 \times 10^{-2}$.
The values of p and r are given correct to 3 significant figures.
Calculate the maximum possible value of $p \div r$.
Give your answer in standard form to an appropriate degree of accuracy. AQA

48 A helicopter leaves a heliport, H, and its measuring instruments show that it flies 3.2 km on a bearing of 128° to a checkpoint, C. It then flies 4.7 km on a bearing of 066° to its base, B.

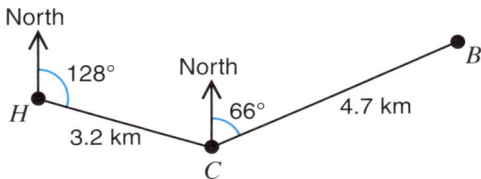

(a) Show that angle HCB is 118°.

(b) Calculate the direct distance from the heliport, H, to the base, B. AQA

49 A survey was carried out to find the average length of a garden.

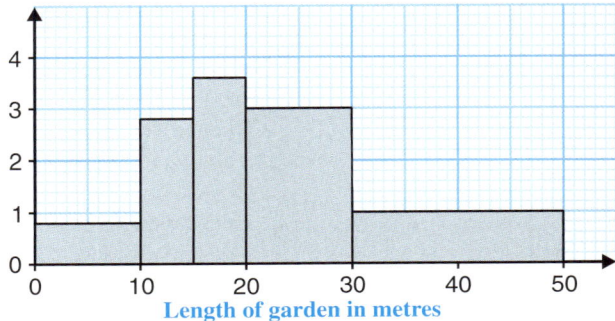

The histogram shows the results.

(a) How many gardens were included in the survey?
(b) Use the histogram to estimate:
  (i) the percentage of gardens less than 12 metres in length,
  (ii) the median length of a garden.

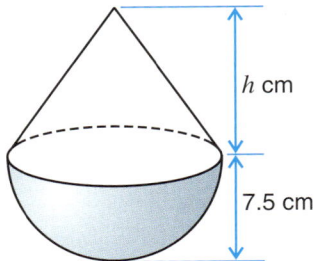

50 A child's toy is in the shape of a cone on the top of a hemisphere, as shown.
The radius of the hemisphere is 7.5 cm.
The volume of the toy is 1650 cm³.
Calculate the height of the cone.

AQA

51 In triangle PQR, $\angle PRQ = 67°$, $PQ = 10.6$ cm and $RQ = 9.2$ cm.
(a) Calculate angle PQR.
(b) Hence, calculate the area of the triangle.

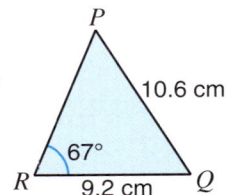

Index